CLOTHED WITH S
A Book of Counsel for ⸜

&

A PRIEST FOREVER

BY
THE RT. REV. WALTER C. KLEIN
Bishop of Northern Indiana

LOS ALTOS, CALIFORNIA
A.D. MMXXI

Author – The Rt. Rev. Walter C. Klein

1ST PRINTINGS

Clothed With Salvation: A Book of Counsel For Seminarians
Seabury-Western Theological Seminary, A.D. 1953

A Priest Forever
Morehouse-Barlow Co., A.D. 1964

2ND Printing – The Seabury Society, A.D. 2021

Edited By – B. James LeTourneau

Cover Art – Nashotah House Class of 1911

ISBN

Paperback – 978-1-7376374-3-1

Hardcover – 978-1-7376374-4-8

THE RT. REV. WALTER C. KLEIN
Bishop of Northern Indiana

The Table

OF CONTENTS

CLOTHED WITH SALVATION
A Book of Counsel for Seminarians

Do not be hasty in the laying on of hands...

—1 Timothy 5:22

Lord Jesus, you are the Good Shepherd who cares for his flock: We ask you to bestow upon your Church the gifts of the Holy Spirit in abundance, and to raise up from among us faithful and able persons called to the ministries of Deacon, Priest, and Bishop. Inspire them to spend and be spent for the sake of the Gospel, and make them holy and loving servants and shepherds of the flock for whom you shed your most precious blood. Grant this for the sake of your love. Amen.

–Book of Common Prayer, 650

FOREWORD

The Rev. Dr. Charles Erlandson

BEING a pastor or priest has never been easy: it is a vocation with innumerable challenges and requires public competency in a disparate collection of skills and talents. Pastoring in the twenty-first century in America is an exceedingly difficult vocation, for which pastors feel they have not been adequately trained.

4 out of 5 pastors will not be in ministry ten years later. On average, they last five years in the ministry, and only a small fraction make their vocation a lifelong career. Most fight depression or discouragement to the degree that they would take another job if they could find one. More than half of pastors interviewed say that seminary did not adequately prepare them, and 9 out of 10 say they have not received adequate training for the demands of ministry. Given such shocking numbers, it's clear that churches need to soberly assess the training, seminary and otherwise, they provide for their clergy.

Written for a different age than our own but wrestling with perennial issues clergy and seminarians face, Bishop Walter Klein's *Clothed with Salvation: A Book of Counsel for Seminarians* is a welcome contribution to providing this much-needed training. Klein was the bishop of the Episcopal Diocese of Northern Indiana from 1963 to 1971. Perhaps more pertinent to his qualifications to write *Clothed with Salvation*, first published in 1953, was his experience in seminaries and divinity schools, first as a student and then as a professor. He served as a lecturer at the Philadelphia Divinity School and, in 1938, became chairman of the graduate department of the Philadelphia Divinity School. Klein was also a professor of Old Testament Literature and Languages at Seabury-Western Theological Seminary and served as the seminary's assistant dean between 1952 and 1959. In 1959, he was elected Dean of Nashotah House, where he served until his death in 1963.

"Do not be hasty in the laying on of hands," St. Paul exhorts the Church, and yet lay hands on men she must. It is incumbent, therefore, that the Church does all she can to prepare men for the sacred ministry of Christ, for this is her vocation. Therefore, Bishop Klein was concerned that future clergy be adequately trained for pastoral ministry and not just academic training. He continually holds before them the high calling to which they aspire, reminding them that to be a priest is a vocation from the Lord, and not merely from men. The vocation of the seminarian is a unique one, for he is being formed, reformed, and transformed as one worthy of a double honor in the life of the Church. He is working out his salvation with fear and trembling in the crucible of the seminary of the Church.

Klein reminds seminarians that while the seminary cannot give men this vocation, "It can foster it, nourish it, fortify it. It can refine it, mature it, discipline it, and direct it."[1] He ever reminds seminarians, as well as any ministers reading his work: "We tremble at the magnitude of the assignment God has given us."[2] He balances this awesome charge with the very pastoral reminder that "we also are men."[3]

Klein is aware that seminarians are a kind of amphibian, that is, they live two intersecting kinds of lives. One life is their present life as a seminarian, a life which Klein sees as preparing men for the ministry not only through a life of prayer and study but also through the sometimes difficult life they have in relation to one another. God is preparing seminarians not in theory but already in practice. The other life of the seminarian is his future life as a priest, to which he must always have an eye.

Throughout his work, Klein observes the many obstacles and enemies that both seminarians and priests are likely to encounter and provides the seminarians the very pastoral counsel that seminarians must one day give to others. He catalogs and diagnoses some of the sins that lie at the door of both seminarian and priest. Though the life of both the seminarian and priest are difficult ones, Klein supplies inspiration to this arduous calling with such words of praise as these: "The versatile, adaptable,

---

1. Page 5
2. Page 12
3. Page 72

mobile, and durable parish priest is the glory and boast of the presbyterate."[4]

Despite the different age in which contemporary seminarians live, they will benefit greatly from Klein's work: in fact, the alien nature of some of the material only makes what Klein says appear more holy and wise. One final virtue of *Clothed with Salvation: A Book of Counsel for Seminarians* is that it is not only a book for seminarians but also for those of us who have so far survived the trials and tribulations of ministry and are still in the battle.

4. Page 94

CHAPTER I

On the Threshold

I N the course of every year that passes, some thousands of young men commence their academic training for lifelong service as clergymen in one or another of the numerous types of association that have come into existence among Christians. Eventually most theological students meet the requirements of their respective churches, denominations, or societies, undergo some manner of ordination, and in the decades of work that follow do, to all appearances, their sincere and faithful best to realize the potentialities of a ministry that ideally embraces the entire world but in prosaic fact operates within pathetically, regrettably, and frustratingly narrow limits. Yet virtually all of these earnest men adapt themselves by imperceptible degrees to their surroundings, making a concession here and accepting a compromise there until they become the irresolute defenders of a theological position or a set of private prejudices rather than the confident apostles of a universal faith. Finally they retire and are free to contemplate their lives in retrospect, and then, unless their vocation is extinct, a gnawing consciousness of loss and failure disquiets them. They recollect a time when they had a seemingly invincible zeal and an intrepid sureness of purpose, and now they sit and wonder at their grievous lack of these qualities. Where are the certainty and the clarity they possessed at the start? If a clergyman engaged in pondering this question concludes, after long and dismal reflection, that his most serious spiritual loss occurred, not in some crisis after ordination, but while he was still a theological student, he is probably to be congratulated on his self-knowledge. Certain it is that the seminary has not invariably proved to be a school of virtue. A good man defeated by evil is worse than a man who has never resisted it at all. Some of the most insidious temptations devised by our gifted enemy the Devil draw their inspiration from the conditions that necessarily prevail in theological seminaries. Impressionable and impetuous young men, ready to learn and eager to teach, are confronted, in an acutely challenging way, with the mysteries of theology, a science that, beyond any other, has produced divisions among men, in the main because it is the most important field of human inquiry. Our very absorption in the quest for the deepest of all verities can betray us if we permit the Father of Lies to bend our interest to his purposes. The trick is not difficult for our experienced opponent. Seminarians know enough about evil to recognize it when it assumes the forms of lust, hatred, greed, and envy, but when it comes disguised as orthodoxy, correct ceremonial, or the most approved church school method, they are promptly seduced by it. Under the Tempter's spell, I mistake my own often eccentric opinions for the potent truths that redeem the world, I seriously argue that God's ceremonial preferences coincide with mine, and I am prepared to dismiss as imbeciles all those who do not perceive the unique merits of my formula for handling the young. Only one misdirected enthusiasm, and that perhaps a very trivial one, is required to transform the devoted man of God into a self-seeking ecclesiastic. This process can get a good start in the seminary, and every time it does there is malicious laughter in hell.

The spiritual hazards that are inseparable from this stage of his progress need hold no terrors for the student if he arrives at the seminary with a vocation. Given a sound vocation, the rest is assured: at the proper moment the Church will examine the candidate's motives, and if he sustains the test, the Church will recognize the reality of his call by ordaining him. The intellectual attainments demanded of him in practice are unquestionably distinct from his vocation. To be sure, a vocation is normally brought to fruition with the help of formal training; but professional education is in no wise indispensable. Some of the most admirable priests in the Episcopal Church have not had the advantage of residence in a seminary. Even today in the Eastern Churches many of the parish clergy are obliged to function with a very meagre store of book learning. Inadequate schooling may cripple us. The lack of an interior call will paralyze us.

It follows from these considerations that the vital certainty, the inward summons to an office that can lawfully be desired only by those whom God has chosen for it, is beyond the reach of the seminary. If the usual evidences of a vocation are wanting, the seminary authorities may urge the student to reconsider his plans, but in such cases the student is the ultimate judge, and he alone can determine whether or not he has been misled. The seminary cannot confer a vocation, nor can it implant one. Still less can it withdraw or destroy a vocation. These are powers that God has not committed to it. Are we then to conclude that the seminary is impotent in this matter? By no means. Notwithstanding the restrictions under which it labors, the seminary can serve a vocation in manifold ways. It can foster it, nourish it, fortify it. It can refine it, mature it, discipline it, and direct it. The disaster it most anxiously studies to avert is the impoverishment of a vocation under its influence. The student's assurance of the divine choice is the one sufficient reason for his presence in the seminary. Nothing he can gain from chapel or classroom compares in value with that assurance, and if, on the last day of his Senior year, his vocation means less to him than it meant on the first day of his Junior year, he has not only made no gain, but also suffered an unutterable loss.

If we lie to ourselves about the past, we shall never be wholly free of the evil that was in it. When God honors us with a vocation, He takes us where we are and as we are. Vocation is unpredictable: God's choice falls on men who have been in the Church since infancy and men who were baptized as adults, on men who have done nothing worse than lose their tempers and men who have murdered, fornicated, and blasphemed, on men who welcome His call and men who shrink from it. Obedience reduces all these inequalities to negligibility. A man with a pious past is grateful for it and recognizes that it is not his fortitude alone that has kept him from sin. The reformed profligate renews his repentance every time he thinks of his vocation and combats sin in his penitents the more effectively for his experience of its ways. It is more profitable to do something with the past than to be depressed at our inability to do a great deal about it. We are never defenseless in those black hours we spend with the memory of the evil we once embraced. All our lives we shall be redeeming the past. Contrition for its defiant sins and thankfulness for its unmerited bounties will remind us how little it entitles us to the vocation that is so marvellously ours.

Acts and events, after all, rank far below persons as factors in the seminarian's earlier life. He belongs, and has always belonged, to a vast and intricate fellowship that, as a whole, is estranged from God. Inevitably, at some point a conflict will spring up between his natural duties and his supernatural vocation, for in that fellowship many wills are at variance with God's and many minds reject the evidence of His activity. The seminarian's father and mother have claims on him that he could not disallow if he would, and when—let us not pretend that it is never so—fidelity to his vocation alienates him, in some measure, from the beloved mentors of his child-hood, he is caught in a clash of obligations. A marriage contracted without refer-ence to spiritual ends adjusts itself imperfectly, if at all, to the exacting standards introduced by a vocation. The friends who knew us as merry pagans are chilled at the thought of what ordination, or even anything preliminary to it, will do to us. In fact, whenever a normal youth grows serious about studying for the ministry, his contemporaries, recalling the apples he has stolen, the girls he has been in love with, and the parties made memorable by his wit and his bottle, predict that he will never make it. Perhaps he never would, if he got nothing but commendation and ap-proval. Some of the persons in our former lives have helped us by assisting us, and others have helped us by opposing us. We may respond to the disappointment of our relatives and the incredulity of our friends by taking a second look at ourselves. Conceivably we shall not be reassured by what we see. There is a devastating truth in the judgments of our intimates, and if objections and derision awaken us to our appalling unworthiness, we cannot resent them. They reveal to us what we must be when we receive authority to preach the Word and administer the sacraments to human beings identical, in every leading trait, with those who at the outset ques-tioned our vocation. Can we aspire to the commanding holiness that will convert even our brothers and sisters and the companions of our early days? The question answers itself. The Incarnation has demonstrated that kinship and friendship can be hallowed. The excesses that we are not at liberty to allow ourselves are a timid dependence on home, family, and other elements of our background and an unfeel-ing determination to spare ourselves the embarrassment of earthly ties. Somewhere between sentimentality and ruthlessness, between complete softness and complete hardness, lies the course of action that will ultimately teach us how to further the salvation of those for whom we once felt a merely human love.

This rarest of all priestly triumphs can be achieved only by men of monumental simplicity. We have no use for the superfluities that other people prize. It is eas-ier to pray in a plain room than in a luxurious one. The man who takes second and third helpings at luncheon nods over his books half the afternoon and finally collapses on his bed or wanders off to somebody else's suite. A nice taste in bow ties and cuff links is not an essential part of the priestly character. An extensive acquaintance with the current shows and the smartest places to dine does not become us. Self-indulgence does not mix with a vocation: it complicates our lives, curtails our usefulness, stifles our devotions, offends decent laymen, and exposes us to the taunts of unbelievers. Admittedly, we add nothing to our value as pastors by being ostentatiously austere, but the opposite of self-indulgence is self-control, not puritanism, and in the absence of the true virtue, which we only begin to acquire during our seminary days, a slight stiffness, or even stuffiness, in these matters is preferable to an unregulated fondness for good living. The well-fed parson of legend may be a delightful person to meet, but in a world of grief and sin even the people who like him must recognize his inadequacy. Simplicity has its roots in the body. Simple quarters, simple clothing, and simple food lead to the simple habit of devoting the greatest amount of time to the most important things. Out of simple concentration on fundamentals grows a simplicity of intention. We are increasingly actuated by a sovereign motive, and if secondary motives cannot be reconciled with it, we abandon them. The energies that formerly flowed in all directions now run in a single channel. Sanctity is, of course, the ultimate simplicity. Beneath the multiplicity of phenomena there is a Will that imparts unity to the world. All things are related in God, and to that extent the universe is exceedingly simple. It is because the saint never forgets this and we almost never remember it that he acts with heroic simplicity and we wallow in confusion.

The new seminarian, as yet unacquainted with the mysteries disclosed to us by the great explorers of prayer, listens to homilies on discipline with a measure of distaste. For one thing, though he may not know it, he is being held back by the reluctance of the flesh. For another, he has probably brought with him to the seminary a rather faulty conception of prayer. Finally, insofar as he is the child of his age, he is dominated by its exceedingly erroneous notions concerning man. Each of these hindrances calls for a few comprehensive observations.

We need not linger over the first of them. The flesh will have its due, and those who wrong it must be prepared for its unsparing revenge. Health is to be sought if we lack it and preserved if we have it. The body is entitled to that amount of attention, but, when it senses any disposition on our part to parlay with it, we may expect it to claim far more than justice allows it. We never win an argument with the flesh. To be trapped into reasoning with it is to yield the advantage to it. It pleads with the eloquent voice of instinct—to our undoing, unless we halt the debate. Surprisingly, it obeys a direct and determined order. If we would escape its fascination, we have only to inform it that the question is settled, and forthwith it retires to its proper place among the forces that govern us. It exploits indecision, but the instant it is confronted with a fixed plan it surrenders.

In a word, the flesh respects firmness. Now human personality, as such, is not invariably firm. The firmest thing in our experience is not a good man, but a good law. Sound laws have a stability that even an exceptionally virtuous man cannot achieve. They are framed independently of the individual will and are not subject to its caprice. A good law anticipates the difficulties that will attend its execution and makes objective and just provision for them, whereas persons are given to making up their minds as they go, with the result that their improvised decisions, forced from them by the panic or passion of an emergency, are usually abortive. Just laws protect principles from the self-interest of persons and persons from the ruthless application of principles. A rule of life performs a similar service in a similar way.[1] It saves us from the folly and futility of those noble but nebulous decisions that embrace virtually everything by implication, definitely exclude nothing, and lead absolutely nowhere. The same decision should be reserved for such rational choices as do not remain mere acts of the mind, but, implemented by suitable measures, develop into habitual modes of behavior, to the profit of the entire personality. Without a rule we do too much on our good days and too little on our bad and our deeds are motivated by nothing more exalted than an impulse to please our idiorrhythmic selves. A rule based on an acute estimate of our capacities and infirmities raises our practice

---

1. The Rev. Bede Frost writes: "Without this beginning nothing can or will be accomplished. The priest who attempts to live a priestly life without a rule which is at once definite, comprehensive, precise, and particular is setting himself an impossible task. No aspirations, no practices, no resolutions will suffice unless the whole life is bound together and enclosed within a rule covering the whole of his normal day and regarded as possessing as binding a character as that of a religious in his monastery. Without such a rule the priest is at the mercy of every wind that blows, and of his own weakness, instability, and waywardness. His life and labour will be dissipated and wasted unless enclosed within its protecting walls, as a great river is of no practical utility, and is even dangerous, unless its mighty power is banked up, canalized, and directed. A great part of the complaints which come from priests to the effect that they have no time for prayer and study is due to the fact that so much time and energy is wasted by any man who does not live and work by rule." (*Priesthood & Prayer, Chapter VI*)

above the plane of whim, appetite, and present interest and makes everything we do a gift to God because we have dedicated it beforehand. Temptation, when it comes, bewilders the brain and stuns the will. If it contrives to gain our complete attention, we may no longer be able to withstand it. In seasons of stress a rule may be the only safeguard we have. By filling our hours systematically with the things we ought to do it reduces astonishingly the likelihood of our doing the things we ought not to do. In short, the observance of a rule gives continuity, consistency, and regularity to our service of God and, in so doing, builds up within us a drive that carries us through periods of aridity and weakness. Manifestly, a rule is indispensable, and the earlier we act on this conclusion, the more quickly do we become expert in the art of capturing the torrent of time and converting it to God's uses.

The discipline of living under a rule embraced as a means of glorifying God gives us in time the self-mastery and the recollection that sustain an unremitting effort to pray. To such an endeavor we are committed beyond question. A few years hence we shall undertake to tell people about a God Who knows and loves and can be known and loved. The God in Whose name we shall soon presume to speak is above all else a Person. We must not talk about Him without knowing Him, and we cannot know Him without praying to Him. We shall pray to little purpose if we continue to regard prayer as the last desperate measure of the defeated. Most of the people who pray at all pray only when they can discover no other way of getting what they want. This view cannot be ours, and if we still hold it in some degree, let us get rid of it. As long as we cling to it our prayers will remain infantile. Prayer must be, for us and for all others who hope to pray with power, a conscious union of wills in the creative pursuit of a common end. In prayer we work with God and with all His obedient creatures. Drawn into a vast, productive harmony, we become supremely creative by collaborating with the Creator. The works of prayer, wrought in God, partake of His eternity and perfection. Prayer helps to fashion life, which artists, however dazzling their genius, merely copy and interpret in paint that fades, in notes that fly down the wind, and in words that time empties of sense. We are therefore under no necessity of apologizing to society for the prayers we say while other men are busy with secular labors. The most useful inhabitants of the world are the unrecognized intimates of God who maintain its welfare and peace by strenuous prayer. Prayer so conceived is not very widely known in our day, and if it were widely known it would still be incomprehensible to the multitudes who, simply and uncritically, live the life of this age. While it would be foolish to maintain that the period to which we belong has made religion uniquely difficult, it must be granted that certain perplexities and frustrations we commonly experience as we grope for the truth about God have no obvious parallels in the past. Modernity, insofar as it refers man to himself for the standards he instinctively demands, is a tissue of errors. By giving man an autonomy that embarrasses him because he is not constituted to exercise it, our culture sentences him to the misery of perpetual confinement within the bounds of his own nature. When humanism, activism, pragmatism, and secularism are in the air, we all breathe them: there is no way of filtering the impurities out of the atmosphere of the age. A great part of American education is technological, and our superlative efficiency, our sheer capacity for getting things done, moves other nations to envy when it does not move them to scorn. American Christianity is intensely activistic: it builds, it organizes, it preaches, it exhorts, and it pauses for prayer only to restore its 'peace of mind,' only to renew its power to act. Our religion exhausts itself in good works and is helpless when good works fail. Effectiveness is the one criterion we all recognize. Never weary of improving our methods, we naively cherish the dream of an infallible technique by which we shall be able to make conversions at will. If we renounce technology and apply ourselves to the humanities, the result is much the same. The religion of pure humanism is the worship of Breasted's absurd divinity, "our Father Man."[2] Here again, man is the prisoner of his own limitations, and he cannot transcend those limitations so long as truth for him is only what men have found out and not what God has revealed. No seminarian is a professed humanist in this narrow sense, but every one of us has a touch of humanism. We do not contemplate the world primarily as a theatre of divine activity. Normally we think of it as man's domain, and we expect human life to interpret itself. Oblivious of man's creaturely dependence upon God, we await the natural emergence of a self-authenticating order, and so we end up in a crude variety of secularism. Until we abandon this illusory hope, we shall not pray with conspicuous fervor for the kingdom of God.

---

2. Dr. James Henry Breasted, Annual Address of the President of the American Historical Association, delivered at Indianapolis, December 28, 1928.

We tremble at the magnitude of the assignment God has given us. Only an irresponsible trifler could be free at this moment of the emotions that oppress us.
Can we do what is required of us? Assuredly we can. The call is a pledge of the
grace. The duties of the priesthood will not be thrust upon us prematurely. For the
present God asks us merely to be good seminarians. He gives us every imaginable
incentive to employ these priceless years to advantage. His gifts–the sacraments, the
daily common prayers, sympathetic company, the wealth stored up in books, skillful instruction, the delights of amiable argument, the gaiety, leisure, security, and
comfort of this favored place –are spread in profusion on every side. In a grateful
response to His generosity we shall find the way to a blameless priesthood.

CHAPTER II

Having Compassion One of Another

THE ordinary man's dislike of prolonged solitude is altogether wholesome. We were not made, it appears, to live alone.[1] Unless we are obliged to retire, periodically or permanently, in order to do our appointed work —and such tasks are allotted to relatively few— isolation from our kind makes us eccentric and eventually drives us mad. The spinster who locks herself up with her canaries sheds all but one or two of her typically human interests and becomes increasingly like her yellow-feathered companions. Every state in the Union has had its crazy hermit who greeted intruders with curses or shots. We preserve our equilibrium by means of intercourse with our fellow human beings. We infer from their conduct that they are impelled and frustrated by the forces that impel and frustrate us. Our bewilderment and our pain, if they were really unique, would crush us. It brings us sweet relief to observe that our tribulations are not peculiar to us. Indeed, a few years of experience cannot fail to show us that we are not singular in any respect. The dark things within us that terrify us are common to the whole of mankind.

A broad and tender compassion ought to spring from the apprehension of this truth. If men were governed by reason alone, they would long ago have made natural sympathy the basis of a world-wide cooperative society. In succoring one another they might have won deliverance from their frailties. It is our misfortune that we prefer comfort to salvation. The redemption we might gain through creative sympathy must be purchased with suffering, but vindication is balm to our self-esteem. Hence we justify our shortcomings by magnifying the deficiencies of others. We succeed in proving to ourselves that we are less wrong than somebody else, and thus we arrive at the conviction that we are right. The conclusions we draw from a comparison of our faults with those of our neighbors are infinitely consoling. If we err, there is an abundance of human precedent for our mistakes. After all, if we

---

1. Genesis 2:18

take a broad view of the question, we are merely stumbling where others have fallen flat. Nor are we satisfied with vindication. We perversely regard all men, not as our co-workers, but as our competitors. No matter how impressive our achievement in itself, if another outstrips us we smart under the shame of failure. Fellow-feeling gives way to a less admirable emotion the moment two human beings simultaneously desire exclusive possession of the same thing. The traits that seem so amiably human in a fellow-sinner are detestable in a rival. The sense of oneness in which at times we find refreshment and renewal is a delicate bloom, and it withers in the hot wind of self-interest. The realists who run the world have an instinctive contempt for humanitarianism. In their own way, they know what is in man, and they reckon, as humanitarianism does not, with the individual's infatuated fondness for himself —an attachment to which politicians and advertisers appeal with all the confidence of long success.

Seminarians have presumably abandoned the unthinking pursuit of their own advantage. Their calling precludes brazen ambition and gross cupidity. The safeguards with which they are surrounded keep the more repulsive forms of selfishness at a distance. In the seclusion of a theological school we are extraordinarily protected, and for that very reason we have to be more sensitive and more watchful than other men. The selfishness of the righteous often looks so much like righteousness itself that only a saint can tell them apart. We can wrong our brother most grievously when we are most innocent of malice.

Paradoxically, one way of doing this is to cultivate a quixotic altruism. Youth has a passion for absolutes, and the passion is more pronounced in some than in others. In the vigor and zeal of early manhood some of us are impatient with the theorists who strive to reconcile the values of the individual life with the values of corporate life. To men of a certain temperament this ancient question, upon which the most acute intellects have lavished the full resources of their genius, presents no difficulty: all they have to do is to prefer the welfare of others to their own welfare. Nothing short of the purest, most undeviating altruism will make their service the sublime thing it should be.

As a working rule, this will be immensely useful. As a principle, it may be disastrous. A reckless preoccupation with the needs of our neighbor lays us open to several deadly dangers. A Christian who never thinks of himself may fail to repent as he should. An inordinate devotion to almsgiving cannot justify the neglect of prayer and fasting. Our duties towards ourselves must be acknowledged and discharged. We are answerable for our own integrity, and we can maintain it only by self-examination and self-correction. Perpetual engrossment in the affairs of others drains us of the interior strength that makes us helpful counsellors. Worst of all, enthusiastic benevolence may prove to be nothing but another kind of selfishness. Altruists often lose their taste for good works when they have to perform them under somebody else's direction.

It comes, then, to this: the individual human being finds neither in complete separation from others nor in complete fusion with them the self-fulfillment for which God has destined him. On the one hand, we have nothing to offer our fellows save our individuality and the grace of which it may be the vehicle: the extinction of our individuality, if it were possible, would end our usefulness and alienate us from our brethren rather than merge us with them. On the other hand, if they fail to attain their full stature, we cannot reach ours. The just and holy life must be a dynamic interplay of our interests with theirs. Self-sufficiency and self-annihilation are equally impossible.

It does not rest with man either to establish or to refuse to establish the blessed order in which our fellows will cease to be, in any sense, our enemies. Such a dispensation must originate with God, and social engineering can never bring it about. Man cannot devise it, cannot deserve it, cannot institute it, cannot overthrow it. In no wise is it a thing that we project for our betterment. We cannot know it until it is among us, and when we perceive its presence we confess that it is totally different from anything we could ever have imagined or conceived. It proceeds from something God has done. It follows upon a divine work completed. It is a favor not to be earned, a happy release from a servitude we had despaired of shaking off, an inexplicable deed performed by God's unbelievable generosity and compassion.

In thus describing it, we assert that it has already come. If it were not a present reality, we should be altogether ignorant of it. The Christian community is under divine

rule and owns no authority save God's. The energy that called it into being during
Christ's sojourn on earth and at this very moment is supporting and inspiring it
is God's unconquerable and inexhaustible love. God loves us without calculation,
and therefore we cannot love our brother by measure. God's love transcends His
justice; hence our love towards our brother, so far from being determined by his
merits, arises simply and exclusively out of the love in which God enfolds him and
us. An attempt to derive it from or to combine it with anything else results first in
its contamination and then in its dissolution.

Usage has involved the word love in a kind of semantic fog: the modest monosyllable has acquired many senses, and only one of them is Christian. Theologians have
sought escape from the confusion of multiple meanings by borrowing the Greek
word agape and agreeing to recognize it as the scientific name of the distinctively
Christian sort of love. One cannot think of agape without recalling Anders Nygren's
admirable study Agape and Eros.[2] In this work Luther is credited with the redis-
covery of agape. The reformer's conception of strictly Christian and evangelical
love is set forth in the following words: "In relation to God and his neighbour, the
Christian can be likened to a tube, which by faith is open upwards, and by love
downwards. All that a Christian possesses he has received from God, from the Divine love; and all he possesses he passes on in love to his neighbour. He has nothing
of his own to give. He is merely the tube, the channel, through which God's love
flows." The undeniable truth here so strikingly expressed is obscured by the unfortunate simile of the tube. It would perhaps not be quite cricket to remind Dr.
Nygren that water probably gained little in purity when it ran through the tubes of
Luther's day. Still, only an archaeologist could be sure of that, and we have a much
sounder reason for challenging the passage. We are not mere ducts for the distribution of a theoretically unpolluted supernatural love. We cannot transmit God's love
without imparting to it some flavor of our occasionally revolting individuality. We
shall do well to discard the tube and adopt a happier image from Shelley's incom-
parable lines:

---

2. Anders Nygren was a Swedish Lutheran theologian who, in his work *Eros and Agape* opposes *eros* and *agape* as
kinds of love. This is in contrast to, for example, Pope John Paul II who sees the two as reconcilable aspects of
divine love. More famously, C.S. Lewis wrote *The Four Loves*, in which he discerns four kinds of love, the three
natural loves of *storge*, *filia*, and *eros* being subordinated to the divine *agape* love.

Life, like a dome of many-coloured glass, Stains the white radiance of eternity.[3]

God's love is more aptly compared with light than with water, and a slight rephrasing, which the poet will doubtless not hold against us, suffices to make these exquisite verses convey our meaning:

Man, *like a dome of many-coloured glass, Stains the white radiance of* **the love divine.**

We have marred the work of a peerless artist in order to state a theological truth, and the only forms of reparation we can offer are a relentless development and an unsparing application of the truth we have stated. We are all unworthy of God's love, and if there are degrees of unworthiness, God does not weigh them and bestow His love accordingly. God does not withdraw His love when we resist it, nor does it increase in volume when we yield to it. Love is not one of God's attributes. It is His essence: God is love. Unless we are ready to concede that in certain acts of love God is not completely Himself, reason does not permit us to argue that God favors some of His creatures above others in the exercise of His love. We can have neither more nor less of a thing that is immutably perfect: it is bestowed or denied in its totality. We affirm with confidence that nobody ever lacks God's love. There are times when our grudging obedience or stiff-necked resistance blunts our sense of its presence, but the love itself neither waxes nor wanes. Under the influence of God's love all comparisons become meaningless. If we are all unworthy, we are all in a sense equally worthy. Love is largesse, not wages.

The concrete implications of such teaching are painful to think about and even more painful to act upon. They crucify us, and our agony is our purgation and our redemption. An active recognition of the universality of God's love is fundamental. My brother's abject need of God's love is identical with mine. The love he receives differs in no respect from the love given to me, since God grants Himself to both of us. Natural or supernatural authority may confer upon one of us some power over the other. If so, the one to whom the power is committed must use it solely towards the realization of the ends that God's love has ordained. The form of the act may not

---

3. *Adonis,* Stanza 52.

be a matter of choice. Nevertheless, the intention remains under the control of the agent's will. The judge who pronounces sentence is himself subject to judgment. In the hands of a humble administrator the law can be employed to convey God's love to those who suffer the penalties of their transgressions. Whether they will or not, men must march to wounds and death at the word of their commanding officer, but the sternest order may contain a suggestion of the love that even the fury of battle cannot drive away. The priest who absolves sinners does so with the knowledge that he, too, is a penitent. Familiarity with the sins of others deepens his own contrition. He shares their need and the love that supplies their need.

In minds long aware of the universal human predicament neither pride nor envy can gain a foothold. Let us suppose that one of my rare seasons of penetration and wit occurs at a time when my neighbor is distracted and dull. The momentary contrast suggests to my elated intellect that, whereas my neighbor has confirmed my low opinion of him, I myself am not quite the fool I thought I was. Unless I really am a fool, I quickly remember how unremarkable God would find me if He did not love me. Ordinarily, of course, my brother outshines me. What do I do when this happens? Do I shun him in churlish resentment of his more brilliant gifts? Is the world darker for the light that proceeds from my brother? Out of His boundless abundance God adorns my brother with beauty, charm, and skill. Am I thereby made destitute? Must honor for him mean shame for me? Magnanimity should be spontaneous in every Christian. Against the background of God's liberal providence envy is the ugliest of our vices. My neighbor's endowments, like mine, are part of the vast capital that all men are invited to use for the enlargement of their righteousness and peace. By an eager and joyful acknowledgment of the love that is at work in my brother I enter into possession of every advantage he seems to have over me. His genius is then no more his than mine. Only his pride can keep him from dedicating his talents to the increase of human blessedness. What but my envy can impede the exercise of his devotion? Our alternative to envy is not a mean-spirited admission of unflattering realities, but the most enthusiastic acceptance of what God has done for, in, by, and with other people.

The choice we have just outlined is implicit in all our dealings with our brethren. Either God's love enables us to collaborate with them in the partnership of the faith and to step aside when their qualifications surpass ours or our self-love betrays us into treating them as rivals. From time to time, in every Anglican theological school, we encounter persons who appear to be laboring under the misapprehension that the Christian life is a contest. They must outstrip their fellow-students, and if eloquence, intelligence, and personal attractiveness fail them, they fall back on diligence, industry, and application. Up to this point they are perhaps guilty of nothing worse than excessive ambition, but too often they are driven farther and in the end their faith is crushed under the weight of countless outward observances. Godliness, in their eyes, is solely a matter of prayers recited, pilgrimages made, candles burned, services attended, and fasts kept. If quantitative religion is true religion, their scores entitle them to the highest prizes. But, unless the New Testament is full of double talk, they will be disappointed when they present their totals and demand the cash value of their merits. The spectacle of this kind of piety proves that the perennial dispute between the advocates of faith and the advocates of works is not a pointless academic debate. Something very important is at issue, and its formulation in terms of God's love settles the controversy. A faith quickened by God's love cannot be anything but a working faith, and faith in works cannot be anything but a want of faith in God's love.

Not a few of us, having escaped this pitfall, blunder presently into another. There are, in the motley congregation of our brethren, some whom we cannot abide. We may esteem them, serve them, and behave towards them with scrupulous justice, but we find, after many years of excruciating effort, that we take no natural pleasure in their company. We must beware of indulging antipathies of this description. They are at bottom irrational, and we waste time in toiling to explain them and incur danger in struggling to justify them. We do not overcome them by passively enduring them. They call for a positive application of love. The observant Christian discovers anew every day of his life that holiness is compatible with the continuance of irritating personal traits. The devoted human personality remains embedded in nature. If I want God's love through my brother —and for my own good I ought to be delighted that I am not likely to get it any other way— I must take it with my brother's moldy jokes, his asinine opinions, his halitosis, and his maddening mannerisms. God has not commanded me to love a bloodless abstraction. Constructive love cannot flourish between me and a human being stripped of the features and ways that repel me and remade to my liking. In loving the work of my own hands, I should merely be loving myself, and in this there is no gain. God is the author of all idiosyncrasies, whether they exist in me or in my neighbor, and in each of them He has wonderfully and inimitably blended the elements of our nature. Simply because the makings of a man are assembled in my brother as they have never been assembled before and will never be assembled again, he has a peculiar grace to communicate to me. I shall never obtain that grace unless I love him, not as I should like him to be, but as God has willed him to be.

If we come up against obstacles to love in our neighbor, we surmount them. If we meet with any in ourselves, we remove them. Nothing in our difficult religion forbids us to correct ourselves with the severity we long to apply to everybody but ourselves. The Golden Rule is a flexible thing, and there are different ways of stating it. Without any sacrifice of substance, we slant it in the direction of the matter under consideration by recasting it in something like the following form: Feel free to do to yourself what you would not think of doing to others. In a healthy Christian personality the growth of lovability keeps pace with the increase of love. If it is hard for me to love my brother, it cannot be easy for him to love me. I will therefore eradicate the imperfections that offend him. I will put far from me everything that renders his duty towards me a burden and a torment. My Christian profession requires this of me as much as it requires me to wear myself out in loving my neighbor. Unless I am in a measure to blame for them, my brother's failings cause me no unrest. God has noted them, and I will not dwell on them. Least of all will I permit them to make a difference in my love. Not so my own faults. These are most vitally my concern, and I will mark for prompt mortification the hardness, the slackness, the meanness, and the aloofness that are the despair of all who are eager to love me.

Only in this aspect of the life we pursue together can we fail calamitously. Whatever distinction we attain in student organizations, in our studies, in our pastoral work, or in exhibitionistic piety, if, when we depart, we are not remembered for our charity, we have accomplished nothing in the seminary. Other things can be taken up and dropped: the demands of charity press upon us all day long. We fall under the discipline of love the instant we cross the threshold of the seminary. There are worldlings who regard charity as the specialty of cloistered clerical perfectionists. There are cynics who dismiss it as an artificial virtue that nobody seriously practices. There are excellent laymen who admire it when they see it, but make no systematic effort to acquire it. One of these attitudes, or something very much like it, has been ours in the past. In the seminary we cannot help learning what love is, and we condemn ourselves to perdition if we do not act on our knowledge. We are bound to the exploration, the cultivation, the assimilation, and the manifestation of God's love. Without it we are the devil's emissaries –a scandal to men and a grief to God.

Love does not disdain modest beginnings. The bare willingness to be taught will serve as a starting-point. Actually, we have all more than once surrendered our own good for the sake of a person or a cause, and none of us is a raw novice in the exercise of self-denial. God's love will transmute loyalty, friendliness, group spirit, and tolerance into the exquisite compassion, tact, and delicacy that enchant us when we see them sacrificially exhibited in the life of a man or a woman who, having attained to utter self-forgetfulness, tranquilly endures the present nightmare of pride and malice in unwavering expectation of the day when the full splendor of our destiny will be revealed. Those who have emptied themselves of self speak and move with a serenity that awes and captivates us. Their touch is potent. Their presence banishes hatred: they are gratefully welcomed as peacemakers wherever they go. We are almost afraid of the light that is in them, and yet we covet it for ourselves. It will come to us as it has come to them. They have developed into the persons they are by relying on love as we have not dared to do. Love has quickened their faculties. It will quicken ours if we submit to it with their humility. A consecrated imagination will open our eyes to the importance of the momentary contacts and casual exchanges that hitherto have meant nothing to us in terms of love. Love points out to us things to do and things not to do, and if we faithfully follow its bidding it will give us wisdom to heal and restore our brother. There are no accidents in a world that is under the dominion of providential love. Our fellow-students and our teachers are here and not elsewhere because God has led them to us and us to them. As our lives expand, human beings beyond count will be enriched or impoverished by what we say and do to them, and it will be so because God has determined the opportunities, if not our use of them. To believe this is, in the judgment of strict

thinkers, bad philosophy and bad science, but the righteous will cherish the conviction in defiance of logic. Men bent on suicide have been turned from their purpose
by a warm salutation or an unexpected act of courtesy. A request for help may catch
us with empty pockets, but we always have leisure to listen, and if we listen with
compassion, we give something better than alms. The suppression of the derisive
guffaw that I too often unthinkingly emit may spare my blundering classmate a day
of humiliation, and who can say what strength he may not gain from that brief freedom? Love is alert and sensitive and ever on the watch for the openings that even a
seminary schedule presents to it. Its compassion springs from its gratitude for the
Passion: can we the undeserving deny our fellow-sinners their portion of the love
that brought the Son of God to earth and raised Him to the Cross?

CHAPTER III

The Courts of the Lord

WE worship a cosmic God, and although we do not equate Him with the universe, we hold that He is absent from no part of it. His power stirs the sands of unknown deserts, and at His touch there is motion in the dark depths of the sea. His friends have discovered that distance cannot separate them from Him: they have met Him in every conceivable place. No boundary arrests Him in the pursuit of His enemies. Those who love Him and those who hate Him must reckon with His presence wherever they may be. According to the stand we take towards Him, He is the Judge Whom we cannot escape or the tender Protector Whom we may trust not to desert us in any circumstances. Live we well or ill, there is a sense in which God is inalienably with us.

Our conviction that God is everywhere is intertwined with other convictions about Him. Let us for a moment set these other convictions aside. The effect of their removal is evident at once, and we readily perceive that a religion based exclusively on the truth of God's omnipresence would, in theory, be able to dispense with all sanctuaries. If we conceived of God's universal presence as undifferentiated immanence, it would be absurd to subject worship to temporal and spatial restrictions. Such a faith, if consistently followed, would either excuse us from worship entirely or hold us to continuous worship. Conscious life itself would be worship, or conscious worship–and what worship is not conscious?–would be the sole occupation of life. In the former case, no effort would be demanded of us. In the latter case, an impossible thing would be required of us. Faith is clearly not the word we want for this type of belief: a faith must have a crisis and a goal, and a religion of mere immanence has neither. Worship as we understand it is the product of dynamic factors. God's pervading presence, as such, is not a dynamic factor. For us the God Who fills heaven and earth is also the God of time and events. God does not confine Himself to a silent indwelling. He struggles with His creation.

The Bible is, in the main, concerned with God as a positive, aggressive being. Nowhere does it attempt an exhaustive or systematic description of Him. The reader is at liberty to infer what He is from the magnitude of His deeds and the boldness of His promises, and the mention of His qualities is incidental to the narrative of His acts. He is represented as thrusting Himself into man's world under all the limitations of the particular. He has allowed Himself to be seen in specific places. He has spoken to specific persons. He has delivered His people at specific times of anguish. The localization of worship is principally His doing, and holy sites are designated by God, not capriciously selected by man. The devout Israelite obediently celebrated his national feasts and offered his sacrifices in the place where it pleased God to dwell. Our own worship has preserved this conception of sacred places, despite the modern custom of building a church to suit the convenience of the worshipers and then inviting God to occupy it. A choice not ours is still remotely implied, even when the spot on which we build is not the scene of a miracle or a vision. The impulse is God's, and in raising a house to shelter the Glory and the Presence we are in some fashion carrying out a command that we have received from Him. We surrender the finished structure to Him by solemn dedication. Thereafter, He is the master and the host, and we enter the house as His guests.

The rules of human hospitality suggest the standards of deportment that should prevail in the house of God. We commonly put on one of our best suits before dining out, and if we forget to shave and comb our hair, we can scarcely expect to be invited a second time. We arrive punctually, ring the bell, and wait for an answer: we do not admit ourselves without ceremony. When our host has greeted us and we have returned his greeting, we make ourselves politely inconspicuous among the other guests. At ease in the knowledge that we are welcome, we eat our host's food with enjoyment, but we do not pocket his silver or put our feet on his table. We ignore or forgive the defects of his hospitality. We do not make a scene over an unpalatable dish. If by accident a bone has passed our lips, we dispose of it quietly: we do not spit it out in the face of the entire company. We overlook the incivility and inefficiency of the servants out of gratitude for our host's generous intention. We do not discuss the dinner or the service, either while we are in the house or after our departure.

It is boorish to offend the person at whose table we dine, and it is a great deal more boorish, and far less excusable, to offend God under His own roof and to embarrass and distract our fellow guests. Seminarians are notoriously lax in matters of this kind. They rush from bed to the Eucharist and barely reach the chapel in time for evensong because they have prolonged their merry conversations until the last stroke of the bell. While the sacred ministers are completing their preparations in the sacristy, late risers who have just discovered anew that fifteen minutes' work cannot be compressed into five are running a frenzied race with the inexorable hands of the clock. The service is well advanced when the last door bangs, and for some minutes thereafter a large part of the congregation is almost audibly out of breath. It is the rare student who pauses at the door of the chapel for a moment of recollection. With no thought of what we are doing we pass from the trivialities of the corridor to the solemnities of the choir, our heads still echoing with the light words spoken a moment before. Once we are in the chapel, our minds are more on the conduct of the service than on the sacrifice of prayer we have come to offer. Few students are so far gone in contemplation that they fail to observe a mistake in reading or a slip in ceremonial. Behind most of the snickers, glances, and smiles that enliven seminary services there is perhaps nothing but a superficial levity, of which the years, as they pile up, will cure us; but at times it is possible to detect a degree of malice, and one looks with dismay at the Christian heroes who feel constrained to make the chapel the battleground of liturgical factions. There is a touch of the diabolical in the man who turns a genuflection into a challenge and the sign of the Cross into an act of defiance.

These years of chapel attendance can be invaluable to men who must someday stand before Christian congregations and guide them in worship. This is the most exacting of all the arts we have to master and practice. We call it an art because it entails the creative use of skill, but it would be a grievous mistake to imagine, as some young clerics do, that skill is the whole of it. Laymen will gladly accept the liturgical leadership of a saintly priest, whether he is a finished artist or not. They prefer eloquence and polish, but if a priest has toiled long for these things without acquiring them and yet discharges his liturgical functions with unmistakable awe and devotion, he will find his people indulgent towards his faults of tongue, gesture, and bearing. The faithful have eyes and ears to distinguish between the priest who is culpably casual and negligent and the priest who is poorly endowed. They are repelled by the smoothness of the accomplished performer who sets up the opaque partition of his own personality between the worshipper and the Lord to Whom worship is rendered. They require of us, above all in the service of the sanctuary, a self-effacing holiness, and when they find it, they recognize, honor, and follow it. They pray best when their prayers are voiced by a priest who says to himself daily, "He must increase, but I must decrease."[1] In the seminary we are so placed that we can fruitfully combine the viewpoints of priest and people. Yesterday we were simple guests under God's roof. Some officiants helped us to worship, and others did not. Tomorrow we shall be responsible servants, acting with the authority delegated to us by the master of the house. May our dignity never blind us to the needs of those who stand where we once stood!

While we are discussing the service that will shortly be the principal business of our lives, let us reflect that we are at present servants in a small way. The lector, the server, and the sacristan are not contemptible underlings in the courts of the Lord. To be sure, they win little glory, but their work is honorable and useful, and, while their faithfulness normally goes unapplauded, their failures can disrupt the peace and recollection of worship. If they chafe at what they view as drab drudgery and tedious training and sullenly or impatiently endure their present obscurity in expectation of their advancement to higher rank among God's ministers, they simply prove their unfitness for promotion. The humble tasks allotted to us in our seminary days are to be prized for their intrinsic desirability and not as mere steps in our progress towards our ultimate objective.

Thus far we have been occupied with preliminary considerations. We are at length ready to come to grips with something far more fundamental than decorum in church. There are Christians who salute God as they salute the flag or any other emblem of common interest and corporate loyalty. When they are in the mood they are uplifted by an ingeniously devised and smoothly executed order of service, and at such times they magnanimously concede to God a certain restricted authority

---

1. John 3:30

over human life. Undeniably, as they see it, we owe God an occasional act of homage, and we lose nothing by doing our duty. Properly conducted exercises of devotion possess definite emotional value, man has his spiritual side, and it is good for busy people–naturally, not too often–to be brought into comforting contact with heavenly things. It goes without saying that it would be absurd to search for any organic connection between the refreshment a man receives in church late on Sunday morning and the refreshment he takes at the country club early Sunday afternoon and perhaps, at intervals, the rest of the day. The church door is the boundary between one world and another. Only fanatics contend that a man should run his business on Monday in the light of what he has learned under God's roof the day before. God is entitled to a discreet and moderate respect. That any sensible man will give Him, but He must not expect too much.

A limited recognition of God may have any of a vast number of motives. In some men stupidity, especially when it is not candidly acknowledged before God and humbly opened to His influence, tends to justify itself by denying truth that even the least gifted human being is capable of apprehending with an effort. In other men laziness is the seat of the trouble: year after year they cling to an outgrown, juvenile conception of God because the abandonment of this notion for a better one would entail a devastating series of reforms in their thought and in their lives. In still others the fault is to be attributed to a strong, proud, malicious will that, estopped by reason from a total rejection of God's claims, nevertheless refuses to concede to God more than a trivial power over human life and identifies Him with the irrational, the unpredictable–the 'Jesus factor,' as American airmen called it in the uncertain days of our war with Germany and Japan. From none of these groups does God receive the one thing He wants of us: worship.

The world is filled with rebels who churlishly withhold from God the offering most due Him, and they are tragically wrong. The confession of their impotence and sin will not result, as they mistakenly assume, in the mutilation of their humanity. Worship will not extinguish the precious individuality to which they cling with doting fondness. Were God to demand that we stop being ourselves, He would dishonor the work of His own hands. Worship is not a strait jacket invented for the confinement and torture of all that we are accustomed to call natural, human, and normal: it is our emancipation, and manumission from a hopeless servitude to nature is the boon it confers upon the natural man. It gives him access to the delights of grace and so completes and perfects what nature has only suggested. It is worship that converts the dissonances of life into the consonances of religion. By sharing in the liturgy we learn to live in two worlds without being disloyal to either. Worship blends the rhythm of creation with the rhythm of God's uncreated being.

Aware, as the most earth-bound of us must be, of our affinity with the things above us and, as the most heavenly-minded of us must be, of our kinship with the things below us, we despair of resolving the antinomies of our position. They are resolved for us in worship. The antinomies are, of course, innumerable, and many of them seem to spring more from the discord of our natural impulses and the irregularity of our development than from the strain of our effort to reconcile matter and spirit. The fact remains that all our disquietude originates in a failure of our synthetic faculties. We adhere to a certain truth or pursue a certain value until we encounter some other truth or value, and when we fix our attention on the new thing we forget the old. In order to be content with the person we are now we must to some extent dissociate ourselves from the person we were five years ago, and the greater the difference between the two, the more vehement our repudiation will be. Although nobody can become an adult without first being a child, each generation is the natural enemy of the next. Were it not for revelation, we should always be strangers to the totality of truths and values, and revelation retains and renews its vitality by becoming, every time the liturgy presents it anew to the faithful, an actual human experience.

The liturgy may be viewed, first of all, as the interaction and harmonization of crisis and routine. If things were as we should like them to be, crises would occur either not at all or only when we needed them to spur us on to fresh exertions. Routine, if we could control it, would sustain us at all times and depress us at no time. Reality does not conform to this pattern. A crisis, while it may galvanize us, is just as likely to paralyze us, and routine has been the grave of many a rare, brave purpose. It does not follow that a union of the two is impossible. We are instinctively certain that we ought to expand by alternating between routine and crisis, doing the same things in the same way for a relatively long time and then, in a shattering collision with the unexpected, finding ourselves able to summon out of the dark energies and gifts of which we have never been clearly conscious. Nothing short of this happens to us when we live by the liturgy. The continuity of worship, a quality emphasized by the fixed elements in the Eucharist and the choir offices, awakens in us a sense of perpetual and both sanctifying and protecting contact with divine things. This is routine, if you like, but certainly the most productive kind of routine. It cannot degenerate into monotony. Long before there is any danger of fatigue or surfeit, a feast or a fast invades the familiar round of psalm and lesson and confronts us with a mystery that searches and judges us, deepening our contrition and intensifying our love. Crisis breaks into routine, and after crisis routine is resumed with an increase of devotion. The ordinary and the extraordinary are wonderfully combined in the annual liturgical cycle, and each of them is experienced as the complement of the other.

Having observed the dynamic of a Christian man's growth under the influence of the liturgy, we ought next to ponder the ancient question of the conflict between the individual and the fellowship to which he belongs. The events of our generation have committed Western individualism, which is a loose alliance of Christian freedom, humanistic narcissism, and political egalitarianism, to mortal combat with a dedicated and—to its adversaries—quite unintelligible collectivism. The struggle can terminate only in a creative synthesis of interests. Again worship indicates the line that we must pursue. Worship disciplines, but does not crush, the individual. His uniqueness is recognized and treasured. Nothing could be plainer than the assurance conveyed to him throughout the liturgy that he loses nothing by becoming irrevocably a member of the Body of Christ. However, this does not mean that he is encouraged to regard the Church as a mere association of convenience. The peculiar beauty of his individuality is inseparable from the power of the Church: he grows, one may say, out of the soil of the brotherhood. Still less does his adoption signify that the Church is a receptacle into which he may dump his responsibilities. The most fundamental of human rights springs from the sovereignty of the individual conscience. Every right is also an obligation. Neither as right nor as obligation is the power of ethical and spiritual choice transferable. None of us can unload upon the Church his responsibility for himself, and therefore each of us hears in the liturgy, along with the voice that speaks to all believers in common, a distinct imperative addressed to him, not, to be sure, apart from the Body of Christ, but nevertheless with direct reference to him as the responsible author of his own acts. The liturgy does not deal with abstractions. It ministers, not to the Mankind that has no life save in the mind of the pedant, but to each man in a setting that consists, in the main, of the lives of men like himself. It takes into account all the needs and aspirations of individuals: it does not promise us, for example, the limited beatitude of a flawless economic order. Without violence and without confusion, it brings believers and the states, institutions, and traditions they serve into obedience to the Will of wills and the Lord of lords. Where else are individualism and collectivism reconciled?

Some remarks about faith and works may not be totally irrelevant in this connection. It is difficult to believe, but unfortunately all too true, that Christians of one sort have been contemptuous of works, while Christians of another sort have at least given the impression that they hold faith in low esteem. Neither error can long resist the truth declared in the liturgy. The liturgy is itself a tremendous work, and all our works are linked with it. The liturgy sets faith in motion, but not if faith is a lifeless profession involving only the mind and confining itself to intellectual assent. Faith is not something we subscribe to; faith is more than something we live by: faith is that in which we live and act. The Christian who remains within the sphere of faith—and he is at its very center when he participates in the liturgy—can do nothing that is contrary to faith, devoid of faith, or even external to faith.

Under the headship of Jesus Christ the redeemed constitute the sphere of faith, the field in which it demonstrably works. Citizenship in this commonwealth of grace is the unutterable privilege of those who belong to Christ by adoption and incorporation. It would be absurd to speak of citizenship if it were impossible to be an alien. We are born aliens, and we are reborn into citizenship. We cannot pretend that baptism makes no difference. The baptized are a peculiar people, a chosen people, a choice people, a preferred people. The ordinances of the Faith are reserved for the faithful: only the hallowed servants of God are invited to partake of the hallowed things. There is a group to which God can say, "You only have I known,"[2] and every verse of Scripture will confirm the statement. The particularity of our religion is not a fault in which we acquiesce because we are not generous enough to transcend our sectional loyalties. Our faith functions in particular places, at particular times, and in a particular society for the single reason that God wills to build His kingdom around the core of the elect. Universality is implicit in our vocation and mission, and the way to the final, triumphant realization of Christ's sufficiency for all men will not be shortened by the premature abandonment of a real and fruitful particularity for an illusory universality. The Eucharist we celebrated this morning held the particular and the universal in admirable balance: it prepared us concretely and specifically for the things we are doing today, and it made us aware of all the worlds that have issued from God's hand and of the long, twisted flow of time that emerges from eternity and sinks back into eternity.

Only in the Incarnation, that is to say, in a divine-human Person, is the interpenetration of the human and the divine perfect and complete. The Church and the liturgy are, as it were, organic developments of the Incarnation, and therefore they partake of our Lord's perfection, with the difference that in them the interpenetration of the human and the divine is impeded by man's resistance and unworthiness. The Church is the Incarnation expanded into a society. The liturgy is the Incarnation concentrated in an act. Worship is the service of the heirs of eternity, who are still in some degree the prisoners of time. The liturgy is framed for beings whose very aspirations to eternity are conditioned by time. Hence it is not by any imperious disregard of time that the liturgy spans the abyss between the absoluteness of the divine and the relativity of the human. On the contrary, the offices of the Church utilize time and convert it into a vehicle of the eternal Will. The shifting seasonal accents of the Prayer Book are the details of a design dominated by the master theme of our progression towards the stupendous unveiling of divine, eternal forces in the dissolution of time. Notwithstanding the collapse of all our efforts to visualize ourselves in eternity–not to speak of defining and describing eternity itself in the language of time–we own with the liturgy that the work God has begun in us will reach perfection, if at all, in His abode, where we, who have so

---

2. Amos 3:2

often found and lost Him in the darkness of time, shall have secure possession of Him and be eternally one with Him; and it is the supreme function of the liturgy to keep this trust alive in us. We have entered upon a life that requires our frequent presence in the courts of the Lord. Some of us will always be able to perform that duty with a simple, eager, hungry delight in contact with sacred things. Others will be able to offer only a devoted will that must struggle unremittingly with a natural distaste for ceremonies. We are not commanded to enjoy what we do in choir and sanctuary. We simply have an inescapable obligation to do it. But ought we to be here at all if it bores us to praise God in His temple?

CHAPTER IV

To Seek by Prayer

THE thing that most impedes the spread of the Church is sin, and next to it, as an obstructing factor, ranks the spiritual infantility of a countless multitude of Christians. Innumerable laymen in middle life or old age–and with them we must bracket a far from microscopic number of priests–have made no material addition to their personal knowledge of God since they were adolescents. The prayers they say reflect this immaturity. Stimulated by the unsparing realities of secular life, we grow up into responsible and competent parents, providers, and taxpayers. We eventually reach adulthood in almost everything save prayer. In prayer we remain children. Apparently time has little to do with improvement. We contrive in time to be moderately effective in most bodily attitudes, but when we assume a kneeling position we cease to function in a manner that does credit to our years. Surely the reason for this lamentable condition cannot be that we have been deceiving ourselves about prayer!

But we have. Christians commonly look upon prayer as a lonely hunt for God, and that is why they give it up so willingly and so finally. It is evident that so terrifying a quest calls for extraordinary enterprise, hardihood, and renunciation, and nature has bestowed these qualities with a niggardly hand. Hence we make a brief and tentative excursion into prayer, and the moment we appear to be losing our bearings we hurry back to familiar territory. It is a regrettable and wholly unnecessary retreat. All that the heroes of prayer can teach us is implied in the things we already believe and accept.

No matter how far away God seems at times, we know that He never abandons us. Prayer originates with God. We do not have to grope for Him in a mist of uncertainty. There are no preliminary questions to decide. We begin with the knowledge that He wants us to find Him. He listens while we pray. He listens all the time we are not praying. His untiring attention, interest, and concern proceed from a will that keeps the world in motion. There are many reasons for the distress good people often feel in prayer, and the pain we suffer in our devotions may well be designed for our correction, but the worst blunder we can make is to be misled by the apparent abortive-ness of our prayers into concluding that God is indifferent. The crudest, weakest, most selfish prayer, if it is meant for God, reaches its destination. God never ignores our supplications. His perpetual awareness is the cause of our turning to Him. Prayer is an act we choose to direct towards God, and if we omitted the deliberate intention prayer would lose its character. Yet in praying we merely restore to God what He has given us. He fashioned us and all that surrounds us. He is equally the author of the occasions of prayer and the author of the organs and faculties that function in prayer. Our contribution is the obedient and grateful offering of our wills. In reality, we are not starting anything. We are charged with a kind of creative transmission. Prayer is not a force we generate, but rather a current that passes through us.

To His own steadfast watchfulness and gracious accessibility God adds the companionship of our living and present friends in Christ and the support of the absent and the departed. We are called to no solitary prayer. When we pray, the Church prays with us. In the strict sense, there are no 'personal devotions.' It is the same person who prayed with the faithful this morning at the Eucharist and tonight, before he goes to bed, will pray for them in secret. His attendance at public prayer is not a reluctant concession to his social character, nor are his private prayers dictated purely by the requirements of his individuality. The prayer that dissociates itself from the liturgy and engages in the cultivation of an exclusive, possessive attachment to God is a selfish, destructive prayer, from which we may expect nothing but ultimate condemnation to the blank silence of our own emptiness. Extra-liturgical prayers are an application of liturgical prayer to ourselves, a kind of personal sharpening of the truths conveyed to us by means of the liturgy. The liturgy, if we adhere to it and pray, at all times, in union with it, protects us from a deadly inclination to indulge our spiritual preferences. The prayers we say in physical separation from our brethren are then sustained and validated by an immense chorus of petition, intercession, and thanksgiving. In all parts of the universe, among the living and among the dead, our comrades and fellow-workers join us in the divine labor of prayer. Neither space nor death can deprive us of their collaboration.

Conceivably a physician can become a criminal and yet retain his skill. History may preserve some memory of lawyers who, after jettisoning their morals completely, have actually shown an increase of professional acuity. Neither of these feats is within the capacity of the praying Christian. The total life of the individual comes to expression in prayer. We cannot keep any part of ourselves out of our prayers. The lies, the lusts, and the ruthless selfishness against which we have taken no measures because we prefer them to God shout us down when, out of a godless life, we venture to raise our voices to God. The evildoer who prays without contrition prays into a void, and unresponsive space flings back at him the discordant, jeering echoes of his iniquity.

Prayer, finally, admits of no confident appraisal in terms of time spent, energy expended, aptitude exhibited, or objectives attained. The remarks 'I pray well,' 'I pray badly,' 'I am now really quite an expert in prayer,' 'I have made incredible strides in a short time,' 'My conscientious meditations seem to be getting me nowhere,' 'I have what you might call a flair for this sort of thing,' 'Prayer is one of my weak points,' and the like show how ignorant of prayer the speakers are. The same amount of prayer may transform one consecrated Christian into a contemplative, gratefully and mightily conscious of a most exceptional vocation, and leave another, so far as all subjective indications are concerned, precisely where he was at the first word of prayer or even more deeply entangled in bewilderment and frustration. If we had a measure of God's insight, we should see that the latter of the two persons is no more a failure than the former is a success. Each has received what God has elected to bestow. Each, after his own fashion, toils to make his will agree unconditionally with God's will. No formula captures the boundless wonder of prayer, but we are close to the central verity of the spiritual life when it dawns upon us that the diversities we observe in those who pray are as nothing compared with the intention that makes all prayer plainly, frankly, and uncomplicatedly the pursuit of God's will.

Prayer can, of course, be made a marvellously intricate exercise, and beginners are likely to find the superficial complexities of certain methods of meditation both coldly forbidding and stubbornly impracticable. Notwithstanding the deficiencies and limitations of particular schemes of prayer, for most of us some method, whatever its character, is indispensable, perhaps merely as an initial aid, perhaps permanently. Usually, after a few months of inquiry and experimentation, we settle down to the practice of a method that is partly borrowed and partly of our own devising. We cannot, with impunity, disregard our collective Christian knowledge of prayer, and, whether our principal source of help is the record left by our forebears or the experience of our contemporaries, not only shall we be preserved from the mistakes of those who have prayed before us, but also we shall become familiar with a considerably broader expanse of prayer than our own unsupplemented resources could have revealed to us. Tradition and authority, if we follow them humbly but not slavishly, will ultimately guide each of us to a just appreciation of his peculiar genius and bent. In prayer we have a freedom that we cannot claim in matters of faith. The Church gives us truth. It is for us to make truth live and work in us, and we have wide discretion as to the means. The prayers we say may be compared with the clothes we wear. In neither is our liberty absolute. Custom prescribes the general form of our dress, and further restrictions are imposed by income, figure, age, and occupation. For all that, we contrive to choose garments that reflect our traits and tastes. Singularity is discouraged, but individuality is not completely suppressed. Similarly, we pray, if we are sensible, not in the style of a millennium ago, but with a modernity that expresses the life we actually lead, and additional bounds are set for us by a host of considerations, personal and impersonal. Nonetheless, our prayers spring from a part of us that no human influence can dominate, and insofar as our needs and capabilities are unique, nobody can tell us how to pray.

Human life in its immensity forms the remote context of prayer. Any situation into which man can fall may move us to pray. The universe abounds in concrete reasons for praying. Our prayers cannot embrace them all, save by a general awareness and a comprehensive intention. Vagueness has no place in sound prayer, and the man who prays for all things impartially prays to no purpose for anything. Effective prayer has for its immediate context some phase or aspect of the contest that good and evil wage perpetually within us. The advantage shifts from one side to the other, and the issue remains uncertain up to the moment of our departure from this life.

Ground is gained, ground is lost, ground is recovered. The daily local reverses cannot, however, arrest the drive towards God that gathers power as we shed our fears and hesitations. Experts have divided the advance into three stages: the purgative way, the illuminative way, and the unitive way. The division would be a dreary academic fiction if it were meant to establish an inflexible standard for all Christians. That is emphatically not the intention. Only the most naive could imagine that everybody moves neatly forward through each of the three stages in turn, arriving, after so many months and days, at secure beatitude. The writers who speak of these main steps of our interior growth are concerned merely to fix a working norm by reference to which we shall be able to determine approximately where we stand and what prayers and auxiliary exercises are best adapted to further the work that God has undertaken in us. In prayer only one difference deserves to be kept unfailingly in view, and it lies in the relative parts taken by the two wills involved. In the prayer of industry, by which we are purged and illuminated, our will predominates: we are the center of consciousness; we act; and we are deeply obsessed with the notion of 'getting somewhere.' We may spend decades in this laudable but imperfect prayer before it gives way to a foretaste of the kind of prayer that will be our occupation in eternity. In the last, blessed degree of prayer God is the center of consciousness, we are acted upon, and the strain of anxious motion is forgotten in the peace that is the bliss of those who are whole and complete in God. We may get very close to this state before we die, and in any event, if we pray long enough and cling fast to the purity and singleness of motive with which we began, we shall find our receptiveness increasing and our ardent desire for the enjoyment of God and His favors turning gradually into an attitude of quiet assent and cooperation.

This consummation may be delayed indefinitely by our own reluctance and sluggishness or by the divine love, which does not confer its bounties prematurely. God may make us wait and toil. Our task, while we are seminarians and for a long time after ordination, will be to keep ourselves praying, and to that end we shall have to know prayer as a science, as an art, and above all as a discipline that normal diligence will enable us to master. In the next few paragraphs we shall attempt to determine, on the basis of the rudimentary rationale of prayer that has thus far occupied us, what varieties of prayer hold the highest degree of promise on the plane of our present attainment.

All prayer that is not actually uttered in the course of the liturgy radiates from the liturgy. Vocal prayer and mental prayer continue and extend the liturgy. If we were sufficiently recollected, the liturgy would in time become a contemplative offering. As it is, we are painfully vexed with distractions, and, more often than not, we leave the chapel with a sense of having received in our common prayers truth and life that must be assimilated at leisure. Thus the prayers we say outside the formal bounds of the liturgy are sustained by the liturgy, and if we deliberately link them with our Lord as He is worshipped in the offices of the Church, especially the Eucharist, we discover that they reinforce our liturgical devotion. We commence with a simple apprehension of the fact that our participation in the liturgy requires of us such self-evidently essential and fitting acts as preparation, formulation of intention, and thanksgiving. Next we see that each portion of the liturgy has a distinctive tone and accent into which we cannot enter without previous reflection. For instance, the first words of the Eucharist contrast the perfection of God the Creator with the inadequacy of man, upon whom God nevertheless lays the obligation to strive for the integrity of uncalculating love. Our reply to the imperative of Christ, Who puts into a single saying the quintessence of the Law and the Prophets, is penitential and more than penitential: we stand before God and dissolve in confusion at the knowledge of what we are. Farther on in the service our "humble confession to Almighty God"[1] confronts us again with our sins, and this time in a very specific way, but the fleeting moment escapes us if we have not made a detailed examination of our consciences beforehand. At each of these points there is a brief opening for an appropriate act. We must not let the speeding instant sweep fruitlessly by. The canticles and hymns can convey our praises, the Prayer for the Whole State of Christ's Church can be heavy with our intercessions, God's majesty can appear before us in the *Sanctus*, if we are ready. We recognize that we are not ready, and even a cursory study of ourselves will show us that we cannot expect to be ready until we prepare for services as we prepare for our classes. A passage of Scripture on which we have meditated speaks to us eloquently the next time we hear it in worship. If we persistently neglect to open our Bibles in private, we shall

---

1. *Administration of Holy Communion*

grow deaf to the voice of Scripture in the liturgy. The mysteries and the verities, the sublimities and the infinities set forth in the liturgy are lost on those who will not pause and ponder them. We cannot assist at the liturgy very often without becoming aware that we are dependent on vocal prayer, Bible reading, devotional reading, and mental prayer for the cultivation and maintenance of our capacity for worship.

We are, at length, sufficiently acquainted with principles to be able to draw up a plan of prayer. This is a very grave matter. Most human beings like to draw up plans, and few like to execute them. We must not become triflers. Our energies should go into prayer, not into redesigning our prayer life every month or so. Once we have adopted a rule, we should leave it substantially unaltered until there is a radical change in our mode of life. The more carefully our first rule is framed the longer it will stand. We do well to construct it with the expectation of keeping it the rest of our lives. It may require little modification even when we become priests.

A balanced devotional life is based on the methodical use –in varying proportions– of three distinct sorts of prayer. We are grateful to Bacon for pointing out to us that "reading maketh a full man, conference a ready man, and writing an exact man." Prayer presents parallels to the activities here named. The devout practice vocal prayer, spiritual reading, and mental prayer. Vocal prayer is consecrated talk, and it carries with it all the profit and all the peril that attend the use of the tongue. Spiritual reading stabilizes, matures, and expands our prayers and shows us how to appropriate our fabulous heritage. Mental prayer clarifies our faith, and in this respect it is akin to competent writing, which clarifies, for the writer as well as for the reader, the subject with which it deals.

The amount of vocal prayer we impose upon ourselves as a daily duty is a secondary matter, so long as this type of prayer does not claim an excessive proportion of our available time, to the neglect of reading and mental prayer. We ought always to recite Morning Prayer and Evening Prayer in private when we cannot say them with a congregation. An attempt to crowd part or all of the Breviary into the schedule of the day will inevitably lower the quality of our vocal prayer. Vocal prayer loses a great deal of its value when we have to perform it at a high rate of speed. It is more profitable to concentrate on a recollected offering of our common prayers and to approach them and depart from them with an unhurried sense of the solemn and blessed work in which we are engaged. Either in the Prayer Book or in one of the devotional manuals so easily procured we shall find prayers that can be committed to memory and used before and after the choir offices. For the Eucharist a preparation, including a statement of intention, and a thanksgiving are indispensable. They may be taken from the Roman Breviary, directly or in some Anglican adaptation. The fixed form may be omitted, as often as one wishes, in favor of impromptu prayers. Every day that does not open with attendance at the Eucharist must be ushered in with an act of spiritual communion. The prayers we used to say as children, just after getting out of bed in the morning and just before lying down at night, may no longer meet our needs, now that we are seminarians, but, if the actual prayers have lost their relevance, we have not outgrown the practice of dedicating the first and the last thoughts of the day to God. Ejaculatory prayers, direct, unadorned, and so frequent that we forget the sense of the individual words, will carry our love to God the first moment we are awake and at intervals during the hours that follow. We ought to have a prayer to say every time we hear a bell or a whistle, every time we drop one task and take up another, and indeed every time we draw a breath. We can acquire the habit of falling into prayer the instant our attention is released from other objects. The day should end with an examination of conscience. To this exercise, which need not last more than two or three minutes, we shall want to attach a confession, an act of contrition, a resolution, and a prayer invoking the divine protection. Finally, we ought to compile an intercession list, allotting to each day of the week a number of persons, groups, and causes. A wide range of intercession is preferable to a narrow one, but, of course, we can wander too far afield and dissipate our devotion in a mere attempt to cover ground.

A relaxed but at the same time vigilant and receptive reading of the Bible and standard works of devotion may be reckoned among our prayers, for it differs in purpose, method, and result from the study to which we necessarily devote the bulk of the day. The latter brings into play the natural abilities with which we are endowed: intelligence, memory, imagination, and, if it is a distinct gift, the puzzle-solving instinct that sustains the scholar's interminable grind. The best of its rewards is the delight of breaking down data and impressions and building them up into a rational structure. Far removed from this is the kind of devotion we are now discussing. The Bible has a divine Word for us if we listen simply, humbly, and expectantly, and when we settle down to read Scripture in this fashion we must shelve the learning that, so far from giving us any advantage, may well burden and confuse our prayers. One young savant of a generation ago became so immersed in the details of New Testament criticism that he found it impossible to meditate directly on the text and was obliged to depend for devotional sustenance on the unscholarly writings of his intellectual inferiors. Let us not join the already large company of single-minded specialists who reinterpret the Gospel anew every day but never address a prayer to Jesus Christ. We need not share their fate: fifteen minutes of Bible reading a day will preserve us from it. No esoteric technique is required for the performance of this common Christian duty. We ask for light, open our Bibles to a passage selected in advance, and read until either the time is up or some sentence or phrase assumes a vivid life and communicates a sharp, personal meaning. We can solve the problem of what to read by keeping a day ahead of the lectionary and so being ready to attend to the lessons when we hear them in the services. A privately devised sequence of readings too often suffers from the fallible judgment of its compiler, while a table of lessons appointed to be read in churches represents the corporate mind of at least a substantial group of Christians. In any case, we should neither consume an undue amount of time in looking for passages to read nor plow blindly through the Bible on the assumption that all parts of it are equally suitable for meditation. Commentaries that aim at a plain exposition of the text may be used in preparation for the daily Bible reading, but we should shut them with decision the moment they threaten to lure us into some erudite quest. We are all capable of understanding Scripture if we approach it with the conviction that the Word still lives beneath the thick crust of controversy and speculation that time has left upon the surface of the Bible.

The literature of Christian prayer is portentous in volume and extremely uneven in quality. Modern writings often contain both old and new errors, and first-year divinity students cannot always detect these errors. Writers who argue that prayer is a nerve tonic or a formula for success do not merit our attention. For reliable direction we should resort to the books–at most a few hundred in number –that have maintained their standing and authority among Christians in face of neglect (or, what is worse, popularity), misunderstanding, and even misuse. By reading fifteen minutes a day we can come close to assimilating, in a year, half a dozen of the spiritual testaments that Christians have not been able to forget.

Vocal prayer and steady reading in the Bible and other well-chosen books are necessary in themselves and necessary also for what they contribute to mental prayer. Vocal prayer gives us a facility in the phrasing of our acts and makes the mind move easily from point to point in mental prayer. Reading accumulates for us memories, ideas, and images, all of which impart warmth and body to mental prayer. In fact, Bible reading as we have described it is an elementary kind of mental prayer. There is great advantage in looking to the liturgical Epistles and Gospels for the subject matter of the first year of meditation. The choice of topics in subsequent years will present no insuperable difficulty to those who have made average progress during the year of initiation.

A meditation, like a sermon, an essay, or a short story, is an organization or articulation of thought and action. It sets out to follow an idea to a productive conclusion. Every serious meditation ends in a tightening-up of some laxity, a tiny adjustment of our lives to the day's enlightenment. The object of meditation is the criterion of its methods. No matter how closely we adhere to a standard method, we shall have to adapt it, at least in a few respects, to our idiosyncrasies.

Anyone who looks comprehensively and exhaustively into methods of meditation will be struck with the essential uniformity underlying their apparent dissimilarities. The validity of the following rules is acknowledged, explicitly or tacitly, by all well-informed and experienced writers:

1. Meditate, so far as possible, every day, in the same place, at the same hour, and for the same length of time.

2. Know in advance the subject and the general drift of your meditation.

3. At the scheduled time go into the presence of God with awe and trust. Be serious about what you are doing and confident that with God's aid you can do it.

4. Be assured that you remain in God's presence until you deliberately leave it. Do not permit yourself to be confused and distressed by involuntary distractions.

5. Think as vigorously and clearly as you can, but do not hold yourself rigidly to logic and order, and do not regard meditation as primarily an intellectual effort. Yield to the suggestions and impulses of the Holy Spirit. The function of reason in meditation is to stimulate the emotions and the will.

6. At the end of your meditation thank God for the conversation you have had with Him. If it has gone well, give Him the credit. If it has gone badly, take it as a favor that He has humbled you.

7. Finish your meditation with a concrete resolution.

In order to meditate to our profit, we have to 'get into the mood,' exploit the mood while we are in it, and conserve the resulting gains after the mood has passed. The word 'mood' is, one must admit, extremely misleading. Its use in this connection is not intended to encourage us in the belief that we ought to wait until a natural inclination enables us to give our minds unreservedly to meditation. The mood of meditation is rather the resolute and sometimes painful orientation of our powers towards God as the heart of all that is. We can put ourselves into this frame of mind, and there are various devices that will help us, but they will not work in a life that is, at bottom, opposed to God. For this reason, the first step in meditation is to live in agreement with God's will. The agreement need not be perfect, but we must hope that God will make it perfect. Thus generally disposed to fidelity and in consequence generally prepared for meditation, we are in a position to execute the first part of mental prayer, thereby consecrating ourselves, for a specific period, to the exclusive practice of an activity in which we are in some manner engaged all the time.

First, contrition for our sinfulness rather than for our sins; then recollection to bring the imagination under control; and, finally, an invocation to the Holy Spirit, Who spoke by the Prophets and will not refuse to speak to us: these three devotions constitute what is known as the 'immediate preparation.' More than this should not be attempted without good reason. An involved preparation shortens the central part of the meditation and may defeat the end for which the exercise as a whole is designed.

The main section of the meditation is made up of considerations and affections, the former ordinarily preceding, and giving rise to, the latter. The whole person responds both rationally and emotionally to the development of the theme, sometimes following the process placidly to its conclusion, at other times halting midway to extract the maximum of profit from some uncommonly meaningful consideration, but always guiding the reflections and the aspirations towards the decision in which the entire effort culminates. For thoughts the imaginative mind will often substitute images. We may, occasionally or habitually, prefer Scriptural incidents to Scriptural sayings as matter for meditation, though word and event are organically connected. We may allow ourselves considerable latitude, so long as we recognize that sentimentality, desire, excitement, and tension are alien to the love that is the supreme fruit of mental prayer. They are a threat to the soul, and it should not take us long to distinguish between these counterfeits and the thing for which they are at times mistaken, namely a complete and genuine consecration of the emotions at their instinctual roots. Affective prayer is of no use if it does not fortify the will and confirm our loyalty to God and His ways. The novice in mental prayer loves God much as he loves human beings. If he is ardent and demonstrative in natural affection, his love for God is full of feeling. Someday he will stop feeling, and then, if he cannot love God with his will, he will stop praying. A dearth of feeling can do us no harm, but an excess of it is something to be alarmed at. Nevertheless, affective prayer, practiced with humility and sincerity, has a place and a function, and a meditation from which it is totally absent differs too little from a mere task of the mind to be very encouraging to an apprentice in the craft of mental prayer.

The conclusion will normally require a little more time than the preparation. The mind will promptly discard most of the considerations, and few of the affections will survive our return to the secular routine of the day. Unless we can select a single thought or impulse and express it, as the day advances, in some manner of action, all that we have pondered and felt will evaporate in the heat of our preoccupation with the things we have to do. By means of a gentle and unhurried transition from prayer to work we can preserve the substance of our meditation and even retain, hour after hour, some measure of the awareness of God we had while we were at mental prayer. At the head of the final series of acts stands the colloquy, an intimate talk with God during which we summarize the points we have covered and implore God to direct us to a suitable resolution. Next comes the resolution, the purpose of which is to implement our meditation. It is less than a vow and more than a remote intention, and deliberate carelessness in its performance cannot fail to have the gravest consequences. Third in order is the thanksgiving, which is in effect a renewal of the colloquy on a note of gratitude. Last of all, we make an act of oblation or self-dedication. The resolution has not fully determined the service we are to render as the day unfolds. God has not told us all that He has ordained for us, and we now signify our readiness to be content with whatever He may send. We close our meditation, not in supine resignation, but with eager confidence in the love that cannot betray us.

Thousands of righteous men and women, some of them manifesting an eminent degree of saintliness, attain, in the faithful use of meditation, the limit of their conscious inner growth. From one year to the next they persevere in mental prayer and have an unbroken and profoundly satisfying experience of its efficacy. To others –and in this group we must place the majority of the devout– a tranquil stability in discursive prayer is not granted. They may meditate for a long time before perceiving any indications of a change, but eventually they will be constrained to reckon with their increasing frustration. The mechanism that formerly ran so smoothly in mental prayer now protests, with creaks and knocks, against further use, and there are times when it does not work at all. The brain has produced many considerations, and the nerves have produced many affections, perhaps even forcing the brain into a secondary role. All this appears to be coming gradually to an end. Mental prayer in the strict sense has passed into affective prayer, sometimes called, with doubtful justification, "the prayer of simplicity," and now affective prayer is either expiring from exhaustion or passing into a third type of prayer. St. John of the Cross has given us a name for this state. We are, as he graphically puts it, in "the night of the senses."[2] Our accustomed means of access to God, Whom we have been in the habit of approaching through images and impressions supplied by our senses, is blocked. It is a suspension of activity, a paralysis, an eclipse. Yet our ordinary use of the senses is not affected. We can make an address that will furnish others with material for meditation, but we ourselves are incapable of mental prayer. Anxiously scrutinizing ourselves, we almost hope to find a fault –laziness, carnality, want of interest– to which we can reasonably attribute this strange freezing-up that has taken place within us. We discover nothing of the sort: we love God more than we loved Him when our meditations were spontaneous and consoling. We are not clinging to anything God has made. Food, drink, friendship, work, recreation, and all the other things that constitute life mean less to us than they have ever meant before. We seem to be able to do nothing for God, and at the same time, while we are baffled, we are not dejected, unless we insist on making a problem out of a gift that should bring us nothing but joy. These are all tokens of our arrival at the prayer of quiet (acquired [active] contemplation). We cannot say that we have finished with meditation. From time to time we may return to it. But in future our normal prayer will be the best that man can attain by striving. We shall spend hours in motionless and wordless, but neither idle nor sterile, contemplation of God as He is. We have gone as far as method and exertion will take us. Beyond lie the abysses and the pinnacles that mystics know but cannot readily describe.

Assuredly God never abandons us to our own resources in prayer, and the ignorant and the indiscreet may rely on Him to preserve them from its pitfalls. The one calamitous misstep we can make is to give up prayer. We shall be safe from that disaster if we bind ourselves, promptly, boldly, and generously, to the observance of some practicable rule of devotion.

---

2. "When the house of sensuality was at rest, that is, when the passions were mortified, concupiscence quenched, the desires subdued and lulled to sleep in the blessed night of the purgation of sense, the soul began to set out on the way of the spirit, the way of proficients, which is also called the illuminative way, or the way of infused contemplation, wherein God Himself teaches and refreshes the soul without meditation or any active efforts that itself may deliberately make. Such, as I have said, is this night and purgation of the senses." (*The Dark Night of the Soul, Chapter XIV*)

CHAPTER V

The Mind of a Theologian

P EOPLE have always been more ready to talk about the Christian religion than to follow its precepts, and among those who prefer discussion to practice it is usually the least qualified who speak with the most uncompromising finality. Our faith has suffered more from pedants, sciolists, bigots, and fanatics than from honest, if not sufficiently contrite, workers of iniquity. Intelligence and zeal have repeatedly exhausted themselves in the service of purposes that could not have survived an instant of exposure to the light of God's countenance. Christian history abounds in impetuous persons who were so forward to utter the truth and demand conformity to it that they did not pause to learn it, and a considerable number of those who have indubitably found it in scholarship have not bothered to look for it elsewhere. If the body must be subjugated and the will reduced to obedience, the mind, too, must be held to a perpetual dedication of its endowments to the God Who formed it. In religion not everything can be known, but the knowledge that is possible must be acquired. Nowhere else are the ignorant under so great an obligation to content themselves with modest silence.

Ordinarily we enter the seminary with a negligible technical knowledge of theology, and, as a result, we are at first unduly impressed with the superior attainments of the teachers and the older students. The awe we feel as neophytes in the company of adepts rapidly wears away, and then we are either depressed at the staggering quantity of information we are expected to absorb or intoxicated with the charm and wonder of theology, particularly the portions of it for which we have a conspicuous aptitude. Thus we step unawares into one of two traps: either we rashly conclude that a formal course in divinity is merely an obstacle that we must surmount or a torment that we must impatiently endure or we become complacent about our studies and equate a theological education with the Christian life. The anti-intellectualists and the intellectualists are both wrong, and both make the mistake of discussing their difficulties excessively, prematurely, and unprofitably. One of the seminarian's most glaring faults is his fondness for talking about the wrong things in the wrong ways with the wrong people. Much instruction now assumes the form of directed conversation, and it is gratifying to any instructor to learn that his pupils take counsel with one another in private about their studies. This, however, is precisely what most seminarians do not do. Instead, they fritter away entire evenings in venting their spleen, propagating their personal opinions, parading their undigested learning, and telling one another what they propose to do when the bondage of the seminary is over. The regrettable consequence of this is that a large number of candidates for the ministry grow more expert in professional small talk than in theology, and when the ministry opens before them they display an inadequacy of which they may well be ashamed, for it arises from their want of the equipment they might have obtained in the seminary. For most of the men whom God sets apart for the exacting service of the priesthood there is one period of genuine intellectual opportunity. The Church maintains seminaries in order to provide that opportunity. If there are some who do not avail themselves of it, the demands of the life they lead after receiving holy orders deny them the luxury of a second chance. No seminary claims to turn out finished theologians, but it is equally true that unless a seminary undertakes to begin in its students a process that, if faithfully continued after graduation, will someday make them competent theologians, it is not doing the work for which, in God's view, it was founded.

Theology is not a specialty. Theology is not a profession. Natural sciences largely aim at the control of natural forces. Theology does not aim at the control of God. It is not a mere tissue of curious speculations about God. It is the mind's obedience to God[1]. It is reason's reverent tracing of God's love, might, and goodness in nature and events. It is the study of God in the immensities that surround us and in the intensities within us. Only a very godly servant of God can be a true theologian. With no effort at all we can be bogus theologians, happily absorbed in cutting God down to our own miserable stature.

One need not be an obscurantist to read Robert Hugh Benson's lines with relish:

---

1. See 1 Corinthians 10:5.

Now God forbid that Faith be built on dates,
  Cursive or uncial letters, scribe or gloss,
What one conjectures, proves, or demonstrates:
    This were the loss
Of all to which God bids that man aspire,
  This were the death of life, quenching of fire.

Such studies as these lead, of themselves, to the faith of the humanist, and not beyond. The more remarkable, then, when we note it for the first time, seems the fact that much of theology is exactly the persistent drudgery Benson has in mind. If only for the defense and vindication of the things received as true in the Body of Christ, the scholar must work sedulously at his little chores. There is no risk in this pursuit for the man who remembers that God's activity in creation forms an organic design, of which the object of a given scholar's studies is an infinitesimal detail. The plodding specialist's preoccupation with 'dates, cursive or uncial letters, scribe or gloss,' so far from betokening a myopic indifference to the things that genuinely count in human life, may be an unobtrusive witness to a modest, but in no wise introverted, faith.

If the small jobs of theology border on the menial and derive their dignity from the whole to which they belong, it is not surprising that their results are rarely of a phenomenal character. Periodically God glorifies Himself by producing a human mind that is capable of writing an epitome of its era and indeed of all the consecrated striving of all times. To a few theologians it is given to achieve a bold, searching, compelling reorientation of men's thought about God. The rest of us may occasionally enrich an eminent masterpiece with penetrating glosses, but for the most part we are disciples guided by, and willingly in debt to, a master.

To adhere, in the main drift of one's thought, to one or more of the titans of theology is not to surrender one's right of judgment. Our obligations to these monumental minds can easily be overestimated, and the classic systems and schools unquestionably owe a great deal to the minor theologians who have filled in the masters' outlines. We ought not to be too diffident about speaking our minds, even if we have irrefutable proof that our minds are mediocre. It is better to be drably and honestly right than to be brilliantly and perversely wrong. Prolonged, determined, and disinterested consideration of a specific question entitles the most prosaic intelligence to views of its own. Productive cerebration is not the exclusive privilege of genius, and we may, on occasion, successfully take issue with the most illustrious of thinkers. Association with intellects of the first order may make our limitations embarrassingly evident, but we cannot permit it to reduce us to a subhuman passivity. On the contrary, it should stimulate us to the confident use of such originality as we possess. Inevitably we shall spend much of our time in reviewing what our forebears and the most significant of our contemporaries have written. The mistake against which we must guard is the acceptance of a formulation of the truth for the truth itself. We are grateful for what our fathers and the pioneers of our own day have discovered, and we do not ignore it, but if God has been able to teach them, He can also teach us. If we want a firm theology, we shall have to erect it on this conviction.

A trustworthy theology is possible because we have the Scriptures, the Creeds, and –not the least valuable of the three– the spectacle of victorious grace in the very process of sanctifying us and those we know. The principal things, the indispensable things, the regenerating and transforming things were entrusted to the Christian community at the beginning and have remained its unique and living treasure. It must be confessed that, in seminary instruction, these cardinal matters do not always receive the constant, evangelical stress they deserve. Zealous young spirits are unsettled both by the prominence, and by the inconclusive treatment, of secondary questions. The prominence, insofar as it cannot be attributed to the conditions under which seminaries must function, proceeds from the student's present want of perspective –and, it may be, partly from the professor's. The teacher lavishes attention on these problems because he is interested in them. The pupil is bored or scandalized by them because he does not grasp the bearing they have on the things he regards as vital. The teacher, if one cultivates him after hours, proves to be a Christian as well as a man of learning, and the pupil, when in later years some argumentative infidel backs him into a corner and assails him with shrewdly selected and vehemently hurled fragments of misinformation, will be delighted to find himself admirably equipped for the defense of the Gospel he thought neglected and slighted in the seminary. Even J, E, D, and P and their little brothers K, S, and L have their uses.[2] We consider them in class year after year without arriving at any satisfactory judgment of their size and importance and indeed without establishing their existence. But they do us a priceless service, for they constrain us to, and confirm us in, a penitential attitude towards the routine that constitutes the bulk of theological inquiry. In frustration we get a milder punishment than our sins deserve, and suspended judgment is patience with a touch of the heroic and the sublime. The Church that delivers us from fear by telling us what we must do to be saved wisely declines to scratch the itch of curiosity by naming for us the author of the Book of Genesis. The crucial questions of theology were answered long ago, and the answers are repeated every day in Christ. As for the questions that are not crucial, it will be a sad day for our science when the last of them is answered. Or, to put it in a way that every good theologian will prefer, it would be a sad day if we did not know that then we shall hear the voice of Christ explaining all mysteries.

Theology thus regarded is more than a study. The sacrificial intention with which we begin each period of work and the submissive, teachable attitude we maintain throughout it invest theology with the character of worship. The mind's best oblation is the thing for which the mind was created: systematic thinking, which cannot but mortify the arbitrariness and emotionality of mere 'reactions.' God does not expect us to offer Him pure reason, because He knows that we are incapable of pure reason, but He will not accept from us a theology fashioned by sloth, prejudice, self-interest, and cleverness, to the total exclusion of the divine forces that, with their quickening and fructifying influence on man's intellect, lift him out of his self-absorption and expose him to the purifying light that God withholds from no determined suppliant. Slovenly logic and intellectual dodges and short cuts dishonor the God in Whose cause they are employed. The only arguments with which we dare to commend Him to the unredeemed are those that represent our own increasing redemption. It is the same man who prays in the chapel and thinks in the classroom, and the God Who receives our prayers as a gift to His love is none

---

2. J, E, D and P refer to the then-popular "Documentary Hypothesis" about the authorship of the Pentateuch. It was not written by one author, like Moses, but by a host of authors representing the Yahwist (J, from Jehovah), Elohist (E, from Elohim), Deuteronomist (D) and Priestly (P) traditions. K, S and L refer to three different theories put forward by Old Testament scholars. Julian Morgenstern proposed a "Kenite source" (K) R. H. Pfeiffer argued for a "South of Seir" (S) source and Otto Eissfeldt theorized a "lay source" (L). In short, these were all variations on the "standard" Documentary Hypothesis.

other than the God for Whom every idea we conceive in His service is a reflection of His intelligence.

Taking liberties with Pope, we venture to assert that the proper study of divinity is God.[3] From the axiomatic truth that everything is related to God it appears to follow that there are no self-evident bounds to theology. In practice, theology has both limits and divisions, and we shall presently define the former and enumerate the latter, but, while the theologian is primarily concerned with the content and implications of what we call revelation, he is more than casually mindful of the divine operations that confront us in nature and in man's combat with nature and with himself.[4] Our concentration on the subjects that constitute the standard seminary curriculum is not a narrowing of our interests, but rather the continuation and fulfillment of a liberal education that seemed lamentably incomplete when it reached its formal close in our departure from college with a diploma. In college some of us learned how to make a living, others learned how to live, and the rest, the blessed few, learned both. In the seminary, as we master the arts of the priesthood, let us make strides towards the breadth and sanctity that will fortify us against the temptation to act mechanically, irresponsibly, or unworthily in our use of those arts.

It is the Judaeo-Christian tradition, more than anything else, that gives our theology its characteristic thrust and purpose and so determines its form and methods. Alien modes of thought have often invaded the tradition, but in all cases they have been absorbed into the monotheistic religion that has a continuous life from Moses to the present day. The essence of the faith so transmitted lies in the conviction that history is a guided process in which a pattern of revelation is evident. Christian theology is the redeemed mind's effort to apprehend the God Who directs the flow of events and, by the aid of the knowledge thus obtained, to help man towards the end God has prepared for him. This definition provides us with a means of deciding what to admit to a theological curriculum and what to exclude. To be sure, there are penumbral sciences, such as the philosophy of religion, moral philosophy, and the history of religions, and their precise status is debatable, but Christians have long

---

3. See Alexander Pope's *Essay on Man*, wherein he writes: "The proper study of mankind is man."

4. The theologian is primarily a master of the sacred page, the Scriptures and only secondarily makes use of those disciplines concerned with the natural and psychological sciences.

been in substantial agreement concerning the structure of theology, in which they recognize four distinct complexes of disciplines: the historical, the exegetical, the systematic, and the practical, or, to employ an almost self-explanatory terminology, church history, Biblical science, theology proper, and the art of pastoral care. This arrangement is both definite and flexible. The lines of separation are clear but not absolute, and such overlapping as occurs is normally viewed less as an occasion of conflict and rivalry than as an opportunity for cooperation and mutual stimulation. The least easily classified branches of theology might even profitably be dealt with by each of the four departments in turn. Whether or not this is done, a very high degree of interdependence must be acknowledged.

Concentricity is the most suitable word for the relation between one form of theological study and another. Wherever we are in the time-swept domain of theology, God is, so to speak, the magnetic pole towards which all indicators point. We are closest to the pole in theology proper, because God is the immediate object of interest and a review of His deeds and His utterances, if it is not misleading to say so, has, from our angle of vision, no more than an incidental importance. Still, a destination implies travel, and our road is marked by those who have preceded us. Notwithstanding the supremacy of pure theology, we invert the historical course of revelation if we try to see what God is before we know what He does. We begin, accordingly, with the tale of His chosen society, an account contained partly in Scripture and partly in church history, and when we have fathomed this narrative and mastered the involutions of law, prophecy, wisdom, and gospel we have something with respect to God to discuss. Not until we are no longer strangers to the God Who was once called Yahweh and is now known to us as the Father of our Lord Jesus Christ do we venture to urge Him, by the application of practical skills, on the people who need Him.

Our comprehensive observations have reached the place where they must be either broken off abruptly or reduced to the form of a digest of the seminary curriculum. We prefer the former alternative. We shall learn soon enough how to distinguish between polemics (for which, please God, we shall have little use) and apologetics and why Christian ethics and moral theology are handled as separate disciplines. Someday our views about what should be taught in seminaries will be as sound as anybody's, and we shall attain that degree of critical acumen the more rapidly the more often we recollect that the theological student works his way through three stages of mastery. In which stage he is at a given moment an intelligently designed course in theology will make abundantly plain to him. Ordinarily he spends the Junior year in being indoctrinated, the Middle year in correlating his constantly increasing capital of facts and ideas and coordinating his development in the several disciplines, and the Senior year in cultivating the field in which he has elected to specialize. The comprehensive examinations are a verdict on what he has accomplished in the first and second stages, and if this ordeal discloses a glaring weakness indicative of subnormal capacity or wanton negligence, his future in specialization is alarmingly dubious. He then finds himself contemplating an intellectual problem that has grave moral and spiritual aspects.

The most secure way of averting such a disaster is to reconcile oneself at the outset to the necessity of severe, self-imposed regimentation in all intellectual activities. The man who ends up with an A in the comprehensives is the man who two years before set in motion, and found out how to maintain, a regulated interplay of at least six factors: intelligence, interest, industry, method, practice, and guidance. The knowledge that stays with us through a lifetime has been assimilated and accepted by every part of us. What the brain has mastered produces no sustained action until it has been learned again and again and again in the remote, dark corners of our being that are the real determinants of our behavior. Distinguished teaching satisfies us because it is compellingly genuine, and it is compellingly genuine because it is the utterance of a complete man, whose entire personality has participated in the gigantic operation of sharpening, polishing, perfecting, and finally harmonizing the insights of the mind, the perceptions of the emotions, and the discoveries of the will. The dilettante is the victim of a fickle interest that is impatient of method. The plodder tries to make industry do duty for the intelligence that has been denied him. The gifted man relies on his wits to give him the appearance of a skill he is too lazy to acquire by practice. The self-willed student persists in his errors because he disdains guidance. How can each of these helps serve us?

Exceptional intelligence must be allied with equally exceptional simplicity if its possessor is to employ it constructively in the priesthood, and by simplicity we mean largely the recognition of intellectual power as one of God's most generous gifts. It is no disparagement of seminarians to say that most of them have little reason to fear the perils that go with an excess of intelligence. On the contrary, the tempests of discontent that sweep through a seminary several times a year are usually, in their beginnings, mass frustrations of intelligence. We suspect that we are simply not bright enough to reason our way out of the jungle of problems, difficulties, and doubts into which the faculty has led us, only to abandon us to our own devices. Actually, in harboring this suspicion we are doing ourselves an injustice. We have, in reality, ample intelligence to meet all ordinary intellectual emergencies, and the predicament we are in will compel us to exercise it, unless we succumb to panic. If the experience reveals a deficiency of mental force, we need not conclude that our inadequacy is beyond remedy. Few men are dropped from seminary solely because they are stupid. If we seem to have been slighted in the distribution of intellectual gifts, our ability to make capital of our limitations offers us an escape from a despairing surrender to our inferiority. God bestows upon one man genius without patience and upon another man patience without genius. The relative achievements of the two are often surprising.

Our intelligence may disappoint us, but our interest in theology, if God has destined us for the priesthood, is never exhausted. The absence of a vigorous, untiring interest, embracing all aspects of theology though perhaps preferring one to another, renders a supposed vocation disturbingly questionable. The few men who shrink in boredom from the reading and cogitation on which a priest's teaching depends for much of its power ought to consider whether or not they are headed in the right direction. Almost to a man we have an invincible interest in the science God has chosen for us. What are we to do with this attraction, which at its best is a blend of the natural and the supernatural? How are we to harness it?

A suggestion on which we willingly act if we can comes to us in a sound piece of folk wisdom: Strike while the iron is hot. At certain moments we respond with spontaneous eagerness to the allure of unsolved problems. The inmates of religious houses are sometimes called upon to make these impulses objects of mortification. The austerity that sanctifies a monk may ruin a seminarian. The consuming appetite we suddenly have for this book or that intellectual project may never grip us again.

If we reject it, we decline a gift God wants us to accept and utilize. It is a poor timetable that keeps us so intent upon routine that we cannot yield to a powerful and promising interest. The best reports, sermons, and term papers are dashed off in a heat of concentration and corrected after the writer's return to normality. Admittedly we cannot work in this fashion at all times, and undoubtedly it would be disastrous to stand idle, waiting for inspiration to descend upon us. A mild interest, reinforced with a determination to perform our duty, will enable us to deal competently with routine assignments. When even this fails, we need to rest or think about something else. No sensible man will remain at his books when application brings an ever-diminishing return.

Our days will be neither too full nor too empty if we adhere to a schedule of working hours. Other people are bound to benches and desks for a fixed amount of time, and the fact that our lives are not wholly subject to the tyranny of whistles and clocks does not release us from the obligation to observe a predetermined order in the use to which we put the hours, days, and weeks of the school year. Industry may deprive us of an occasional pleasure, but it makes amends by protecting us from periodical overwork, with the happy consequence that we complete our labors calmly, unhurriedly, and comfortably in advance of the deadline. Our rule must provide a margin for illness and unforeseen interruptions, and the best way to defend oneself against the unexpected is to follow a plan that is several days ahead of the schedule. Anxiety has its physical concomitants. It is practically every time the unorganized and therefore distracted and often hard-pressed seminarian who has trouble in maintaining his health and alertness.

Industry, nevertheless, cannot operate alone. It has to be coupled with method. Problems that defy mere energy yield with gratifying submissiveness to a calculated attack. Analysis pierces the complexities with which we cannot deal and identifies the elements, which can be dealt with one by one. The correct analysis of a question will often, of itself, suggest the answer. There may be a multiplicity of answers. There may be no answer at all. There may be no problem. Analysis will, in any case, indicate the possibilities. When there is some prospect of achievement in further concern with the problem, we move forward to a criticism of the material under consideration. To a tiny knot of conservatives in every Junior class criticism means

the ruthlessly rationalistic study of the Bible, and in view of this we may as well employ Biblical criticism as an illustration. We shall try to keep the illustration from
growing into a long-winded digression.

If Biblical criticism terrifies us and appears to menace the simple faith of our child-
hood, we commit no sin in taking a long and careful look at it. We shall discover
that it is a branch of study, a discipline, a science. It has its laws, its techniques,
and its well-defined field of operation. A critic is a man of considerable special
knowledge who toils over the problems that can be solved by reason and is ready
to change his mind whenever reason gives him a reason for doing so. There is no
finality in the findings of Biblical criticism. The critic busies himself with questions of date, sequence, context, contact, cause, and effect, and his techniques and
standards are essentially the same in all historical and literary areas. The Bible is
literature, and there is no reason why it should be exempt from the application of
the methods that are pursued in the study of literatures not viewed as sacred. The
Bible contains history, and honesty requires us to examine its history as sharply as
we examine any purely secular record. What is the critic's procedure? He gathers all
the evidence he can find and chooses the explanation that most commends itself to
his intelligence–an intelligence sharpened by experience. The critic may be unable
to make a choice, and if he decides on a solution, the solution may be wrong. The
thing to observe is that he uses his reason. Even the fundamentalist is endowed with
reason, and if he thinks that the Bible is not subject to reason, he falls into two extremely perilous sins: he denies that God is reasonable and he denies that God has
a right to be worshipped with all the powers and faculties that man possesses. The
Bible is not a bloodless collection of dogmatic pronouncements. It is the work of
living men and women, each of them fallible after his or her own fashion. God does
not communicate with us by taking possession of the vocal organs of certain chosen
sages and prophets. Inspiration is not dictation. Scriptural truth comes to us by way
of human personalities. The redeeming certainties of religion are formulated for us,
not in the abstract, but by the human beings who experienced them in times that
lie far beyond the horizon of our own immediate knowledge. Every affirmation in
the Bible has its setting in time and space. Criticism strives to recapture that setting.
If a writer's words have been altered, it seeks to restore them to their original form,

and it finds the primary meaning of the original form in a concrete situation. The moment the Bible ceases to be our only textbook, we become critics—nay, we cannot read the Bible itself without comparing one part with another, and to do this is to criticize. Since criticism is required of us, let us come as close as we can to being professionals.

Having apprehended the constituents of a problem and scrutinized each of them with a critical eye, we turn to the work of synthesis. Ultimately everything we know must agree with everything else we know. Many of the present ligatures of knowledge are only provisional. A mind committed to the study of God works without weariness at unification, in which it sees the objective that God has set for man's reason. We aim at that serene, total grasp of creation in which we shall find the power to demonstrate that every apparent 'although' is really a 'because.' A useful Friday evening exercise is the threefold operation of sorting out, fitting together, and summing up the intellectual gains of the week. Conflicts cannot assume menacing proportions in a mind that takes stock of itself at the close of each round of learning.

We have mentioned planning more than once, and here we ought to view it for a moment against the background of method in general. The role it plays in actual study is scarcely a matter of debate, but we habitually overlook its protective power. The life of a scholar is necessarily a somewhat insulated one, and the seminarian will not get beyond the first step towards scholarship unless his life also is insulated. We should not permit people to take it for granted that they may occupy our time whenever they choose. Above and beyond our specific plans for getting things done there is the indispensable comprehensive plan that excludes many useless things from our lives, keeps our engagement books as empty as possible, and gives us the courage to deal firmly with the man who is bent on killing time and invites us to become his accomplices.

We expect our teachers to avail themselves of modern techniques in the exercise of their profession, and if the instruction we receive has not been laboriously and solicitously prepared for our consumption, we feel wronged. The instructor has a grievance at least equal to ours if we fail to employ a technique of assimilation. No engine–least of all the human brain–is perfectly efficient. Every day we dissipate quantities of our energy in unproductive effort. God has created engines according to His good pleasure: this one to race smoothly along the track of destiny and that one to chug and puff in immobile futility. Two things can be done for a poor engine. It needs, first of all, a radical overhauling that will check the loss of power in smoke and friction, and then, when its principal faults have been corrected so far as they can be, it will do its best only if a practiced hand is at the controls. Our failures in study stem from the clogged state–in rare cases, also from the unsound construction–of the machines with which we think or from our inexpert way of running them. A seminarian who is uneasy about the meagre amount of work he is getting done may be suffering from a lack of the requisite intelligence, from an inner difficulty that absorbs his vital forces, or from a quite ordinary ignorance of the steps to take in turning the unknown into the known. The ament has been admitted by mistake and must be invited to leave. For neurotics and psychotics psychiatric service is available. By far most of the men whose grades are not commensurate with the time they spend in study are laboring under nothing worse than a want of communicable craftsmanship. American genius delights in contriving increasingly economical ways of doing things, and the country abounds in experts who can teach us how to handle our minds without strain and without waste. The accomplishments we admire in readers of phenomenal intake and infallible memory, in linguists who quickly become skilled in the most outlandish tongues, and in note-takers who catch every word are, more than we suspect, matters of technique. This kind of professional knowledge is sold at a price, and while the purchase of it may impose mild hardship on students of slender means, the cost is negligible compared with the gain. The tendency to attach excessive importance to technical attainments can always be curbed by the reflection that technique alone does not make a theologian.

The fifth of our factors is ordinarily a potent incentive to seminarians. Academic instruction puts them to sleep. Practice wakes them up. The prospect of effectiveness in the practice of the ministry supports them through weary terms of attendance at exercises that sometimes seem designed solely to delay ordination. As a matter of fact, practice is not a pleasure that must be postponed for three years, but a duty that is binding from the outset. If by practice we mean the application of Christian truth, it is the daily business of the faithful, and we are doubly pledged to it, since the life we have embraced makes us simultaneously God's pupils and the teachers of His children. The plan of study under which we work provides for a broad variety of practice, all of it putting our theories to the most severe kind of proof. This, however, does not exhaust our experience of practice. In the prosaic sense of drill, practice has a claim on many of the hours we spend in the seminary. The manual and verbal disciplines of theology demand literally unceasing practice, and if, as our studies approach their close, we become aware that we are halting preachers, sloppy celebrants, and indifferent Grecians,[5] we shall be forced to recognize that we have not offered to God the toil and fatigue that would have made us all that we ought to be.

When learning and life are closely allied guidance is one of the chief avenues to knowledge. A little of the store we are now accumulating as students will have to be discarded. The bulk of it will be incorporated into the living design of a devoted priestly life. After ordination we shall go on learning, and the new knowledge will in part supplant the old. If any of our memories survives untarnished, it will be the recollection of the moments when the tension between teacher and taught was relaxed and guidance came to us in the ready understanding with which our confidences were welcomed. The impact of an idea may move us to spend an afternoon in the library. The touch of a personality may determine the tone and achievement of a whole life. A decent reserve keeps our teachers from offering us unsolicited help. If we can conquer our own diffidence, we shall find them happy to place their resources of thought and prayer at our disposal.

The theological student is a dedicated man, and as a dedicated man he spends three years in pursuit of the professional knowledge without which he cannot make a free and rewarding use of his ministry. He has a clear and not very remote objective. Before three full years have passed he will face his canonical examiners, and only the most unremitting application from the first day to the last will enable him to approach the ordeal with serene confidence. However, the instruction he receives in the seminary is not designed merely to prepare him for canonical examinations.

---

5. Klein's phrase "indifferent Grecians" is a reference to the seminarian's ability to use the Greek language and, therefore, limits their understanding of the New Testament.

When the Church finally puts the stamp of ordination upon him and sends him out to do its work, he will be fighting an intellectual battle. He will find that the faculty has not answered all possible questions for him in the seminary. His intellectual enterprise will then become perhaps the supremely decisive factor in his ministry. His teachers try to develop a high degree of intellectual enterprise in him while he is under their care, and they do it by putting the facts before him and encouraging him to attempt an interpretation. They urge upon him the cultivation of reason as part of his submission to the discipline of the Faith.

Chapter VI

It Appertaineth Not unto Thee

THE seminarian who studies his theology and says his prayers with an unmixed desire to serve and please God will presently become convinced that God is redeeming the world for him and making all things new. This is not auto-suggestion, for the wayward human will corrupts creation and there is, in sub-rational creatures, a beautiful natural purity to which the holiest human beings are acutely sensitive. As our attachment to God approaches the relative perfection of genuine unselfishness, the universe assumes a radiant freshness that reflects our interior purgation but exists apart from that purgation. We are granted the enjoyment of everything because we claim nothing. It is the sinner who is subjective. For him the world is discolored by his own envy and lust. He covets the possession, the management, the control, and the unbridled use of nature, in which he perversely beholds, not the manifest omnipotence of God, but the disorder of his own imperious appetites and affections. God has made nature harmonious and lovely in its vast obedience, and those who love God see it that way.

We shall go on seeing it that way if we attend to our own business, which is never of cosmic proportions. The world is full of matters that, whether taken singly or viewed collectively, are no affair of ours in the sense that we are under obligation to take action with regard to them. If something has to be done about them, God has selected others for the task. Somebody else's failure, in our eyes, to carry out the commission we think God has given him may indicate, not that God has transferred the responsibility to us, but that we have all along been mistaken concerning the other man's vocation and duty. May God deliver us from the estimable men and women who look upon themselves as His confidential trouble-shooters! The suggestions they volunteer are irrelevant, impertinent, and distinctly unhelpful, and the steps they take, on their own initiative and with headlong assurance, are uniformly ruinous. We must take care not to be numbered among the zealots who are perpetually occupied with other people's business to the complete neglect of their own. Here lurks a temptation that few seminarians wholly escape. We are defenseless in face of it if we do not know it for what it is.

The identification of this malady is one of the easiest tasks of a seasoned director of souls. He knows that an excessive and, in not a few instances, censorious interest in the behavior of others is characteristic of those who have only recently begun the serious practice of the Christian religion and are still somewhat dazzled and bewildered by the experience of conversion. For such persons the total subjugation of man's will to God's is the least palatable requirement of the faith they have embraced. They imagine that a perfunctory gesture of renunciation suffices, and, having made it, they blithely resume their former manner of life, with a few immaterial changes, and call it Christianity. In the early phases of our transformation into true and faithful likenesses of God's perfection we are simply too naive to recognize the reappearance of the natural selfishness with which even the most righteous men must contend until they reach the grave. The diseased will that is our unfortunate heritage reasserts itself with surpassing cleverness. It maintains its strength against indefatigable piety and, convincingly made up to look like something else, enlists our instincts in its service. This is the source of all our enthusiasm for the improvement of others, and so engrossed are we in the chastisement of our neighbor that our own faults flourish, undetected and uncorrected. Many a misguided movement of reform has originated in somebody's refusal to reform himself. This passion for remaking people, as though one were the Creator, belongs to spiritual adolescence. In priests it is detestable and insupportable. In seminarians a mild form of it is normal and tolerable, but the sooner we leave it behind, the better.

In truth, there is no essential difference, except perhaps one of temperament, between the man who is always pushing dubious causes and giving pointers to presidents, kings, and bishops and the man who keeps himself complacently happy by exposing his neighbor's deficiencies. Both these men are evading the duties God has allotted to them, and for every one of us the first of those duties is his interminable combat with a will that values its own gratification above every other achievement. Power is not given to men to glorify them: its purpose is to implement their loyalty to the ends set for them by the very constitution of the world God has made. We have the custody and use of wealth, but not the title to it. These considerations impart sense to the Christian practice of renunciation and the Christian virtue of detachment. When we speak of sacrifice we do not mean heartbreaking, crushing, inhuman self-denial: we mean simply getting rid of the things that stand in the way of an undistracted response to our vocation. When we speak of indifference we do not mean not being interested in what happens to us: the adoption of such an attitude would empty existence of the purpose that gives it coherence and direction. We have in mind rather a willingness to work with the means God furnishes and to remain where providence, which may look deceptively like accident, has placed us. The consecrated person, so far from fretting at the limitations of his vocation and nosing about in matters that God has committed to others, is absorbed in the labors that are properly his and, as a result, has no inclination to broaden his field of activity without a manifest command from God. He is either diligently exploiting the openings that present themselves or alertly and patiently waiting for fresh openings to become evident. He does not forsake his vocation and plunge into something else because he is momentarily thwarted. If that were a Christian line of conduct, most priests would desert their parishes. More often than not, a young priest realizes, soon after taking up a new work, that his people are fundamentally and well-nigh incorrigibly reluctant to accept and use him as a priest. Three courses are open to him in his disappointment. If he is a trimmer and a time-server, he will become what his people want him to be. If such things as self-development and "being true to oneself" represent the supreme values of his life, he will leave his stupid parishioners to their fate and look to his secular interests for solace. If he is that great rarity, a priest who is all priest, he will study to accomplish by prayer and example what God for the time being does not permit him to accomplish by actual ministrations. Look into the history of the faithful priest, and what do you find? He is not the aggressive seminarian of a few years ago, the brilliant malcontent, the iconoclast and faculty-baiter, the virtuoso who so enjoyed putting his teachers right that he never discovered what they really meant. The seminarian fulfills his vocation by minding his job, which is to lead a life that it is the job of others to plan for him with more attention to what the Church requires of him than to what he, at the moment, prefers. Here is a theme that admits of the most detailed elaboration.

The first of the things no seminarian need worry about is the curriculum. It may be stated categorically that no undergraduate theological student is a competent judge of what constitutes a proper course in theology. Until he has completed such a course, his opinions ought to be exceedingly tentative. He must be taught a variety of things before he can acquire the standards that will enable him to pronounce a just and valid verdict on a theological discipline or on the manner in which it is presented.

Frequently the value and significance of a subject are obscure at the time of study, only to be revealed in luminous clarity when we are at last in a position to make wide and discriminating comparisons. These obvious considerations do not deter the brash beginner, whose meagre attainments give him a cocksure-ness that is impressively absent from the attitude of riper theologians. He knows what the faculty ought to be teaching, but he rarely approaches the faculty with a modest suggestion. Instead, he harps persistently on the single string of his dissatisfaction and so keeps himself upset and stirs up others. Presently he has raised a veritable tidal wave of disaffection, and its destructive power is felt throughout the seminary. Of course, at a reunion years hence the culprit, reminiscing in the fatuous manner of old grads, will laughingly confess that he was wrong, but his long overdue regret will then avail nothing. Thoughtless complaints lead to grave mischief, and the calamitous effect of an academic upheaval is more permanent than the emotion to which such disturbances may commonly be attributed.

Occasionally, to be sure, a student in search of a grievance hits upon a serious weakness in the curriculum. If he will go quietly to the Dean and make courteous inquiry about the matter he will be surprised at what he hears. The Dean will assure him that the faculty has long been conscious of the fault in question and is applying all its resources to the quest for a remedy. Moreover, the real defects of the curriculum cause the faculty more concern, discomfort, and grief than its supposed imperfections cause the most unsympathetic student. If effective action were possible, the faculty would long since have taken it, and undergraduate enthusiasm is not likely to succeed where experienced skill has failed.

If students are quick to detect flaws in the curriculum of a school, they are even more keenly–and unnecessarily–alive to the inadequacies of its administration, its morale, and its discipline. In all of these matters their judgment far surpasses that of the authorities. The simple and cordial cooperation of the students will keep a school going satisfactorily in spite of the most slovenly administration, but mere conformity is too obvious a course for the subtle seminarian to follow. He finds greater delight in pointing out how badly the school is run, and then, of course, he can relax in the knowledge that it is absurd to support a poor system. The morale is his to maintain or break, and the surest way to break it is to whisper in everybody's ear that it is going to pieces. Control of the tongue has no match as a safeguard of morale. One's spirits are best kept up by being infrequently mentioned. And what of discipline? Here the elusive mean will remain forever beyond our grasp. The discipline of a school is always too severe for some, too lax for others, and just right for nobody. The ordinary seminarian finds this an altogether welcome state of affairs. Naturally, he reasons, if the school does not provide a suitable form of discipline one is not bound to practice any discipline at all. Give him a free hand, and he is very generous with his discipline. He knows that others need it far more than he does, and therefore, noble fellow that he is, he imposes it liberally on them and has virtually none left for himself.

God seems never to spare a body of undergraduates in theology the torment of enduring in their midst the student who voluntarily takes charge of everybody's piety and manners. Long before he is a priest he is a model of what, according to his inflexible convictions, a priest should be. Like an army officer whose scale of living anticipates his next promotion, he is perpetually one step ahead of himself. He never gets a theological education, because his devotion to the Breviary and to the spiritual direction of his fellow-students gives him no leisure for study. He distributes his unsought counsel impartially, whether it is appreciated or not, and every novel twist of ceremonial that has its brief day in the school can be traced to him. He knows precisely how everybody ought to pray and what everybody ought to wear, and in his opinion the faculty is deplorably sloppy. The only things he does not know are dogmatic theology, church history, the Old Testament, the New Testament, ethics, moral theology, practical theology, and his own limitations. He will become a priest without ever having been a seminarian. All through his life he will defeat himself by trying to do today what he will not be ready to do until to-morrow. Of him this may confidently be predicted: as soon as he is a priest he will buy himself a mitre and an episcopal ring, and whenever he grows tired of being a priest–a man of his type quickly becomes the victim of a monumental weariness–he will put them on and admire himself in secret.

Another error into which seminarians fall is a premature interest in the affairs of the Church. There are undeniably events and trends in ecclesiastical life that deserve all the intelligent attention we can give them, but no seminarian has time to follow all the little parochial doings that are reported in the church press, and the student who becomes an accomplished retailer of pious gossip will inevitably fail to become something more important. Even if we confine ourselves to broad issues, we should, while we are seminarians, be cautious about drawing fixed conclusions and taking sides. We are in the seminary, not to make decisions in great matters for which we have at present no responsibility, but to prepare ourselves to deal with great matters in future. The more we learn about principles while learning is our privileged occupation, the steadier our hands will be, later on, in the application of principles.

A seminarian engaged to perform a specific task in a parish must make a nice distinction between what is his business and what is not his business. The rector will usually issue explicit instructions, and the seminarian will expose himself to considerable unpleasantness if he does not observe them scrupulously. It is the rector, not the seminarian, who frames the parish program and takes the lead in its execution. A discreet seminarian can make himself inestimably helpful. Rash aggressiveness on the part of an assistant simply multiplies the rector's problems. The seminarian is employed neither as a consultant in pastoral methods nor as a political agent. If there are any strings to be pulled, it is not for the seminarian to pull them. The most harmless-looking string may be in reality a highly charged wire, and the seminarian who impetuously grasps it may get even a greater shock than he deserves. In every parish innumerable booby-traps await the meddling hand of the curious stranger. The seminarian who springs too many of them is a marked man before his career has clearly begun.

Minding our present business does not preclude an occasional sober thought about the business that will be ours in future. We want particularly to know what things are incompatible with that business. If surrender is demanded of us, we prefer to make it gradually. We come to the seminary with the customary personal equipment of educated young men: hobbies, favorite writers, developed aptitudes in athletics—in short an assorted lot of graces, preferences, and accomplishments rightly dear to us because they enable us to be ourselves. Many seminarians, besides, are not happy at the thought of saying farewell forever to their former professions. How much of all this must be laid aside permanently at ordination?

The question is settled partly by realism and honesty and partly by our ordination vows. A man of intelligence and good will can be trusted to reach the right conclusions without much assistance. The priesthood gives us dignity, honor, position, and influence far beyond our natural deserts. It also assures us, if we prove our competence, of all the support we really need for ourselves and our dependents. In material matters we are less subject to uncertainty and worry than the majority of our parishioners. Justice requires us to work at our task with devoted attention and undivided energy. The priesthood has priority over everything else. Surplus time, if we have it, may be used for any purpose that is not in conflict with our principal aim. However, the more zealous a priest is, the less vacant time he will have on his hands. Immoderate enthusiasts become so deeply immersed in the routine of the priesthood that their horizons contract and, in consequence, powers that were intended to be used generously and widely have only the most straitened outlet. Presently those powers will cease to have any outlet at all, for people do not welcome a pastor who sees in every person he meets, not a human being to be sanctified without any loss of humanity, but merely an actual or potential object of priestcraft. In a word, the priesthood must be patently and unmistakably our chief occupation, but we make it a vain occupation the moment we begin to regard it as our exclusive business, either in the sense that we are interested in nothing else or in the sense that the priesthood belongs to us alone. The best safeguard against crippling narrowness is a periodical review of theology. What is the purpose of the divine gifts we are authorized to dispense? Is it to impoverish life or to enrich it?

In the belief that it is good for us, so far as our vocation permits, to look and act like other people, the Church allows us marriage, discretion regarding our dress, ample latitude in recreation, and the freedom to select our reading without reference to an index of forbidden books. This by no means exhausts the catalogue of our liberties. External authority deals very gently with the Anglican clergy, and in all but a few cases the absence of compulsion is abundantly justified. The men who abuse the want of external restraint have not taken the trouble to understand and apply their ordination vows. When we receive the priesthood we undertake, among other things, to "be diligent in prayers, and in reading the Holy Scriptures, and in such studies as help to the knowledge of the same, laying aside the study of the world and the flesh."[1] Sincerity finds these words neither obscure nor ambiguous. They must have substantially the same meaning for all priests. The implementation of the promise is committed to the individual. Prayer gives us a fine sense of right and wrong with respect to our vocation. Priesthood, in one of its aspects, is personal attendance upon God, and one look at our Master's countenance should suffice to scatter all doubts as to how we stand in His sight. The intimacy and regularity of our service keep us in the divine presence, and when we have forfeited, or are in danger of forfeiting, God's confidence, we know well enough what has happened. Because our ministry is no longer single-minded, God is no longer pleased with us. Disloyalty has crept in, and until it is rooted out, trust will not be restored. "The world and the flesh" are comprehensive terms, not necessarily always of the same meaning to the same people, to say nothing of different people. If a list of things to avoid were substituted for the present broad promise to "lay aside the study of the world and the flesh," our religious practice might, it is true, become considerably more definite and uniform, but the closer definition of our duty would afford slender compensation for the loss of the opportunity for heroism that goes with the uncertainty now confronting us. We are given, as it were, a blank that each of us fills in according to his conscience. Whatever specific things we do or do not give up, the vow means for all of us unconditional self-abandonment. More precious to God than any particular surrender is our limitless readiness to enjoy or abstain at His command. We do not develop that willingness overnight, and therefore the

---

1. *The Ordinal*, Priests.

seminarian is well advised to ponder these matters before the necessity of action is thrust upon him. Again and again there will be unforeseen chances for the use of his gifts and attainments, and the question for him will always be: Does this opening constitute a hazard to my vocation?

For example, it is at all times desirable to bring the Faith to bear on man's economic pursuits, and there may be times when we cannot escape the obligation to do so. We cannot always be content with the enunciation of principles. Now, if a pastor finds his entire parish paralyzed by a ruinous strike, what is he to do? Should he make it his business to take aggressive action for the relief of his parishioners or, more broadly, for the reconciliation of the clashing interests of employer and employee? He should not act unless his parishioners want him to act, and they will not want him to act unless they know that he is qualified. In this and other recurrent conflicts between one group of human beings and another a priest who knows what he is doing may render priceless aid. Such struggles are not for the blundering amateur, and the priest who, despite his incompetence, elbows his way into an industrial argument has a better chance of uniting the disputants against himself than of settling the question at issue. Clearly a problem like this cannot be solved by the application of an invariable formula. Even the priest whose fitness to arbitrate is universally acknowledged will, in a given case, have to determine whether or not the role of economic peacemaker militates against the obligations of his priesthood. Perhaps the most inclusive observation we can make is that the special knowledge we possess has a claim to use, and, when our qualifications are unique, that claim may assume the character of a divine command. In practice, of course, a priest is almost never placed in the position of being the only person who can end the strike, save the state, or lead the army to victory. Priests who divide their time between their priesthood and economics, politics, education, business, or some other non-priestly employment must have an exceptionally sound reason for leading so difficult a life. Few can endure it very long, and in the end it is the deeper interest that prevails.

By virtue of his office a priest is an apologist constantly engaged in commending the Faith to non-Christians. He is also a resolute opponent of all error that is serious enough to do demonstrable harm to his fellow-Christians. These functions are undeniably his, and it would be cowardly not to exercise them at all, but to say this is not to assert that he is bound to exercise them on all possible occasions. In all cases, he should hold his peace until he has made a sympathetic examination of the false teaching he proposes to attack. This study may indicate that tact and forbearance will prove more potent than denunciation. We have no right to take it for granted that it is our business to raise our voices loudly on behalf of the Faith every time we encounter unbelief or heresy.

The culture of our time conditions us and our efforts. We must speak its idiom. We cannot disregard its tricks of thought. It is a human achievement, and we owe it respect and a certain prudent admiration. It is our business to master the media it offers us for the transmission of a faith that can be made compelling in any tongue. It is not our business to indulge ourselves recklessly in the amenities of an efficient but not conspicuously godly civilization. Human culture is at best a vehicle through which and a framework within which religion pursues its ends. The temper of the age is always in conflict with the imperative of Christ. Novels studied for their analysis of human behavior refined a celebrated English bishop's pastoral touch. Novels have been the opiate of many a disgruntled cleric. We utilize the techniques of civilization, but we do not permit it to dictate our standards. If we meet it with an established attitude, we shall be proof against its seductions. A Christian stand towards the culture of our day cannot be improvised under the pressure of actual contact. In the seminary we have time to assess the secular values by which our contemporaries live, and out of this unhurried criticism grows an intuitive fidelity to our mission, which is so often confused with the glamorous causes of this world. The 'indelible character' of the priesthood is an awful reality. It is important to preserve the external tokens of our dedication. It is more important to cherish and develop the dedication itself. When the time comes, we can put on the uniform of the priesthood in a few minutes. We cannot make a complete offering of ourselves to God on the spur of the moment. It is not too early to ponder the questions the Bishop will put to us on the day of our ordination. They became our concern on the day when God invited us to seek the priesthood.

CHAPTER VII

We Also Are Men

BELIEF in the humanity of the clergy has never been formally enjoined upon the faithful, and since all persons in holy orders were at one time laymen and the laity are presumably convinced of their own humanity, the Church might well be accused of putting itself to gratuitous trouble if it made explicit proclamation of the undeniable truth that its ministers are in all respects men. Nevertheless, a brief, direct pronouncement on the subject would serve a purpose. People, when they think about their clergy–and we need not flatter ourselves that they devote much time to this kind of cerebration–, grow sadly muddled. Some of them regard us as subhuman: they see in us a pallid breed, devoid of vigorous appetites and, as a result, well qualified for a life of unnatural virtue. Others hail us as superhuman and treat us with a reverence that embarrasses and sometimes horrifies us. Among those who admit that we are human there are two classes. The larger group is made up of frail human beings who enjoy being frail and are infinitely comforted at the discovery that the clergy share their foibles. It is useless, they tell themselves, for mere laymen to struggle against infirmities that defeat men of God. To the remaining handful we look for an understanding of our true character. They require their clergy to stand for a new humanity in Christ, and we offend them when we are human in the wrong way.

For many years after we make our submission to Christ–indeed, in a few unfortunate cases, throughout life–we cling to two irreconcilable conceptions of humanity and live in the hope of hitting on a working compromise between them. On the one hand, it seems to us exceedingly human to do things for the pleasure they give us (and therefore not to do them when they fail to yield delight), to crush, without sentimentality or scruple, the people who stand in our way, and to deal with such matters as illness and death only when we cannot side-step them–in short, to act upon the conviction that human life contains the ends for which it exists. On the other hand, we are motivated, sincerely if rather intermittently, by the belief that human life reaches its final fruition in God. If we are worn out with trying to be Christians, it is because we are squandering all our ingenuity on the futile task of making these two principles appear to function together. We deceive nobody, except perhaps our gullible selves. The false fervor, the preoccupation, the fatigue, and the anxiety that betray our worldliness make it evident to all who watch us that we are being torn and broken by a double allegiance. A prophet with one eye on his temporal welfare is only mildly convincing. Everybody is afraid that, in a crisis, he will decide for the lower, more immediate loyalty, as far too many prophets have. Such a man talks frequently of 'legitimate ambition,' 'a sane and normal life,' and 'avoiding extremes,' and we do him more than justice when we say that he works at least as much for his own advantage as for the love and glory of God. People who turn to him for help are disappointed to find that something vital is missing.

This vacillation is irrefragable proof of the helplessness of unregenerate man. We are neither angels nor brutes. With each of these orders of creation we have real affinities, but we do not bring our humanity to perfection by pretending either that we are all spirit or that we are all flesh. Nevertheless, a man left to his own resources will gravitate towards one of these false views of himself. If he does not, though lacking the properties of the angels, deny his body and attempt to live like a wholly spiritual being, he repudiates the spiritual element of his nature and tries to be a mere animal, despite his inability to pursue the purely physical existence that in beasts is a dignified and beautiful thing because they possess an innocence and an instinctual sureness that can never belong to man. In fact, the only thing that makes us genuinely human is association with the divine. Only in fellowship with God can we learn what He intended us to be when He made us. Only in reliance on Him can we remain faithful to that knowledge. As Christians we first become aware of what it means to be a man.

Our spiritual security demands that we refuse for ourselves all honors that belong properly and exclusively to the God we represent. We must be firm, and at times brutal, with the foolish souls that will not listen to any teaching but ours. Admiration turns easily into adoration. An absolutely unique mediator of grace and knowledge becomes, in effect, a rival divinity. A person who can reach God only through a particular clergyman is in dire peril and puts the clergyman in dire peril. Such an attitude, inasmuch as it is tantamount to a denial of God's sovereignty, must be condemned as the most vicious form of false worship. It is not enough to refrain from encouraging it. Even to tolerate it is a grievous sin. Whatever the consequences to them or to us, we must, if necessary, roar at people again and again that we are nothing but men, and if we unfeignedly believe what we are saying we shall eventually make our point. We need have no patience with the perverted loyalty that would convert the parish into a local high-place and the rector into a local Baal. The salutes, the reverences, the privileges, the titles, and the applause that are showered upon us so lavishly should be inspired, not by the men we are, but by the God Who has chosen us. Every seminarian will do well to watch, candidly and without morbidity, his reactions to immoderate praise. If he accepts it eagerly and neglects to pass it on to God, he is preparing for himself a defeat that will overtake him at some unpredictable point in his ministry. An apostate forsakes his God because he has always, at bottom, been his own god. Our power as priests depends on our ability to remember the difference between our humanity and God's divinity.

A priest's vocation does not dissolve the ordinary ties in which he is involved by the simple fact of his humanity. Moreover, since he continues to be human, he is permitted to contract such new ties as promise to further his vocation. What the Church allows us we may take simply, humbly, and without shame, if we are convinced that we need it. If we do not avail ourselves of the Church's generosity, our self-denial gives us no right to hold others to our severe standards. A sober consideration of these elementary truths would soon silence the debate between celibates and non-celibates. The only sound reason any of us can have for not getting married is the inner certainty that marriage would impair the quality of his priestly service. It undoubtedly has that effect on some people, and they do well to avoid it, but they must not suppose that the seemingly austere form their vocation has assumed confers on them any manner of preferred status. Holy matrimony, as every genuine celibate knows, is not an ignoble surrender to the flesh. A priest's marriage is justified solely by the prospect of increased holiness and usefulness for him in the state of life he has elected to embrace: in the quaint language of Article XXXII, "it is lawful for [bishops, priests, and deacons], as for all other Christian men, to marry at their own discretion, as they shall judge the same to serve better to godliness." Certainly this motive is not inferior to the celibate's. What, then, is the argument about?

If a priest can serve Christ acceptably by following, for His sake and to His glory, the ordinary patterns of life, he is also free—always, it must be understood, in obedience to Christ—to deviate very widely from the norm. We affirm, in recognition of the wonder of our own daily growth and in defense of God's omnipotence, that there is boundless sanctifying power in everyday things. This assertion must not be permitted to upset the equilibrium of Christian truth. We must declare, with equal conviction, that a few extraordinary Christians gain holiness by their renunciation of the things that are the principal and normal means of sanctity to most Christians. The exceptional vocation is neither less human nor less divine than the common call. One of the least excusable faults of Anglicanism is its reluctance to do justice to unusual vocations. Behind the reluctance is a suspicion that needlessly questions many a manifest act of the Holy Spirit. Perhaps this accounts as well as anything else for the curious blindness that enables many Anglicans to regard themselves as models of sane spirituality when in fact they exhibit nothing but a prudent mediocrity.

At the risk of seeming to dwell interminably on a matter to which we cannot yield the supreme place in our lives, we venture to subject marriage to further examination, since, as the most intimate and tender, and therefore the most perilous, union that two human beings can contract, it leads us very directly to an understanding of social ties in general. Four attitudes towards marriage are represented in the typical body of theological undergraduates. First of all come those who, while fairly certain that they will eventually marry, have not as yet selected the girl. Next we must consider the men who retreat as far from marriage as possible. Then we shall discuss the unduly eager, who are inclined to plunge prematurely into matrimony. Finally, there is the currently large class of those who are married when they enter the seminary.

The first type of man is in danger of being too casual about a question that should never be left to chance. He has probably not bestowed adequate thought upon an alternative to matrimony. He is disposed to relax and allow nature and circumstances to solve the problem for him. He looks upon marriage as vaguely inevitable and has no clear ideas about the sort of woman he ought to marry. He is, of course, eminently eligible and will grow more so right up to middle age. If he has difficulty in making up his mind, several women stand ready to relieve him of the responsibility. Unless he is very circumspect–and by definition he is not–he will drift unawares into a position that has hideous possibilities. It may turn into what was called, two or three generations ago, a "sinful attachment": this has happened to seminarians and to priests. It may issue in something only slightly less calamitous: long years of frustration in the company of a wife who recognizes no bounds in her claims upon him. Sorrow is in store for the lighthearted youth who does not look far, far ahead.

If some men are content to allow things to take their course, others, sometimes even before they begin their theological studies, are under the impression that they have rejected marriage. Seldom is the question completely settled, though the student, in his enthusiasm, may be entirely certain that it is. A mind made up too early is not likely to stay made up. Admiration for celibacy in the abstract or for the courageous Christians who have chosen it under divine guidance is not identical with a vocation to celibacy. For every genuine vocation there are scores of merely romantic and emotional attractions. If our interest in celibacy is of the latter sort, it will soon wear itself out, but not before it has worn out some of our closest friends. The militant promoter of celibacy is the most pestilent kind of bore. He puts his faith in a scheme of life and forgets the God Who sustains, not schemes of life, but human beings. The artificiality and unreality so evident in his views are strikingly absent from the thought, speech, and conduct of a person who is really called to live unmarried for God's sake. If a man suspects that he has the celibate's vocation, let him say little about it and, after his ordination, put it to the proof in a religious order or under the supervision of a qualified director. Occasionally a seminarian tries to close the question by taking a vow of celibacy. This he must do, of course, in secret, for no confessor in his senses would lend it his approval. Although such vows are of dubious validity, one can never be sure that they are totally invalid. To what extent they bind the conscience nobody is really competent to say. A seminarian who makes God a promise and subsequently discovers that he is incapable of fulfilling it will always be uneasy about his broken word. It is therefore better to take no irrevocable action during one's seminary days.

Here, as usefully as elsewhere, we may deal with the restive, and often impetuous, seminarian who makes a grievance of any official restriction his school may place upon his freedom to marry. Where such control exists it is designed to protect both the institution and the student. Before it can grant the student permission to marry, the school must satisfy itself that there is no possibility of its being called upon to maintain an impecunious couple. Far more serious than this is its obligation to safeguard the student's future happiness and usefulness by making certain that the proposed match manifests substantial promise of becoming all that a Christian marriage should be. Unless its rules absolutely prohibit a student's marriage before the completion of his course, the seminary will commonly give the desired leave if the marriage is not open to objection on economic or spiritual grounds. The unsettled student who expects marriage to provide escape, refuge, or release and imagines that it will, in some magical fashion, impart stability to an undisciplined and confused life should be curbed before he assumes responsibilities that are more likely to aggravate than to relieve his distress. Stable persons make stable marriages, and wedlock is a hazardous undertaking for those who have not gained a high degree of self-mastery. For Christians there can be no irresistible desires. The man who feels that he must be married at once is merely proving that he is not yet capable of marriage as the Church defines it.

The married student has established himself as a permanent and valuable type of seminarian, and the esteem he enjoys has been earned very largely by his wife, who, self-effacingly accepting the restraints and even hardships imposed upon her by her husband's call, has so devotedly identified herself with his interests that she has contributed incalculably to the confidence and power with which he exercises his vocation. The exquisite tact and mature spirituality displayed by the majority of these young women accentuate the failures and rifts that sometimes occur in the lives of seminary couples. A man who aspires to the priesthood can make no headway against his wife's invincible opposition, and if she cannot be prevailed upon to alter her attitude, he must yield to her claims, which have the divine authority of holy matrimony behind them. She has much to answer for if her selfishness robs the priesthood of a promising recruit, but it seems better, in such cases, to preserve the marriage, which is clearly in possession, than to allow it to be overridden by a supposed call to which an unreserved response cannot be made without the woman's consent. While a matter of this sort should be, and usually is, settled before the student enters the seminary, neither pride nor shame may, at a later time, be permitted to stand in the way of a decision against the priesthood, if it becomes evident that there is no practicable alternative to this bitter and seemingly tragic sacrifice.

Happily most married men who reach the seminary at all are there because their wives have undertaken to stand steadfastly by them during the difficult years of training. No product of grace is more impressive than a marriage that is in truth a potent and creative concord of two wills united in the pursuit of natural and supernatural ends. When husband and wife belong to each other in this fashion they are wholly God's and there is nothing they need despair of accomplishing in His service. A Christian family is a little world of grace, and the life to which it is dedicated is the germ of the divine kingdom for which we all labor. No matter how sincere and eloquent a priest's admonitions may be, they do not compare in sheer instructive force with the demonstration of fortitude and love he gives his people in his own family life. His home must be a triumphant proof of the reality and practicability of the things he preaches. All who enter his house should sense at once that it is the abode of something more Christian than complacent, uninspiring domesticity. The process that transforms an ordinary household into a compelling example of what Christian marriage and parenthood can be must begin the moment the family comes into existence. Married seminarians frequently live under distracting conditions, and the pressure of innumerable chores gives them little leisure for the relaxed cultivation of fireside pleasures, but no schedule is so loaded with other obligations that it leaves no time for family prayer, and no quarters are too crowded to be a school of forbearance and consideration. The head of a Christian household is a priest and a pastor to his dependents, and we do not lay aside this office when we become priests and pastors to the whole flock of Christ. Rather, since the old priesthood is enlarged by the new, we are more strongly bound after ordination to minister to our own flesh and blood, and we should all be aware that our priestly vocation undergoes its gravest trials and achieves its most brilliant victories in the sphere of our family life. The married seminarian has, for the present, only the narrower priesthood, but he has also the chance to use it patiently and fruitfully and thus to show the Church that it can confidently entrust to him the wider powers of the office he seeks.

It would be absurd, of course, to view Christian society as a mere federation of Christian kinship units, but it remains indisputably true that the vital fellowship of Christ, which is the Christian life, expands by the extension of hallowed family loyalties to persons who do not, according to the flesh, belong to the family and whom, in consequence, we cannot treat as brothers until we have transcended the natural limitations of family and clan and converted these institutions into agencies of adoption that function, no longer purely to maintain and protect themselves, but much more to gather all men into the brotherhood of salvation. Natural associations are safe for those who utilize them in this manner. Like other men, we marry, beget children, deny ourselves to feed, clothe, and teach them, keep in touch with our relatives, cling to our friends, and, in general, prize the values that underlie a rational human life, but, whereas other men are disenchanted and embittered by the failure and decay of these things, we attain, through the same experiences, to an assurance that surpasses the solace of earthly love. The most human of all men is he who explains humanity to itself. In the deceptive light of a self-contained society, man, though everybody he meets reflects all his essentials, remains incomprehensible to himself. He fathoms the arcanum of his nature only when he contemplates the image of himself as he once was and, by his own choice, may again be. Words are of no service to him: he must behold the concrete actuality in a creature of his own sort refashioned by grace, yet still demonstrably and comfortingly human; and precisely this, and no caricature of it, a man ought to encounter in the priests who pass his way. It is our fault if he does not recognize it. Mannerisms can distort it; poses can hide it; self-indulgence can dim it; pride of place can conceal it; vulgar familiarity can obscure it. We shall have to be on our guard lest by our carriage, our accent, our dress, our habits, our prejudices, our learning, or our wealth we become aliens to our people. If our purpose is to be disastrously, calamitously, and fatally human, we can realize it very easily by putting birth, fortune, education, or some other accidental thing before our priesthood. This is not what our people mean when they praise us for being human: they mean that we make their sorrows and difficulties our own, glory in their virtues, and repent for their sins. They respect our humanity when we share their troubles generously and their pleasures discreetly. They expect to see in us some gleam of the Word made flesh, some promise of a perfection that their secular leaders cannot give them.

Chapter VIII

Sin Lieth at the Door

IDEALLY, sin has in every priest a watchful, indefatigable adversary, never caught off his guard by a sudden hostile movement and always prepared with counter-measures. The office for which we are in training may be relied upon to furnish us abundantly with arms and armor, but none of the equipment God issues to us is foolproof, and ordination will not deprive us of the liberty to mishandle, by ignorance, stupidity, or slackness, the weapons and safety devices placed at our disposal. Moreover, in the Christian service rank enjoys no absolute immunities, and the loftiest brass may occasionally find itself entangled in the closest combat. No position is more curious than ours, for in the very act of leading our commands to victory we may suffer a secret personal defeat. We have at least three types of struggles to coordinate: the corporate struggle of the Christian group committed to our keeping, the separate struggles of our penitents and other persons whom we advise, and our own struggle, which tries us with special difficulties. It is primarily the last of these efforts that will engage our attention here, and yet we cannot ignore the others. While for divinity students as distinct from priests they still lie ahead, we already have the priestly outlook, and therefore it is clear to us that in our war with sin we are both objects and, by God's favor, agents, of redemption.

We cannot fail to observe, even before we are priests, that the priesthood bestows upon us a priceless blessing simply by making the conflict with sin easier, in certain respects, for us than it is for unordained Christians. We are powerfully upheld by unmistakable indications that our people expect us to prevail over sin. To push the matter down to the lowest possible plane, the certainty of irreparable ruin as the result of a serious lapse puts a curb upon the most self-seeking priest. Happily, few of us need to consider the question at that level. It is generally true of the clergy that they are decent enough to respond to the generous trust that demands high spiritual attainment of them. If they had no positive inducements to virtue, their reluctance to disillusion their people would, of itself, provide no small degree of protection. Justice alone would forbid a betrayal of those who take our goodness for granted. Our tendency to become what people think we are may owe more to nature than to grace, but we should not, on that account, undervalue it. In our more carnal moments we may have to use it as our last defense.

Another safeguard is our perpetual occupation with holy things. This intimacy becomes unbearable to those who are not themselves holy. We spend the bulk of the day in the performance of priestly labors, many of them sacramental acts. We write sermons, read theology, and say our offices. We visit people for the express purpose of talking to them about God, and seldom do we return from such a call without the feeling that the Holy One has purified our utterance. If we are conscious of what we are doing, the willful violation of the holiness that touches us in so many ways must become for us a constantly receding possibility. We simply cannot be false to the things we cherish, the things that constitute our life. We either resist or absorb the holiness that surrounds us, and if we resist it, we cannot long abide its presence.

Then, too, we know sin precisely and extensively, and the frequent sight of its devious malice should sharpen the sense by which we detect and reject those delicate degrees of evil that flourish unrestrained because they are normally unobserved. The uninstructed can sincerely say of many an act that they do not know whether it is sinful or not. Experience and study give us a nice judgment in these matters, and, save when we are confronted with one of the heartbreaking dilemmas that sometimes occur, we do not have to think laboriously before pronouncing a given act bad or good. The indications of sin that are invisible to the amateur in morals are plain to us. This is not the limit of our discernment: we pierce the confusion of human behavior and penetrate to the unacknowledged drives and loyalties from which conduct springs. We can do more than identify a sin: we can give its life history. Hence, if we have any illusions about ourselves, they must be deliberately cultivated. We are as open to the incursions of sin as anybody else is, but we have resources that are denied to the ordinary combatant. We often hear the furtive footfall of sin; we catch its foul scent on the wind; we drive it away from those who, unsuspecting, are about to become its victims. To us sin betrays its omnipresence, since vigilance on behalf of God's people is our duty. This being so, when we fall we cannot protest that we have been surprised.

Notwithstanding our debt to the sobering influences of habit and environment, we are not interested in deterrents as such. We have many, and it is both comforting and a little humiliating to consider how liberally God has provided them, but we are not long in making the discovery that rectitude rather than sanctity is the condition to which they lead. It is a precarious virtue that is based upon nothing more substantial than a man's regard for his health, his credit, his earning power, his good name, and his professional standing. One can be conspicuously upright and still yield with astounding readiness to the pull of a desire that momentarily makes all self-mastery seem pointless. Persistence in the belief that we are born with sovereign authority over our own being nullifies any advantages we may possess. This wrong-headed attachment to the illusion of our independence is the primal sin, the archetype of sin, the common father of all sins, the essential sin of which every conceivable act of sin is fundamentally a modification or variation. Therefore our need of regeneration is deeper than our need for any gift, benefit, or privilege in the war with sin. The priest is preeminently a recreated man. At our conversion we relinquish our fancied rights, and from that moment on we are hampered by no preconceptions about what ought to happen to us in this world. We are so lost in God that sin cannot find us, and if from time to time we are frightened by its shadow and alarmed at its nearness, we have only to recall that it cannot enter the Presence in which we dwell. We live on God's bounty, and a thankful joy in that abundance precludes covetousness, envy, and theft. Our honor is a reflected honor, and it cannot make us proud, for we exist to mirror God's perfection. We convey God's love to our fellow-creatures: how, then, can we hurt them? Our lapses prove, not that temptation is irresistible nor that we are worse than other men, but that our conversion is incomplete. We need not feel defeated: there are many ways of completing it. They will become evident as we grasp what theology means by certain words that, on the lips of careless thinkers, lend themselves to arbitrary and misleading uses.

For example, we can spare ourselves much unprofitable anguish and a considerable amount of futile toil by learning once and for all the difference between temptation and sin. Every seminarian is capable of distinguishing between them on paper, and we are all so sure of our soundness on this point that we resent a reintroduction of the subject, but how firmly has the sub-rational part of us apprehended the difference? Each of us harbors an unreclaimed self that detests travail, conflict, and effort far more vigorously than it yearns for the peace promised to those who endure these things. We meet many Christians who profess Christianity for the sake of the calm they hope to get from it, and we ourselves may well deserve to be numbered with them. To persons of this mind temptation is an impertinence, and under its pressure they take an increasingly tolerant view of sin. They prefer the trivial certainties of a shielded life–and a shielded life always entails a compromise with sin–to the boundless pain of temptation. Our reluctance to suffer blurs the distinct line we must overstep in our transition from temptation to sin, and when we are no longer sure which side of the line we are on, the relief of a discreet concession to sin seems better than the intolerable bewilderment in which resistance involves us. The Devil is an experienced horse trader, as the downfall of countless harassed and fatigued Christians has proved. At no time is he unwilling to negotiate a settlement that appears to be much to his disadvantage. He is patient and does not mind waiting a long time to collect his gains. His analysis of our predicament is very plausible. God, he points out, has not made Himself quite clear about this matter of sin. He has commanded us not to sin and at the same time has denied us an infinite capacity to stand up under temptation. Either He is monstrously cruel or He is playing a kind of joke on us to see whether we are bright enough to get the point. It would be an affront to Him to believe that He is our inferior in sympathy and broad-mindedness. This possibility eliminated, we are free to recognize that His requirements are less grim than we in our simplicity have hitherto assumed. We may now venture to entertain the thought of a little arrangement with the Prince of Darkness. In return for free access to us on stated occasions, he will undertake not to challenge God's right to our devotion the rest of the time. We are going to sin in any case, and it is silly not to do it with an unagitated conscience. Perhaps we are not quite stupid enough to accept that argument. In a flash we are confronted with another. Some sin that we long ago dismissed as forgiven is summoned back from oblivion to torment us, and it is suggested to us that God has put us on His black list, from which no amount of repentance can remove us. Perdition is our destiny, either because our sins are too bad for pardon or because God has never had any other intention with regard to us. God has disowned us. We may as well console ourselves with a few sins. The indulgent God Who figured so prominently in the eloquent logic we were listening to a moment ago has, most curiously, become incredibly brutal. Again, we refuse the lie. Thus far we have been treated with gentle urbanity. Swiftly a change occurs, and before we can collect our shocked wits, the Supreme Hater plunges us into the most excruciating temptation. All we can do is to cry, "I won't, I won't," and each time we say it we despair of our power to hold out any longer. Then we hear the voice, intimate, sorry for us, worried about us: "You are going to break if you go on this way: no human being can stand it. Nobody has ever been subjected to such torture before. You have been very brave. Now give up. The time comes when a man must think of himself. Suppose you go crazy or have a nervous breakdown. You say that is of no importance, and you are wrong, but, of course, one knows how idiotic good people can be about these matters. I am only trying to help you, and if you weren't so muddled up, you would thank me for telling you the truth. While we are talking about truth, you may as well have the real thing, since apparently nothing else will make you change your mind. Here it is, if you can take it: You are continuing a battle that is already lost. You have never felt so dirty in your life. You have the best of reasons for feeling as you do. You have never been so dirty in your life. Could you feel so empty of volition, purpose, interest, confidence, fortitude, and all the rest, if you were still merely being tempted? The saints, they tell me, have a very different feeling. This proves that you have sinned, and–there can't be any question about it–nothing can make you guiltier than you are. This is the kind of reward you get from God. Now, from me you would get justice." These things seem mad as we read them. Actually, they are appreciably more rational than many of the thoughts that dart or float through our minds even in the course of a few uneventful hours. A sound and active mentality drives this evil nonsense away with laughter and suffers no harm. Grief, boredom, discouragement, fright, worry, shame, and similar states and moods increase our vulnerability. During periods of crisis we find out just how well we have assimilated the Christian faith, particularly the portion of it that explains temptation and sin to us and shows us how simple a matter it is for a Christian man to tell them apart, unless he permits his glands, rather than his intelligence, to make his decisions for him. Any mischief is possible if we assent to the manifest falsehood that sin can be forced upon us. If we repudiate this untruth and abhor sin as God abhors it, we shall be absolutely safe.

A life controlled by these considerations and regularly offered to God will be practically free of serious transgression. Prudence compels us to insert the adverb. The time never comes when any of us may presume to say, "I can no longer sin."[1] Our emancipation will not be complete until we are beyond time. Time is the element of growth and decay, and all the while we tarry in it we are capable of losing what we have gained. We cannot climb to a certain eminence of sanctity and settle down there for the rest of our lives. We cannot live indefinitely on accumulated goodness. We thrive on effort, and that is why temptation is indispensable to our interior soundness. The stimulating prick of temptation exercises our inner powers and so conserves and increases them. We go on being weak and unwary long after we have ceased to be actively wicked, and the injury done to our wills by the sins of our careless years is not necessarily healed when those sins are remitted. Temptation springs largely from what we have been, and we are beholden to it for a knowledge of what we are. Its severity is principally our fault. Its existence is a priceless blessing.

Some of our temptations are universal. Others are confined to the priesthood. The latter overcome us by slow infiltration. Sacerdotalism, institutionalism, sacramentalism, and paternalism—pompous words for pompous sins!—Are habits into which we drift more than misdeeds we deliberately commit. They are four not materially different ways of converting an approach to God into an object of worship. They halt us far short of our destination by the artful device of making us believe that we have arrived. The high rate of success in the application of these tactics bears witness to the determined cunning behind them.

It is solemnly believed, in certain fortunately narrow clerical circles, that the Christian religion was founded in order to provide a setting for the priesthood. This is sacerdotalism. Sacerdotalism is so gross an overvaluation of the priesthood that it

---

1. "After we have received the Holy Ghost, we may depart from grace given, and fall into sin, and by the grace of God we may arise again, and amend our lives. **And therefore they are to be condemned, which say, they can no more sin** as long as they live here, or deny the place of forgiveness to such as truly repent." (*Article XVI*)

cannot help being a dangerous undervaluation of everything else. Where it prevails familiar things suffer a remarkable change. Faith is esteemed primarily for its power to make men tip their hats to the clergy. Hope is the expectation that the astute practice of politics will bear fruit in preferment. Charity is the naive tolerance that enables the laity to overlook the flagrant faults of their pastors. A preference for vocal prayer is a conspicuous mark of sacerdotalism. Perhaps the best thing that can be said for prayer (we are now listening to the voice of the sacerdotalist) is that it gives us a reason for putting on ecclesiastical vestments. Congregations are so tiresome with their perpetual complaints about the inaudibility of the services. They can see the vestments. Why should they expect to hear all the prayers? Has nobody told them that we aim at a mystical mumble because we know that it is vastly more productive of devotion than plain words plainly spoken ever could be? If they are so bent on praying, we suggest that they share with us the burden of reciting the Breviary. Let us at least show them how hard we have to work. They will find it profoundly edifying, when they drop in to say their prayers before the Blessed Sacrament, to see us, breviary in hand, doffing and donning our birettas and emitting a gentle susurration as we perform the least inspiring of our sacerdotal chores. We must not, however, always read our offices indoors. The best use to which we can put a fair day is to whip out the old breviary and, happily absorbed in it, pace up and down in front of the rectory. The whole neighborhood is edified at the sight. That will do for prayer. Fasting can be disposed of even more quickly. It is an old-fashioned custom that the Pope will probably abolish when he has completed the Creed, but, since it is a part of the Catholic religion, we have to recommend it. Far too much fasting is required of priests, and it interferes seriously with their work. The fasting demanded of the laity is quite another matter. Possibly they don't get enough of it. Something must be done to make them more liberal in almsgiving and, at the same time, less curious about what happens to the money they give. Thus speaks the sacerdotalistic mind. May it expire in derision!

One encounters here and there a priest whose ministry is circumscribed by his inability to discover in the Church anything more supernatural than an organization, a corporation, an interest. This is institutionalism. It does not matter which of the Church's accidental qualities particularly kindles the enthusiasm of the misguided cleric. We obey the Church, not for its antiquity, its efficiency, its influence, its universality, or its beauty, but because it is the community of Christ.

A large measure of pastoral work is based on a willful misconception of the nature and purpose of the sacraments. This is sacramentalism. We may venerate the sacraments so deeply that, for fear of seeing them profaned, we deny them to people who need them. We may feel so sharply man's hunger for them that we resent the restrictions the Church has placed upon their use. We may be so convinced of their unfailing efficacy that we prescribe them indiscriminately. We may be so dependent upon them that we cannot live the Christian life without them. We may be so fond of administering them that we regard this as our only priestly function. Sacraments become vain forms when they are dispensed without reference to the Lord Who ordained them.

A superficially mild but at heart abominably vicious person is the pastor who asks of his people nothing but complete docility. This is paternalism. Father always knows best. A parish can have only one head, and that head is the seat of the only original mind within the parish bounds. The laity have no duty but to consult the oracle and follow its directions. The instant a layman presumes to have ideas of his own, slap him down. A few years of this policy and the autocrat has only himself to rule.

These portraits are drawn from life. They depict sinful attitudes into which we can slip with little consciousness of what is happening to us. In order to escape a resounding downfall we shall require something like a saint's familiarity with repentance and mortification.

Repentance, we are quick to admit, is more searching and exacting for us than for our people. They see sin darkening an hour or, at most, devastating a life. We see its handiwork in a cosmic disorder. Behind the deeds and words of sin we discern its previous conquest of our thoughts, and that is not the limit of our vision, for we recognize that the purest saint can still reasonably and realistically lament his sinfulness. Here is a thought that should give us pause: We are deeply entangled in the totality of human sinfulness. Here is a thought that should give us longer pause: We are answerable, in part, for the sins that come to actual maturity in other men. The latter consideration will always give an edge to our penitence. Perhaps, in the last month, we ourselves have done little that can be called evil, but how many souls have we led into sin, encouraged in sin, or failed to keep from sin? If we are in perpetual contact with sin, we are also only a step from the Cross, and we can quickly put out a hand and touch the wood on which we were redeemed. For others attrition must often suffice, because they do not habitually behold sin and the Passion in compelling contrast. Contrition should come easily to us: we measure every sin by our Lord's agonies.

But for the habit of self-examination, which our first repentance will establish and all subsequent repentance will confirm, we should remain, until the moment of death, in complacent ignorance of our most flagrant sins. The worldling knows his gifts and his dynamic possibilities, but not his iniquities–a term he avoids out of respect for his well-kept personality. We kneel at night and review the day in all its aspects. We remember the rude words uttered and the gentle, healing words we were too busy to utter, our forgetfulness of God, our profane preoccupation with the motions of living, our impatience in prayer and our eagerness for gossip, the envy beneath our admiration, the secret fury, the unclean glance, the inward sneer, the childish love of things denied us, the adoration of gods that do not exist, the stuffing of the body and the starving of the soul. Every penitent arrives eventually at his own way of performing this exercise. Whatever our preferences, we shall not be able to adhere indefinitely to an invariable form. Where shall we find a form that will serve us day in and day out? The commendations and denunciations of Scripture are suggestive rather than exhaustive. The Precepts of the Church, the Beatitudes, and the Theological Virtues give us, at best, mere diagrams of the Christian life. We learn the elements of repentance by confronting ourselves with each of these in turn and surveying our lives today from this angle, tomorrow from that. Bound, as we unhappily are, by angles, slants, and points of view, we gain no comprehensive sight of the utterly righteous love that cannot perfectly be set forth in law or maxim. Even so, it does not take us long to find out where to seek the authority of the regulations and exhortations that guide us. It resides in the Lord of heaven and earth, Who fixes our standards and is our standard. With Isaiah we are stunned, crushed, and confounded by the impact of the ineffable glory, and the holiness we cannot bear to gaze upon shapes our repentance. We were created with the freedom to dishonor the glory and the holiness of our Creator, and nobody's choice is quite identical with anybody else's. In self-examination we look most keenly for the sins that are most dreadfully and distinctively ours. These sins are not likely to be brought to light by a ready-made form of self-examination.

A thorough scrutiny of conscience cannot be accomplished in a few minutes at bedtime. Before Sunday communion, before sacramental confession, and at the retreats we should make once a year or more frequently, a special inquiry into our current habits and tendencies will provide a broad check upon our progress. No priest is at liberty to exclude the administration of the sacrament of penance from his ministry, and any priest who denies himself the blessing of absolution and the benefit of the specific, pertinent, and objective guidance that only a brother priest can give will be justified in his neglect of these things only if he has proved to himself that he is not relying unduly, and perhaps proudly, on his personal resources. The penitent's kneeling-pad will always be the best school for confessors. Besides making us better at our jobs, regular appearance in the role of penitent adds a salutary pain to our supplications for forgiveness and brings us at last to the place where, recognizing that it is much harder for our people to acknowledge their sins than it is for us to acknowledge ours, we presume to offer a certain lowly reparation for the defects of their repentance.

Having received pardon, we are inclined to expect God to sweep up after us. The truly excruciating part of repentance begins when we set out to undo the wrong and the harm that others have suffered by our misdeeds. Knowing that we cannot really restore what our selfishness has ruined, we now feel, for the first time, the cleansing and restraining hurt of sin. There can be no tranquility for us until we have made such amends as can be made. Although the sin lives on to shame and warn, if not to accuse, us and therefore things can never be again as they were before the deed was done, it is gloriously true that apologies can be made, explanations can be offered, wreckage can be cleared away, debts can be paid, lies can be corrected, and, most comforting of all, we can mortify the "evil imagination" that produced the sin. A godly priest is a mortified priest. Mortification does its most admirable work in small ways. It is better to surrender a tiny thing at the moment of greatest desire than to punish ourselves on a grand scale. The saint's mortifications are scarcely noticeable. He substitutes a banality for the witticism that might have wounded somebody. He welcomes the loquacious, time-devouring caller. He does not shrink from doing a thing because he does it badly. He gets out of bed whether he has had a good night's sleep or not. He eats the bacon that has grown cold while some sorehead detained him in the sacristy. He wears the collar that has come back from the laundry with a spot on it. He is as courteous to the person who calls him Mister as to the person who calls him Father. The diligence of his preparation is not determined by the size of his congregation. His approval of his wife's new hat is so spontaneous that she does not suspect what his real feelings are. If he has a headache, nobody knows it. He unconsciously takes a cigarette out of the pack, and, consciously but unobtrusively putting it back, makes himself wait half an hour for a smoke. He does nothing that we cannot do. He accomplishes something that we do not accomplish. He cheerfully chips away little fragments from the hard rock of his selfishness, and finally not a trace of it remains. We have hazy plans for a big blasting operation, but for some reason they never materialize.

CHAPTER IX

According to the Gift

For the third time spring comes to us in this privileged spot, and we know that when it comes again we shall not be here. What has happened to the untutored, diffident, suspicious youths who came here in all their rawness the fall before the fall before last? We do not recognize ourselves. The old miracle has been repeated in us. Once again God has touched willing men, and no longer are they abjectly unfit to be sealed and bound to Him forever by His anointing and by their vow to spend themselves at His bidding.

God, in showing us our congenital insufficiency, has imparted to us the secret of its remedy. They serve Him best who maintain before Him an openness, a passivity, an emptiness, an accessibility, an expectancy. The wisdom of a priest is not an inborn trait, but a daily gift. In each perplexity we inquire of God concerning what is true and right, and to each inquiry God gives a specific reply. Asking without shame and waiting without impatience, we give ear without distraction. When we came here we were self-propelled. Our conversation was salted with such expressions as 'my life,' 'my career,' 'my vocation,' 'my communion,' 'my Bible,' and 'my meditation.' They gave it its flavor. Three academic years later we find ourselves led. We have erased the 'my' and written 'our' or 'God's' in its place. We have become increasingly attuned to the seminary and its ways, and we must ascribe this mounting sympathy as much to unlearning as to learning. We have discarded a great deal that impeded God's approach. These days He can reach us. We have stopped using Him to sanctify our decisions. Having made the greatest of all decisions, we are sincerely interested in what He desires of us. We invite His judgments and welcome His commands. We have actually acquired a faint resemblance to Christ, the Supreme Priest, and this is the promise of our ultimate sanctification. God has made us strong enough to take the insults with the salutes, the frustration with the success—in short, to practice the indifference that is so far from being another name

92

for apathy. This is not the priesthood for which we originally volunteered, but we prefer it to the illusions that once moved us. We were drawn to something we did not understand, and now that we understand it we can embrace it with enduring love. Our patent infirmities and glaring deficiencies do not distress us, as they did a short time ago. There is plenty of vacant space within us for God to occupy, and we know how to keep it uncluttered.

In April and May the Seniors are undeniably in an overburdened state from which only graduation and ordination can liberate them. Many of them seek relief in an inward dissociation from the seminary, and the interval between this and their physical departure takes on the character of an ordeal both for them and for the faculty. It is true that the remaining weeks can neither add materially to gains already made nor redeem the blameworthy omissions that are now so unpleasant to recall. It is at least arguable that the rights of the future have priority over those of a life now virtually concluded. At the same time, the seminary has one more truth to communicate. Our obligations to a post or a condition continue until we are released by authority. At graduation we exchange the duties of undergraduates for the duties of alumni. At no point short of graduation may we act as though the seminary rules were relaxed in our favor. Now and hereafter we shall have to be on our guard against an error that is the cause of a stupendous quantity of shoddy service. The fact that, at a given moment, we are not going to stay much longer where we are does not automatically put us on a reduced schedule. The outgoing incumbent's last day should be as fresh, enthusiastic, and vigorous as his successor's first day on the job. The seminary tries to breed clergymen who will not stop earning their pay before they stop drawing it.

We have, on emerging from the seminary, a broad but still very superficial mastery of theology. Our horizons have been stretched to the limit of their elasticity, and further expansion, if forced upon us immediately, might hurt us. Our new task is to strike downward and bring to light the wealth beneath our feet. For a few years each of us must concentrate on his own little patch of the Kingdom of God. The place to which God directs us may be in a lush, fertile, well-populated part of the realm, but it will more probably be an obscure, uninspiring corner productive of nothing but trials. Wherever we are and however we happened to get there, whether at the behest of our superiors or by our own election, interest and application will make us specialists. Even though it be keenly distasteful to our temperament, the cure committed to us perfects our natural parts by means of a combination of emergencies, problems, vexations, and mere tedium, and in this manner we are prepared for coming achievements. Providence sees to it that we gravitate towards the quarter in which our talents can operate with no more hindrance than is good for them.

The last year of training is a suitable time for a painstaking study of the varieties of the priestly vocation. Despite the indispensability of specialists, the individual can make a sound choice only by exploring all the complications of a delicate question. The rarer and less readily marketable specialties are cultivated at no little risk, except when the specialist can draw on private means. The placement of the more common types of specialist is determined as much by personal considerations as by professional. Expertness becomes a harmful thing as soon as it gravely impedes the practice of the priesthood. Every priest should be consciously and gladly engaged in the work of redemption. The time must never come when we are dejected at the prospect of a return to a general ministry.

The versatile, adaptable, mobile, and durable parish priest is the glory and boast of the presbyterate. In him no virtue is wasted, no accomplishment is superfluous, no grace shines in vain. The larger his parish is, the more it sustains him. The smaller it is, the more it requires of him. He must be audible, affable, and accessible to everybody. The bohemians want him to relax, and the puritans want him to maintain his dignity. Loving both, he disappoints neither. He gives a courteous hearing to insurgent youth and censorious age. His sermons have the polish of print and the intimacy of a familiar conversation. On the one hand, the professor, the doctor, the lawyer, and the senior executive are impressed with them: on the other hand, they are not lost on the tiniest child in the congregation. Why should we celebrate his admirable life in a multitude of words? We all know him, we all revere him, and we all aspire to be like him. Disdaining compromise, he is a master of synthesis. He does not reconcile the interests of factions. He lifts the reluctant and the willing, the bright and the stupid, and, after much patience, his followers and his opponents into a harmony of faith, prayer, and work. Renowned preachers may outpreach him. Financiers may pronounce his budget unsound and his accounts unmethodical. It may seem to accomplished administrators that his parish is inefficiently organized. Directors of religious education may be able to offer him aids that he would never have been able to devise for himself. Professors of theology may find his scholarship shaky. Hospital chaplains may be more at ease with the sick than he is. Foreign missionaries may make his life seem drab. The monastic clergy may surpass him in their knowledge of the anatomy of prayer. His inferiority to these persons does not render him miserable. Although he would be the last to make a point of it, he possesses something that they have not acquired. When we say that he excels in no branch of his ministry we must add that he neglects no branch of his ministry. His specialty is the resolute, and therefore necessarily mediocre, practice of all specialties. His individual performances are unremarkable. The sum of them is distinction. He symbolizes the Church as the widely applauded preacher and the rest do not. What he does in his parish the Church does in the world. The best thing God can do for us is to make us plain, plodding parish priests, and that, in fact, appears to be what He has decreed for most of us.

The total absence of the pastoral impulse is an impediment to the priesthood on any view of the objective effect of ordination. The fulfillment of the urge to minister admits of much diversity. The parish is not every priest's element. One can always find in the American Church a handful of flourishing and brilliant non-parochial ministries, each of them exercised by a priest to whom a parish would have been a strait jacket. It is essential to the vitality of the Church that we have among us some personalities that stiffly resist standardization. One desirable figure of the kind, the social servant, insists that we make at least a token effort in a field that has fallen, all but completely, under the control of the state. Another is the prison chaplain; a third, the hospital chaplain; a fourth, the industrial chaplain; a fifth, the military chaplain; a sixth, the college chaplain: operating in radically dissimilar spheres, they must wonder by what logic the word chaplain can be applied to all five of them. Next comes the foreign missionary, erecting the fabric of the Church in unfriendly lands, taking root in alien cultures, and forcing primitive tongues to yield words for Christian realities. His domestic counterpart is not his inferior in the mastery of folkways. Add to these the teacher and the religious and you still have not named every extraordinary minister known to the Church. When you ask such persons how they came to be what they are, you will learn, more often than not, that the groundwork of the life in question is an infirmity acknowledged, accepted, and disciplined. A natural liking or aptitude may suggest the path our priesthood is to follow, but rarely does God permit our tastes and abilities to function in the way we prefer. Our gifts would run away with us, were it not for our recognition of our incapacities. Therefore, our sense of some menacing weakness may be the dynamic of our priesthood. Perhaps the first intimation of the work we are someday to do will strike us as we listen, indifferently or with a positive disinclination, to a speaker who has come to the seminary to tell us what can be done in the slums, in the jungle, in the Air Force, or in a monastery.

When we depart from the seminary we must carry two intentions with us. The priest who resolves to remain a student all his days and to lead men to the priesthood cannot fail to make some return to the seminary for what it has given him. Every week, if not every day, contains certain hours that can be used for nothing but study. Study must have a fixed and secure position in our timetable from the moment of our entry upon our first pastoral charge. By no other means can we keep alive within us the prayerful, hardworking, truth-loving critic, the new self born and nurtured in the seminary. Diplomas and degrees may be treated either as monuments or as ladders. After all we have been through in the seminary, we cannot help knowing that they are the latter: the very word degree implies progress. Far above us is the cold, bright summit of perfect cognition, and if we climb steadily towards it, brave, ready, and righteous young men will follow us into the clouds and up to the Glory beyond.

A Priest Forever

If any presbyters have been advanced without examination, or if upon examination they have made confession of crime, and men acting in violation of the canon have laid hands upon them, notwithstanding their confession, such the canon does not admit; **for the Catholic Church requires that only which is blameless.**

–Nicæa I, Canon IX

Almighty God, the giver of all good gifts, in your divine providence you have appointed various orders in your Church: Give your grace, we humbly pray, to all who are now called to any office and ministry for your people; and so fill them with the truth of your doctrine and clothe them with holiness of life, that they may faithfully serve before you, to the glory of your great Name and for the benefit of your holy Church; through Jesus Christ our Lord, who lives and reigns with you, in the unity of the Holy Spirit, one God, now and for ever. Amen.

–Book of Common Prayer, 634

PREFACE

The Rt. Rev. Walter C. Klein

ABOUT a decade ago I published *Clothed with Salvation: A Book of Counsel for Seminarians.* Some hundreds of seminarians have found it pertinent, and it has recently been reissued. The present volume, designed to be a companion and sequel to the earlier work, has been written at the suggestion of a former pupil of mine, now a priest, who, like many of his contemporaries and like myself, does not disdain a modest word of counsel about things he is supposed to know very well already. The burden of this book is that nobody knows all about the priesthood. I have not sought to duplicate treatises on pastoral care or manuals specializing in priestly spirituality. My endeavor has been, rather, to suggest how a priest can remain a priest in spite of an almost universal conspiracy to turn him into something else. I have learned more about priesthood from I Corinthians 4: 1-5 than from any other passage of Scripture. St. Paul is my mentor, and I owe him the substance of my work. My debt to other priests cannot be expressed in detail. Their insights are scattered in this long discussion of the vocation they so faithfully followed. What they so generously gave me I now pass on to my juniors in the greatest of all offices. I am indebted to Mr. E. Allen Kelley, Managing Editor of Morehouse-Barlow, Inc., for many excellent suggestions.

CHAPTER I

The Wings of the Morning

THE day of a man's ordination to the priesthood is a day of attainment. He has actually reached the point that, that, a few years ago, seemed alarmingly remote. At first he could not believe that he was capable of becoming a priest; his vocation frightened him. Then, as he submitted to it and pursued it, he found himself marvellously reassured and fortified, though there were hours when uncertainty haunted him. It was not all a strenuous, anxious struggle. A great deal of it was uninspired–if, on the whole, fairly obedient–waiting. Papers had to be signed, courses had to be completed, and officials had to act. These things did not happen smoothly. He had to cope with delays, oversights, and misunderstandings, and at certain moments he felt that he was immobilized and forgotten. This sense of being discarded did not, however, remain with him very long. In turn the initial reluctance, the recurrent doubts, and the continuing reservations disappeared. At least he knew that, when the time came, he could make the prescribed answers truthfully and embrace the new responsibilities willingly. Now the time has come. He is a priest. His will is irrevocably engaged in the life for which he has been chosen. For the moment his vocation possesses him. Presently we shall discuss the perplexities that will soon assail him.

Before we turn to them we ought to contemplate briefly the priesthood itself, apart from the eccentricities of the individuals on whom it is conferred. It is a very objective totality. Between the priest who was ordained a few hours ago and the priest who is celebrating his jubilee there is, as any first-year seminarian will gladly tell you, no radical difference of authority, function, or dignity. The freshly ordained priest, in his essential priestly character and powers, will never be more a priest, no matter how long he lives, unless he is raised to the episcopate. He is diffident and ignorant, and perhaps also crude and clumsy, but the germ of all his future competence and serviceability is in him already, waiting only to be developed and fulfilled. He may never develop it. He may betray it, dishonor it, and repudiate it. Nevertheless, it is there and will remain. If it fails, no attempt will be made to renew it by ordaining him again. From the very moment of his ordination he possesses everything that belongs constitutionally to the office of priesthood.

The priest, in short, is complete at the instant of his ordination, so far as any act of the Church can make him so. If he really understands what he has received, he will assume the duties of the priesthood with invincible confidence. It will not be any manner of reliance on himself as a human being, but simply the certitude that he has been branded, as it were, with a mark that nothing can efface. Henceforth, self-doubt will have only a limited power over him. To remember always that he is a priest will be his unfailing defense.

The saintly Canon Carter wrote thus of the priesthood a century ago: "A Priest is one who, not by any merit, or virtue, or power of his own, but by the will of God, has been made a necessary link in the chainwork of the Divine purposes. Himself as ineffectual as the words he speaks, or the inanimate creatures he may employ in his ministrations, he has nevertheless received, no necessary superiority indeed over his fellow men, but an attribute of grace, distinct from them, though given for their sakes, by virtue of which they are brought into such relationship with God, that through his instrumentality, they obtain the promised blessings of the covenant under which they live."[1]

The accent here falls in precisely the right place. The necessity that makes an elect man a priest forever is of God's decreeing. God calls us, prepares us, ordains us, and tells us what to do. Doubt cannot unsettle us unless it is so fundamental that it extends to God himself. Once we are priests, our priesthood stands or falls with the totality of our faith. If we lose the belief that we are priests, we lose also the belief that there is a God who has made us priests. As the Old Testament says, God is our Rock. On this Rock our priesthood rests. We have the solid security of an office that, by God's will, is indispensable. We have reached the place to which God has been leading us.

---

1. T.T. Carter, *The Doctrine of the Priesthood in the Church of England*, 2nd ed., p. 99

The first few weeks after ordination are, like a honeymoon, to be enjoyed. The thing long desired is at length ours, and it would be inhuman and ungrateful to fight our exultation. We are conscious of a vast access of grace, an influx of power that lifts us high above the banal, the petty, and the drab, as though we were mounting on the wings of the morning. Of course, what the psalmist really said was "the wings of the dawn."[2] It is genuinely a dawn for us, a sudden, fleet diffusion of light in a universe never before so illuminated. The regeneration of baptism and the unction of the Holy Spirit in confirmation are now remembered and perhaps for the first time understood, as we undergo a third renewal and behold the world with priestly eyes. This ecstasy comes but once to most of us. Let us not give it up before we must.

While there is much godly joy in the elation we are now experiencing, relics of our earlier selves are still evident. One thing we unquestionably feel at this season is plain, natural relief after the grinding ordeal of training. Over forever, we hope, are the familiar tribulations of the theological student. No professors will demand papers of us on or before a certain date. The prospect of an examination will no longer darken our days and disturb our nights. Most of us have known little exterior discipline in the seminary, but now we are emancipated even from this, and from now on we shall be undisciplined unless we discipline ourselves.

Moreover, we have emerged from that impecunious state in which all but a few favored theological students spend their harassed years of study. We have debts, but they do not seem so formidable as they did when we lived precariously on student aid and summer earnings. Our families, if we have them, are delivered from the discomfort and awkwardness of student quarters. The seminary wife, after three years of doubling as a teacher, a secretary, a nurse, or a receptionist, enters overnight into the possession of a home and the means of sustaining it without perpetual worry and calculation. Yesterday we vegetated in semi-poverty. Today we luxuriate in a discreet prosperity. Compared with the hazards of student life, the restrictions of our brief diaconate have been merely a pleasant introduction to the boundless beatitude of the priesthood. We have arrived, we can relax. For some of us, alas!, the relaxation proves to be a lifelong laziness. Then there is pride, which is as human

---

2. Psalm 139:9

as relief and far more dangerous. Forgetting the providential encounters and influences that have guided us to the priesthood, we are inclined to take credit for our ordination as though it were our own achievement. Society is less deferential to the clergy than it used to be, but, particularly in small communities, some remnants of rank and prestige cling to our office. Tradition and convention have prepared a clerical mask for us. Young men assume it too eagerly and wear it too arrogantly. It sometimes hides the lack or the death of a vocation. When titles are of more concern than prayer, salutes and tributes interest us more than service, and self-assertion precludes all forms of self-oblivion, we are scarcely more than sacerdotal robots, exercising authority, to be sure, and conveying sacramental grace, but converting nobody. People make much of us at first; the air is heavy with compliments, and triumphs are freely predicted for us. The impulse to encourage beginners is universal. If we are stupid and selfish, our egos expand under this kindly praise until the smallest incident becomes a matter of self-reference.

We are the Lord's stewards, however, not his competitors. A morbid and incurable case of megalomania can begin in the early months of one's priesthood. The best way to escape it is to assess, candidly and unsparingly, our original motives. Possibly at the outset we sought the priesthood in order that we might improve our standing among men, and that may be what ails us now. At all events, pride is poison to a priest. This is the time to abandon it to the uncompromising heat of zeal and love. Whatever our motives used to be, we know what they ought to be now.

One of the graces of ordination is the power to do what we do for the right reasons. We may have personal, tempera- mental, or psychic reasons for being priests, but these are secondary and must be subordinated to the theological reasons, which underlie all true priesthood. "He must increase, but I must decrease,"[3] said the saint whose role was to introduce the Christ. He states the cardinal reason for the ministry committed to us: we are priests in order that God in Christ may more and more be recognized, loved, worshipped, and served; and if we are loyal priests, men will ultimately forget us as individuals.

No person working on the natural level relishes being looked through, as though

---

3. John 3:30

he were not there. Not so the priest; he learns to glory eventually in this very lack of personal notice. It is his assurance of the only kind of success that is permitted to him. The paradox of his life is that the more he fails, the more he triumphs. Although failure in duty is as culpable in him as in anybody else, his failure in the common struggle for riches, reputation, and power is precisely the means of his accomplishing the mysterious labors that God has allotted him. The only way to prove that men ordinarily seek the wrong things is willingly to abandon these things and to be blessed by the loss of them. By theology, the knowledge of God, we find our proper place in cosmic history, and this is dignity enough for anybody. Absurd, wretched, and damned is the priest who, wherever he looks in creation, sees only himself and his illusory greatness.

Thus to describe the self-effacement that should characterize us is not to suggest that contrived impersonality becomes us. Such an attitude would be ridiculous in any priest, above all in a young one. Nobody can strip himself of his personal traits, for, if personality is not the sum of those traits, it is visibly marked by them and cannot dispense with them. In fact, the more we merely humanly try to change our personalities, the more we reinforce and accentuate their most repulsive features. The last thing that will do us any good is an attempt to evacuate the personality completely and to purge it of all that may make our treatment of one person different from our treatment of another. When we essay anything of the sort, we either happily fail or–may we never be so unfortunate! –infatuatedly persist until we have converted ourselves into zombies. In some such manner arise the automatisms that are not the least ruinous of clerical faults. It takes more than an assortment of clichés, formulas, and stereotypes to make a pastor.

The bestowal of the priesthood rejuvenates us, whatever our age, and youth is normally spontaneous. In this respect we should never grow old. The studied approach, the shrewd maneuver, and the wary circumlocution are not for us. By day and by night, in our calls, conversations, and contacts, each of us is necessarily an undivided person, representing the wholeness of God to people who can see life only in fragments. When we speak we ought not to give the impression that we are calculating what we should say before we say it. The kind, healing word should spring readily from our lips, even if sometimes it is awkwardly uttered. It is better to be reckless, tactless, and blundering than to be a withdrawn, incomplete human being with whose entire personality nobody ever becomes acquainted. Old parishioners no doubt laugh in secret at a young priest's transparent enthusiasm and unthinking courage, but they laugh compassionately and enviously, with a sigh for their own loss of youth's disarming candor.

Ordination to the priesthood is both an end and a beginning. To be a priest is also to become a priest, to grow with progress, regression, and resumed progress to the full stature of the priesthood. We have reached one objective only to set out towards another. In short, we are still human beings and we are still alive. We have yet some distance to go.

The first year after ordination to the priesthood is a period of experiment and discovery. We test the rule we kept in seminary and the sciences and crafts we learned there. We find that a priest is not merely a completely matured seminarian. A measure of discontinuity separates his present ways from his former ways. Survival entails adaptation.

The difference is perhaps most perceptible in our prayers. We are much closer to the altar than we used to be. The service of the altar is our daily occupation. A devotional reorientation occurs in the transition from the choir to the sanctuary. The seminarian's prayers are certainly not inferior to the priest's; but as the priest and the seminarian have not the same office, so their prayers are not the same either in content or in emphasis.

The priest, while still a recipient of grace as he has hitherto been, is now also consciously, willingly, and happily the mediator and minister of grace, by sacrament and sermon, and by the simple fact that he is a priest. He prays for and with the whole Church, and the whole Church sustains him in his prayers. He quite literally and concretely offers the prayers of the people, the prayers they mean to offer and the prayers they fail to offer because they do not know or will not recognize that they need them. He adds to their prayers what is lacking, and if much is lacking, he is in some measure to blame. Such prayer as this presupposes that the priest is accurately familiar with the good and the bad in his people, and this he cannot be without unremitting pastoral industry.

The recollected and faithful priest is therefore the voice of a multitude, and the more he identifies himself with the multitude, the farther he will be carried in the divers directions that prayer can take. In the ordinary performance of his duty, if he knows what he is doing, he will pray with unwonted depth, breadth, and intensity. And then, after a time, the unwonted will become the accustomed, the repeated, the accepted.

At this point the priest will either lapse into a routine, which may lead him to prayerless discouragement, or go back, as we all must periodically do, to his spiritual origins. If he makes the right choice, he will consider himself a raw beginner, just as he did in his seminary days when he first embraced a rule of life. He will lay aside all preconceptions and empty and open himself to receive the wisdom and instruction that God will not forever withhold from him. The light will come, and it will show him what form his personal and private service of God can most advantageously take. He will frame a new rule of prayer, mortification, and stewardship—new, not because he regards the old rule as unprofitable, but because of altered circumstances. Like all other rules observed by people who live in a world of surprises, the rule on which a priest decides a few months after his ordination should be practicable, stimulating, and flexible.

Most parishes and missions present a certain pattern of activity. Before long the bulk of our work becomes predictable, and we can foresee when we shall barely have time to pray at all and when we shall have more than anybody but a saint would welcome. To this extent we can commit ourselves realistically to definite devotional chores, such as meditations, retreats, intercessions, and spiritual reading. These are things that can be done. We are gravely remiss if we do not maintain this kind of practice with few omissions, and those of a very trivial kind. This is one of the things we are being paid to do.

Neglect of the acts to which we are pledged leads to slackness in us and almost immediately to slackness in everything we touch. In order to do them we do not have to feel like doing them and we do not have to be satisfied with them when they are done. This, at any rate, is the advice we give to our penitents, and we are not serious priests if we cannot take it ourselves. Here is a service that is substantially independent of emotional fluctuations.

We must have things to do, but they must not all be things that can become painless with habit. There are many devices for making a rule stimulating. Baron von Hügel used to lengthen his prayers when he found them difficult and abbreviate them when they were easy. Such mortification will not weaken our health, and it is so directly aimed at self-will that, no matter how often we resort to it, it will never cease to be mortification in the strict sense of the word. For that reason it will continue to be stimulating, whether or not it is at the same time entertaining, comforting, exciting, or bracing. Stimulation means many different things to people. A wise priest attaches only one meaning to it. A rule is stimulating if it presses, prods, and goads us towards sanctity; and what is sanctity but the absorption of our aims in God's?

A rule that is practicable in terms of a priest's actual life in a specific sphere will also be flexible. An absolutely unyielding rule will not do. A well-conceived plan of devotion provides for emergencies and thus, besides preventing wasteful interior conflicts, preserves us from the pride of perfect regularity. Let us establish a minimum to which we are obligated save in the event of sheer inability to act. Beyond this our devotions can be extended as the day permits or suggests. Theoretically a set maximum is neither necessary nor advisable; we never do enough. How then can we do too much? The only excessive devotion in a priest is devotion that cools his zeal or impairs his efficiency. It occurs so rarely among our clergy that we need not dwell on it, and when it does occur, retirement to a contemplative monastery is indicated. Addiction to prayer is not likely to put our souls in jeopardy.

A seminarian's rule can ignore study, since he has a curriculum to follow and is told in detail how to follow it. The supervision of deacons' studies is increasing, and if it became universal the Church would gain immensely. Then with our arrival at the priesthood, we enter upon a perilous freedom in this regard. A void opens before us, and we ought to put something in it at once. Otherwise we may fall into an abyss of triviality, idleness, and boredom. A decision about study is required of us.

Here, as in prayer, what was good for the seminarian will not suffice for the priest. The latter is no longer served by that convenient band of 'resource-persons,' the faculty, differing among themselves in their respective degrees of *expertise*, but all of them more knowledgeable than he. He is now his own teacher, and every day's ministry is replete with theological problems that clamor for responsible investigation. Realizing that he is still only a student of theology, he embraces a discipline that will eventually transform him into a theologian, however modest his ultimate attainments. He is charged with the total interpretation of human existence, a task that does not consist solely in the repetition and exposition of authoritative formularies.

There is a dynamic in the mind of a real divine; in his limited way, he is, like his Lord, prophet, priest, and king and has the redeeming knowledge that goes with his tripartite character–a knowledge that is more grace than information. This is the priestly learning by which men are saved, and we have no use for any other. Each of us increases in it by discipline, though not always the same discipline.

Accordingly, while we allot a portion of the day or week to study, we do not exhaust our duty by reading a predetermined number of pages in a certain span of time. Our purpose is not so superficial; we can fulfill it only by growing faithfulness to the most serious theological and pastoral interests now proliferating within us as we grasp the magnitude of the gifts we have received. Work is not an impediment to prayer. Study does not reduce our pastoral efficiency. Prayer is not an interruption of any of the other things We are bound to do. We pass quietly from one activity to another, content in everything to do with submission what the hour asks of us. That is the life of a priest who knows that he is a priest and does not want to be anything but a priest.

The first year is a precious year because then the crucial choices we have to make as priests are easier for us than they will be if we postpone them and allow failure and infidelity to accumulate. For a brief time, partly because we are young and partly because God lends a peculiar grace to our freedom, we have the courage to make decisions and the wisdom to implement them. As yet cynicism has not weakened us and disappointment has not dulled us. We have not begun to lose the joy of priesthood, and why should we ever lose it? We are eager, idealistic, reckless, and generous. These qualities must be conserved in our growing practicality and discretion. To the last we must stand at the altar with the wonder, reverence, and gratitude we experienced the first time we celebrated the Eucharist.

CHAPTER II

Separated unto the Gospel of God

J AMES Thurber is the discoverer and the historian of "the war between men and women." It is a fundamental, perennial, inescapable conflict. We are all involved in it, with or without our consent. Similarly, the contemplation of parochial life often gives us the impression that we are ineluctably engaged in an unlimited series of hostilities between the clergy and the laity. In this unacknowledged war there are lulls, truces, and even intervals of almost complete peace, but the contest is always renewed, and virtually every parish can make its own addition to the lamentable record of furious clashes and irreparable casualties. Indeed we have among us some cynical extremists whose conduct suggests that they regard the strife in question as the expression of a purely natural, and therefore an unavoidable, enmity.

We cannot simultaneously entertain this vicious determinism and believe in the efficacy of the love that we have learned from Christ. By the mere exercise of charity, which is the freest thing in the world, a Christian puts himself out- side the reach of brute necessity. We need no further proof that the difficulties so often occurring between clergy and laity do not spring from any semblance of natural law. To what, then, can we trace them? To the acerbities of history? To poor theology? To bad or- ganization? To defective communication? One can think of other possibilities, but these, the first to cross the mind of any priest, will suffice.

A large literature on the position and potentialities of the laity has grown up during the last few years, and the authors of some of the works produced have shown a great interest in Christian history as a record of lay achievement. This kind of em- phasis is both salutary and dangerous. When we read these eloquent champions of the laity, we are obliged to recognize that historical vicissitudes have encouraged false conceptions of the layman's vocation and proper Christian work. At the same time, we need not reject the whole of post-apostolic history in order to obtain for the layman what is due him. We have had some exceedingly radical utterances, of late, concerning past attitudes towards the laity. Dr. Hendrik Kramer introduces a chapter headed "The Theological Status of the Laity in History" with the prediction, "We will find the amazing fact that, notwithstanding the often great, even crucial significance of the laity, they have never become really *theologically* relevant in the Church's thinking about itself."[1] If this dictum is true, we may as well discard the bulk of Christian history, which, in that case, negates revelation in a very essential matter. If Dr. Kramer is right, the Church has so long been so wrong about its constitution and membership that it can have no lingering hope of putting things right in these late times.

Nay, worse than that, the failure at its most profound level –so says Dr. Kraemer– is theological. The Church, historically impotent, also has been theologically sterile. For one who thinks even mildly in Catholic terms such pessimism is exceedingly hard to assimilate. On the contrary, we know that an authentic theology repairs the disasters of history. Theology is not a mere epiphenomenon of history, nor is history as such the primary material of theology. Theology both yields (in its concrete expression) to history and resists history. It is our protection against the disenchantment that darkens the vision of those who contemplate history for nothing but its own sake. In history but not out of history we have received an authoritative norm of Christian teaching. It belongs to the Church, "the people of God," because of "the mystical union that is betwixt Christ and his Church"[2]; that is to say, Christ the Truth is the teacher. Christ in each atom of time renews in us the knowledge of truth, partly through special organs of teaching within the Church and partly through the universal life of the ecumenical and eternal Church itself, with its bible, creeds, sacraments, and ministry. The question of the layman's place and apostolate cannot safely be posed in detachment and abstraction. We are accused of paying too little attention to it in the past. Now we appear to be obsessed with it, to the exclusion of all theology that cannot be pressed into support of our narrow interest.

Theology and polity are closely joined both in history and in logic. We must therefore ask whether, perchance, the organization, government, and administration of

---

1. Dr. Hendrik Kraemer, *A Theology of the Laity*, 48.
2. *Form for the Solemnization of Matrimony*

the Church have in some wise subjugated the layman and withheld his heritage from him, thus in effect demoting a son to slavery. Many Roman Catholic laymen feel that they are being kept in a kind of servitude. Possibly they are, and possibly the Same thing has happened to hosts of laymen in the last two millennia. We are, however, not prepared to concede that anything like that is happening to the Protestant Episcopal layman today. It would be preposterous to argue that the polity of the Episcopal Church is designed to keep the layman in subordination to the clergy. In our church assemblies he debates and decides on equal' terms with the clergy, and our eagerness to hear his views and to count his vote some times gives him an uncomfortable sense of being out of his depth. Former times may have done the laity the injustice of expecting too little of them. This age errs, not in expecting too much, but in expecting the wrong kind of thing.

In fact, with some brilliant exceptions, lay people do not know very much history, theology, or polity and can only rarely be persuaded to consecrate any energy to the mastery of these disciplines. Hence one can plausibly contend that history, theology, and polity have really not very much to do with the matter and the thing we most have to worry about is communication. Communication, even when it is very tenuous, precludes alienation. We have to find out why, in some cases, the shared idiom is wholly lost. A broad look at clergy and laity gives some promise of putting us on the track of an answer.

If priests are still men —and of course they are— they are men with a difference. Let us disregard, for the moment, all theological formulations of that difference and ponder, curiously and naively, the emotions with which church people view their clergy. There are laymen who have a theological knowledge of priesthood and value a priest simply as a priest, whether or not they can add any personal enthusiasm to their recognition of his ecclesiastical character. Most lay people, however, are regrettably swayed by their private tastes and distastes and feel that they cannot benefit by the ministrations of a priest who is in any respect or degree repulsive to them. Violently partisan in their attachments and antipathies, they fairly smother their favorite clergy with affection and delight in denigrating or ignoring all the rest. They may even fall into a superstitious awe of the beloved priest's person.

It scarcely needs to be mentioned that such excesses, though rarely worse than fool-ish in the laity, are monstrous insofar as the clergy have any positive share in them. Some of the devotion we are offered has to be rejected. We can exercise no godly ministry towards those who cling to grossly false ideas about us. Still less may we in any way suggest such ideas to them. A purely personal following, unless we contrive to sanctify it, will ruin us.

These aberrations and disorders merely indicate that priests and laymen need not be rivals. If they will, they can be close, productive partners. The most certain way to prevent unhealthiness in our relations with lay people is to define with real theo-logical accuracy the character and powers of the baptized and confirmed Christian —and then to convey to this Christian the intelligence of what he is. Lay people have boundless honor and worth in Christ. Every one of them is infinitely important to him. He listens to them without fatigue, and their most puerile trivialities never irritate him. They belong to him because he lived, died, rose and ascended for them. Consequently, a priest who understands his priesthood has a veritably sublime con-ception of the reborn human beings to whose service his priesthood is directed. Moreover, his ministrations communicate to them the reverence and the love that Christ has taught him to feel for them. We need look no farther for the crux of the misunderstanding that can so quickly turn Christian striving into unchristian strife. When priest and people are at odds, Christian recognition has been withheld by one side or the other. Either the priest does not encounter Christ in his people or the people do not discern in him the traits of the Christ he represents.

Whether it be the former or the latter, whose fault is it? If the priest does not meet Christ in the good and evil of his people, it is because he does not want to find him. If the people observe nothing in the priest to remind them of his Master and theirs, the reason may well be the priest's loss of all resemblance to Christ. Let us be very sure of our own innocence before we put on the laity the chief blame for the troubles we have with them.

The analysis of the difficulty is also the discovery of the solvent. Instruction will not suffice, nor will efficient parish administration. Not even pastoral devotion, in a casual, loose sense of the term, is enough. What is required of us is that interest in our people –in all people– shall have a distinctive priestliness in its essence and motivation. Therapy, counsel, protection, encouragement, inspiration, and an interminable series of other benefits can be procured from experts who are not priests. To us it is reserved to communicate to men the elusive mysteries of life and death, to tell them what they are and what by grace they can be, and to put this truth before them not entirely by the words we address to them, but more abundantly and more convincingly by the unverbalized candor of complete charity. Our separation unto the gospel of God entails a literally unrestricted abandonment to mankind in its manifold situations of distress and impotence. Anybody should be able to come to us, test us, judge us, and detect in us nothing ambiguous, obscure, or devious. Our integrity in the Gospel will disarm all assailants.

The people of God is both prophetic and priestly. Moses, the unique prophet, generously wishes "that all the Lord's people were prophets"[3], no matter how this may seem to detract from his own preeminence, and the realization of the Mosaic ideal is part of the eschatology of the Book of Joel.[4] Christians constitute "a chosen generation, a royal priesthood, an holy nation, a peculiar people";[5] hence priesthood, like prophecy, is a common possession that ultimately becomes active in individuals. Our identification with Christ makes us all in some sort prophets, priests, and kings. The laity participate in the Church's prophetic proclamations, in its priestly action, and in its exercise of the authority that God has conferred upon it.

All this has been said again and again, and it is so patently true that the majority of theologians will readily agree to it. Then each, according to his persuasion, will qualify it. The present writer can most handily register his own amendments by quoting a succinct statement from Dr. Alden Drew Kelley's valuable little work *The People of God*, and offering a few observations. As Dr. Kelley ably puts it:

> To summarize, the church in its aspects of nature and mission is an indivisible whole and should be regarded as that. The church understood as the People of God is for the world in what it is and what it does. Accordingly, the laity is to be defined theologically by defining the church; not by *con-*

3. Numbers 11:29
4. Joel 2:28-9
5. 1 Peter 2:9

trast to the church regarded as clerics and monastics, nor as a *part* of the church, nor as an *order* of the church. The laity is the church, period.[6]

Most of this is acceptable as it stands. A cleavage between clergy and laity is wrong. It is wrong to ignore the world and to disclaim responsibility for its redemption. We cannot understand the laity apart from the Church. But do these propositions logically culminate in the final assertion? And can we follow the author when, farther down the page, he says, "It would be more accurate perhaps to speak of the clergy as 'the other laity'"?

Semantically the phraseology here employed is misleading. If *laity* simply means "the people of God," the laity are (*or* is) coextensive with the Church. *Laity, Church,* and *People of God* are interchangeable terms. Now this is precisely what they are not in the usage of our time. Dr. Kelley and others have shown in detail the indignities to which the term *laity* has been subjected and the corruptions of meaning it has undergone. Yet we think that the three words should be treated as synonyms. Such a situation, unless we are very careful, involves us in an ambiguity. A rigid uniformity of usage will have to be maintained if the discussion is going to get anywhere at all. For example, one falls into absurdity when one juxtaposes the two propositions that "the laity is the church" and that the clergy is "the other laity." There cannot be two "peoples of God" as there must be if the clergy can be "the other laity." Writers in this area must decide what a word is to mean, and, once the decision is made, they ought to be strict with themselves in their use of the term. The effect of darting from the broad sense to the narrow sense (or reversing the direction) is both to startle the reader with what looks like a paradox and to upset him with a quite indubitable semantic inconsistency.

If we are going to be biblical, we cannot say that the Church is solely "for the world." It is equally for God. Worship is a terminal good. When we have attained it we cannot go farther and we are not impelled to go farther. Much of modern theology is suspicious of the delight of pure worship. Utter concentration on God does occur in man's distracted existence, and it would be a pity if these fleeting ecstasies were spoiled by this curious new puritanism, which appears to view the enjoyment of

---

6. Dr. Alden D. Kelley, *The People of God,* 32.

God in praise and adoration as the most reprehensible self-indulgence. The Church is a serving community, but it is also a worshiping community, and worship is an absolute, requiring no justification by reference to practical effects.

We have heard the word *relevance* often enough to be completely tired of it and unconsciously to resist it. In the vocabularies of some theological writers it is scarcely more than a fancy name for convenience and usefulness. Under the cover it provides we adjust all religious teaching to human limitations. Only by an abuse of language can we pretend that our technique is biblical. If the God for whose "pleasure [all things] are and were created"[7] is not relevant to our deepest fear and bewilderment, there is nowhere in the universe any relevance to anything. So, at all events, says Scripture; here the majesty of God is the organizing truth. From the meeting of God and man as creator and creature spring the austerities, and in their train the comforts, of religion. Those who try to reverse the order, perhaps with a secret hope of escaping the hard things, find no balm for their wretchedness.

All the words we use in our efforts to characterize the laity are awkward. Dr. Kelley is right to object to those he mentions, and no doubt language will always defeat us in this endeavor as it does in all others. The unavailability of a completely satisfactory term need not, however, deter us from experimenting with any phraseology that strikes us as suggestive and promising. Expressions denoting or implying groups can no longer stimulate us; they are old, worn out, and flat. Only by merging can groups cease to be separate, and a merger of clergy and laity is emphatically not the remedy for which we are groping. Expressions based on the concept of fluidity are, in contrast, highly congenial to much modern theological thought. All moorings are abandoned, and we and our vocations are unpredictably shaped by an incomprehensible 'process.' On these premises, anything can happen to the relative positions of clergy and laity. The past counts for nothing, tradition is discarded, and Christians attack the perpetual problems afresh each day. The old way of thinking freezes our institutions, and the new dissolves them. Clearly, we must look for a middle course.

Clergy and laity are both united and divided by their respective interests: This is a

---

7. Revelation 4:11

broad, yet not nebulous, term; when we speak of interests as factors in the relations of persons and aggregates of persons, we have a reasonably lucid idea of what we mean. Interests have a creative power over individuals and communities. A consuming interest in any specialty whatever will eventually turn a man into a very special type of person, with rare attainments and rare limitations. An economic interest will dissolve natural alliances and forge unnatural ones. Because it penetrates so close to the springs of human behavior, interest may well prove to be the most flexible and provocative term at our disposal. At any rate, we are going to put it to the test. This we mean to do as concretely as possible.

What we have to say is simply this: the typical interests of the clergy and the typical interests of the laity are reconciled in the common priesthood of the Church. The priest habitually and characteristically sees the Church in terms of *leitourgia*: the primary duty of the Body of Christ is worship. The layman puts the accent on *diakonia*; he expects the Church to be active, efficient, helpful, and successful. In order to be able to use the terms consistently and constructively we restrict each of them to what we conceive to be, on the whole, its main sense. The nuances that emerge in their intricate semantic histories will have to be disregarded. *Leitourgia* is to be understood as most inclusive rendering is "worship." For *diakonia* the most inclusive rendering is "service."

Leitourgia and *diahonia* do not constitute an absolute antithesis, for if they did the Household of Faith would long since have succumbed to its own interior strains. There are laymen who have a better conception of the priesthood than most priests have, and to that extent they prize *leitourgia* more highly than *diakonia*. With at least equal frequency priests become so engrossed in *diakonia* that their *leitourgia* deteriorates and eventually is completely subordinated to the purely active part of their ministry. Neither the sacerdotal layman nor the laical priest embarrasses our thesis, but rather both by their eccentricities accentuate the truth that will serve as the chief premise of our discussion. That truth, which is a matter of observation, can be conveniently restated in this wise: practically every priest puts worship above service, and practically every layman puts service above worship.

We believe that the priesthood is Christ's gift to the Church. We hold that it is inseparable from the very constitution of the Church. The Church cannot be other than priestly. We maintain that the Church is most truly the Church when priests are most truly priests and laymen are most truly laymen. We argue that it is always Christ who explains to the Christian, clerical or lay, the latter's distinctive role in the vast work of adoration with which the Church is charged.

Since the universe belongs to God, it can be contended that no place is holier than another. Yet this appears not to be a principle on which the Bible would have us act. Some places, by divine appointment, are holier than others, and so are designated times, persons, acts, and other elements in the involved economy of salvation. In consequence, we may legitimately ask whether there is a time or an act in which a priest is most unmistakably a priest, and to ask is forthwith to answer with certainty that priests completely realize their character in the celebration of the Holy Eucharist. Be this a daily or a weekly *leitourgia*, it is supremely the thing for which the priest was ordained, and no priest has ever been permitted to spend his life in oblivion of this nuclear fact of his priesthood. Routine may dull our sense of the awfulness of the place we occupy and the work we do when we lift our hands before the altar, but our insensitivity cannot exceed the bounds that discipline and grace set for it. No practicing priest is so slack that these moments at the altar mean nothing to him. Offices may be neglected, meditation may be abandoned, pastoral care may degenerate into a series of automatisms. For all that, before the altar the priest remains alive to his priesthood.

In the light that shines upon us in the sanctuary the quality of our interest in *leitourgia* is unsparingly exposed. The selfish sacerdotalist is known by his exhibitionism and ceremonialism, which distract and offend the people and confirm them in their belief that *diakonia* is the only thing that matters. The self-effacing priest has the opposite effect on the congregation. He facilitates its worship and thus leads it to the glad acceptance of things that at first were strange and forbidding. He may have the gifts of tact, persuasion, and eloquence, but these are not indispensable, and by themselves they will never produce the concord that prevails in parishes guided by clergy who are truly conversant with *leitourgia*. Fundamentally the Eucharist is Christ's sacrifice. Secondarily, but also necessarily, it is the priest's personal sacrifice: the oblation of many of his private preferences; the offering of his embarrassments, misjudgments, and overlooked opportunities; and finally the surrender of the very desire to present a pure and perfect sacrifice.

It is, of course, not wrong to worship God with all the concentration, fervor, and generosity we can command; we underline the obvious in order to prevent misunderstanding. What is injurious to us and irreverent to God is the prideful insistence that the sacrifice be performed precisely as we think it ought to be performed –and the disappointment that ensues when it is not performed that way. A Eucharist humbly offered with blunders that arise from human weakness is better than a flawless Eucharist offered with self-congratulation on the part of the celebrant. It may even be said that we exercise a certain *diakonia* through our mistakes in *leitourgia*. Our general competence in liturgics should never be open to question. If we are not deliberately slovenly, our slips and lapses can forthwith be added to the sacrifice and so at once forgotten.

The more we lose ourselves in penitence and intercession, the less prone we shall be to inadvertent liturgical errors. This, too, is a way of proving that we understand *leitourgia*. Sins are never heavier than when we carry them to the altar. We know what we ought to do with our sins before we celebrate, and presumably we are not willing to increase our guilt by venturing on this solemn exercise of our office without preliminary contrition. The contrition should not cease when we reach the altar. The remembrance of forgiven sin has a salutary, remedial, restorative influence upon the personal devotion we contribute to our *leitourgia*. It would be morbid and crippling to recollect the sin without the forgiveness. Sin repented of and pardoned is a different matter. The sin itself is evil, and we cannot lay it as such on the altar. The offering we do make is the sorrow and gratitude of a sinner emancipated from sin. Our joy in liturgy is the deeper for the assurance we have that our sins have been remitted. Our humility will be the deeper for our abiding mindfulness of the sins themselves, those acts, so incredible in a priest, for which in strict justice we deserve to be driven out of God's service. We never go to the altar without the need to smite our breasts.

A priest who moves about in his parish always arrives at the altar with a considerable load of intercessions. His mind is full of yesterday's calls and the visits he must make today and tomorrow. These pastoral efforts of his engage his emotions profoundly and powerfully, giving rise to seeming distractions even at the climax of the Eucharist. Such preoccupations are not threats to spirituality. A simple interior act converts them into occasions of intercession. The range of that intercession can be as wide as we please. For the most part it will have to do with the weal and the woe of our people, for whom we are mediators by God's appointment. Often this will be our only way of finding out how we are to serve the stricken, the harassed, and the tempted. We ought never to be ashamed of what we have to present to God for the action of his wisdom and mercy. All things human are pertinent at the altar. We offer realities, not illusions. An honest plea for the wayward and the tormented is no small portion of our *leitourgia*.

In the cluttered hours or days that follow each Eucharist we celebrate, a Eucharistic radiance should linger about us. We should be noted for our cheerful gratitude and our invincible charity. Men must observe that we magnify God in everything that befalls us: in the delectable and the detestable, in the toward and the untoward, in the merited and the unmerited. The offering we make is not a momentary gesture; it embraces every circumstance and event of our lives. *Leitourgia* is our element, but always with an infinite amplification that preserves it from snobbery, pedantry, and bigotry. Let us recall daily that, for the most part, our unordained brethren will not find God adorable unless they find us at least likable.

We have finished, for the present, with *leitourgia*. Now We shall take a long look at *diakonia*.

The impulse to service is universal. Man is born with it, and everybody has it. Our instincts teach us that it is monstrous to live for oneself alone. Seldom will a man admit that he has no interests except those that refer to himself, and when he makes so sweeping an acknowledgment, we do not wholly believe him. If we lacked altruism, it would be necessary to simulate it, because we cannot live in society without contributing, or seeming to contribute, our stint of service. The Communist serves, the politician serves, the soldier serves, the merchant serves —nobody escapes service, be it sacrificial or servile. Service was not invented by Christians, nor is it now monopolized by them. Yet Christians have given it a distinctive turn.

Our task is to identify what is unique about Christian service. Many, if asked, would assure us that Christians are always disinterested in their acts of mercy and thus are distinguished from the heathen, who exhibit no such sincerity. If only it were so! We are disenchanted to learn that it is not. There is a broad streak of self-seeking in the bulk of human helpfulness. We may genuinely aim, most of the time, at the relief of a fellow human being, but how often are we content to do him an act of unadulterated, unrewarded kindness? Hidden somewhere in the deed or its consequences is the benefit that attracts us more than any purely altruistic urge can move us: self-approval, applause, or the pleasure of knowing that somebody is dependent on our bounty or subject to our authority. Our ability to purge ourselves totally of self-regard is debatable. We read of some Christians in whom the love of self was supposedly extinct. We do not presume to make this claim for ourselves, and we should hesitate to make it for any of our contemporaries. Self is ubiquitous, protean, and resilient. We vanquish it only to fight it again.

A year in any parish, mission, or institution will prove the justice of our remarks. The simplest, and for that reason the most convincing, example is the new subur- ban mission, a socio-ecclesiastical unit peculiar to this generation. In such a setting, if anywhere, the Church should be able to make a fresh start, avoiding the blun- ders that are so conspicuous in the history of missions and eventually raising the Christian life to the level of millennial harmony. The mission, like the community surrounding it, fairly effervesces with enthusiasm for *diakonia* of divers sorts. This congregation has no idle members; everybody wants to do something, even if what he wants to do is only to get somebody else to do something. We have a brilliant array of specialists, each convinced that the exercise of his specialty will be the making of the mission. The treasurer, not very liberal himself, knows a lot of people who with the right magic could be persuaded to give lavishly. The carpenter gladly builds an altar according to his own specifications and takes a few Sundays off to rest from his exertions. The merchant donates some shopworn merchandise and sends his wife to represent him at the family Eucharist. The salesman makes a small pledge and attempts to make a large deal with the bishop's committee. The teacher is willing to teach so long as she is permitted to teach as she pleases. The president of the altar guild steams off in pursuit of her own ends, with the rest of the altar guild following reluctantly, uncertainly, and presently not at all. The ladies in general organize themselves with a view to fund-raising and in a short time have an incredibly large amount of money, but the vicar's suggestions concerning the use of their wealth give rise to strident discord. The organist plays, the choir sings, the advertiser advertises, and the critic criticizes, each in his (*or its*) own fashion. The result is not the concord we envisaged. In one short year, old churchmen have introduced their prejudices into this virgin congregation, new churchmen have developed into ferocious partisans, and the mission is whirling with violent centrifugal motion. Our dedication to *diakonia* is driving us into disaster.

Admittedly, our sketch, as it stands, is in some respects a caricature of life in suburban missions rather than a candid description of the 'typical' or 'average' mission. We apologize for the injustice we may have done to the great company of those who are contributing unselfish service to the growth of these missions. Our point, bluntly put, is that egocentrism cannot for very long be kept out of Christian service. Christians are human as well as Christian, and they cannot escape this infirmity. All that man builds up is finally pulled down by people who put themselves first.

The Christian's safeguard against this abiding peril is submission to such guidance as he has the grace to accept. The supreme truth about Christian service is that it is guided. It is guided to our salvation if we are receptive, attentive, and obedient with respect to our allotted work, as Christians know they ought to be but ordinarily are not. It is guided to our loss if we are competitive, possessive, and imperious about it, as men who know nothing about vocation. In both cases God controls it and, without violation of our freedom, draws out of it the fulfillment of his designs.

The ultimate school of Christian service is the house of God. Worship is the greatest of our works upon any same evaluation of work. In the end all *diakonia* is absorbed into *leitourgia*. That is why the priest is always the leader and the layman properly his assistant and supporter. An imbalance results when they try to exchange roles. In the idiom of modern philosophy and theology, what is required is a perpetual dialogue between priest and people. This entails an absolute freedom of criticism in Christ. It does not, however, permit either party to deny his character or desert his trust. The priest must abide in his priesthood, and the layman must exult in his laymanship. Each must see himself as the complement of the other, the bond between them fructifying their differences. Neither of them has any reason to envy or suspect the other.

Uncertainty is the blight of this age, and our nerves are betraying us. An alert layman should be able to observe for himself that, as matters now stand, sacerdotalism is not likely to prevail in the Episcopal Church. The clergy are too unsure –inwardly unsure– of their position to be arrogant about it. For this very reason they are the principal authors of a false laicism that could gravely weaken the Church. So far from arrogating privileges to themselves, they are abdicating some of their responsibilities by trying to unload them on the laity. The laity have concerns of their own to worry about, and they cannot be expected to relieve us of our mission. They will perform their assignment if we perform ours. They are necessary to us, and we are necessary to them. We discharge our ministry to them partly by being separated men. We have been ordained to do a work that laymen cannot do. The "lay apostolate" is not a substitute for the priestly apostolate or the apostolic apostolate, and neither clergy nor laity can exercise an apostolate independently of the bounds set by Christ himself.

Priests do not exhaust their priesthood by ministering to laymen; they sometimes minister to brother priests. Only by unremitting effort can a priest maintain a pastoral posture towards those who share his vocation. He wants some of the things they want, and thus they are his rivals. Some of them are his superiors in priestcraft, and the constant sight of their competence may occasionally prove too much for him. Others resort to him, as to a master, for instruction and advice, and a wrong response to them may be his undoing. Rectors do not always refrain from bullying and exploiting their curates, and a crushed curate readily retaliates with venom.

How loyal, how cooperative, how sympathetic are we towards our fellow-priests? We could make much more of the solidarity of our calling than we ordinarily do and yet not be in any degree a caste, a fraternity, or a club. Councils, conventions, conferences, and clericuses are intended to renew and edify us, and this they will accomplish if we adhere to the proper business of such gatherings. They give us a chance, not only to make inspired decisions, but also to consult one another concerning things that puzzle and thwart us. The conversation should revolve about our sluggish prayers, the intricate cases of conscience presented to us, and the imperfect rapport that still prevails after all these centuries between clergy and laity. Bawdy stories, snide gossip, and shoddy intrigue transmit no grace and do not appertain either to *leitourgia* or to *diakonia*. They are an offense to good priests and a multiplied scandal to laymen. Let *agape* begin with those who are supposed to define it, teach it, and exemplify it. Its power is never greater than when one priest receives it through another.

The priesthood is a mystery, but there is nothing esoteric in the nature or proper practice of priesthood. The priest is more in bondage to the layman than the layman to the priest. It is a willing bondage and therefore not a bondage at all. We cannot say which fares better, the priest or the layman, in the order of faith and love. The interplay of *leitourgia* and *diakonia* makes such questions superfluous.

Chapter III

The Charge of the Sanctuary

THE present chapter and the one just completed will overlap in some measure. Here we shall abandon the terms *leitourgia* and *diakonia* and devote ourselves to liturgical problems as we encounter them in the helter skelter of parish life. This, we trust, will be a very practical chapter. It centers upon the family Eucharist. It embraces much besides.

The family Eucharist has grown partly out of reinvigorated theological and liturgical teaching and partly out of a change in the conditions and the routine of ordinary living. Theologians have undertaken to relate the liturgy, more closely than before, to the actual structure and movement of contemporary life, and liturgical scholarship has stressed the unitary character of the Eucharistic action. Formerly, in many a parish, a devout churchman went to one mass to make his communion and to another for Eucharistic adoration. The family Eucharist theoretically combines these and the other elements or aspects of the supreme Christian offering, and the most enthusiastic among us are confident that Eucharistic unity has been restored. The rest of us cannot completely banish a certain skepticism concerning the alleged perfections and triumphs of the family Eucharist.

We have no intention of advancing arguments for the abandonment of this service, which we value as highly as anybody does; but we do think it could be conducted with a little more decorum, a little more reverence, and a little more recollection than is commonly the case; and, in our opinion, if it were, it would be more instructive to the people than the hasty homily that too often adds to its confusion. The family Eucharist has multiplied communions without visibly increasing conscious, intelligent worship. The "numinous," about which theologians talked so much in the heyday of Dr. Otto's famous book,[1] seems now to have been forgotten in the

---

1. Dr. Rudolf Otto, *The Idea of the Holy*

distractions of the most popular service the Episcopal Church has ever known.

In the seventh chapter of the Book of the Prophet Jeremiah we have a summary of one of the most eloquent sermons known to us. With impassioned vehemence Jeremiah hurls at a deluded people the truth concerning its corrupt worship. His argument has classic force and point. The condition of God's presence in the house erected for him is the righteousness of the people who resort to it with their manifold petitions. God is not, as these worshipers insolently imagine, endlessly indulgent towards the selfish and iniquitous who pay him a perfunctory visit from time to time and maintain his cult in lavish style. Religion cannot be a cover for ways that are a denial of all that religion asserts. A sumptuous church does not sanctify man's pursuit of his own designs.

Far be it from us to suggest that the suburbanites who flock to the family Eucharist have committed the enormities of which Jeremiah accuses his auditors. Some of them, we dare say, have committed some of them, if we may express ourselves loosely. At all events, we are not here primarily interested in flagrant sins. What troubles us is the close resemblance, in fundamental dispositions and intentions, between Jeremiah's congregation and the congregations in our own churches. Now as then, popular religion, when it is not merely a matter of unblushing self-interest, is something less obvious and not more admirable. It is a precarious bulwark against all that man does not understand. The least reverent of men can speak of a 'Jesus-factor' in human life, and those who recognize cosmic uncertainties must be extraordinarily brave and self-reliant not to take precautions against them. Religion composed of precautions is an exceedingly dubious religion. The bulk of folk religion has always been of this character, and even in the various Christian persuasions there are multitudes who give God a minimum of worship simply because they do not know of a way of proving that he does not exist. Only a very unrealistic priest can be confident that he has elevated all his people above the level of the tenuous faith we have summarily, but we hope not inaccurately, described. A little of this crypto-paganism may even creep into the family Eucharist.

Our sole defense against the inroads of spurious religion is worship that is an unambiguous implementation of the creed. Neither in the Apostles' Creed nor in the

Nicene Creed is there any mention of the specific needs of those who assemble in God's house. These symbols confine themselves to what God is and what he has done, and our assent to the faith as it is delivered to us activates within us the promise of salvation and security. Upon those who believe that God can give remission of sins, resurrection, and eternal life, these gifts are eventually bestowed; and in our present partial possession of these things and our prospect of enjoying them in their plenitude, we are emancipated from our sensitive, anxious selves, and our misdeeds, illnesses, and failures shrink to manageable dimensions.

If our prayers are mere blind petitions for deliverance from immediate difficulties, the difficulties will abide with us in some shape even when the prayers have been generously answered. Worship, and nothing but worship, will give us our real heritage, which is a share in God's freedom. The adopted sons of God, who in worship continually rediscover the glory that absorbs all suffering, are indestructible. They are preserved, not because they want to be preserved at any cost, but because worship joins them to the source of life. All ministries that do not contribute to this end are futile. Presumably the young priest has assimilated the lessons of liturgics, pastoral theology, and parish administration. Each of these disciplines after its own fashion influences his creative regulation of worship and its ancillary activities. Liturgics accentuates the centrality of God in worship. Pastoral theology saves the director of worship from a false absorption in rites and ceremonies by reminding him that they also minister to man. Parish administration ought to have something to say about the care of the sanctuary and the discipline of the sacristy.

At the altar and on the way to and from it the priest is –at least for the moment– the undisputed leader. Nowhere is his example more potent. If he smokes with his vestments on, the acolytes and the choristers will do the same. His breathless unpunctuality will be reflected in the tardiness of his assistants. An unprepared, hurried, irritable priest will infect with his low spiritual tone a scandalized, if still respectful, laity. A service ought to be a unified act, and a preoccupied priest cannot make it that or anything resembling it. In the liturgy the priest makes not only an official, but also a personal, offering. He offers his preparation, his undivided presence, and his thanksgiving.

Some services are planned, others merely happen. The reverent service of the sanctuary commences with the priest's devotional preparation, which should be made without fail even if it has to be made some hours in advance. He offers the training he has given to choristers, acolytes, and lay readers; the foresight that has made him check every detail early enough to prevent a serious omission; and the silence and seriousness on which he does not have to insist because in his person he exhibits them so convincingly.

When he is in the sanctuary or in choir he is all there, patently with no thought that is alien to the service in which he is engaged. This, rather than any rare *expertise* in communication, will save him from the clerical eccentricities and the unpriestly slovenliness that still mar so much of our worship and unduly bind the prayers of our people to this world and its desires.

The cordial hand at the door is important. Our thanksgiving may have to be postponed until the congregation has been dismissed with all the courtesies to which it is entitled. Then, if we are capable of such simplicity, we imitate the Syrian Orthodox and take leave of the altar,[2] with thanksgiving for what God has done for us and an apology for our faulty response. When we have acknowledged our shortcomings there is nothing presumptuous in the reflection that the Numinous is also the Compassionate.

All that has hitherto been said we regard as belonging quite essentially to a priest's liturgical duty. Less than this is negligence, but more is not necessarily supererogation, save in the eyes of a priest who has a loose and low notion of his office. Liturgical perfection should be our ideal, our obsession, and our delight. It is not easily attained, and the pursuit of it sometimes bores us. At first the charge of the sanctuary is the most congenial of responsibilities. After a time we find it onerous and monotonous. At that point perfection comes within our reach.

Let us note that the perfection we are discussing is always relative. There are almost no absolutes in the realm of liturgics, and only fanatics will dogmatize about the details that God has left to man's discretion. Voice, temperament, tradition, and taste all come into play. It is not for any of us to say that one style of worship is

---

2. The Rt. Rev. Walter C. Klein, "The Syrian Orthodox Liturgy," *The Holy Cross Magazine*, Vol. 64, 313.

intrinsically superior to another when reference is made solely to secondary features. Accordingly the purpose of the next few pages is not to provide space for a
series of ukases on liturgical matters. We shall present nothing more coercive than
observations and suggestions, and any idle words we chance to speak can quietly
and quickly be forgotten.

One can be relaxed and permissive about many things in a parish, but not about
the sacristy. The advantages of a taut sacristy can be so convincingly exhibited that
everybody will presently be aware of them and nobody will venture to withhold
his co-operation. The priest need not be a martinet. It is simply a matter of firm
and persistent training. All those who have access to the sacristy should be made
to understand that it is reserved for the appurtenances of worship, as properly and
necessarily as other parts of the premises are reserved for other uses. Brooms and
pails should not be kept in the corners of the sacristy; its cupboards, cabinets, and
drawers should not be cluttered with church school supplies and the overflow of
the tractable; some other grave- yard should be found for defunct signs and other
oddments that nobody can bear to throw away; and, in sum, alien gear of all sorts
should be stopped at the door. Exceptions may have to be made in exceptionally
small churches, but they should be made with penitence and a resolute purpose of
amendment.

Within the bounds of the sacristy there should be a quite perceptible atmosphere,
compounded of cleanliness, tidiness, silence, and devotion. The mere absence of
gross dirt will not suffice; a competent altar guild keeps everything washable im-
maculately washed and everything susceptible of a polish dazzlingly polished. Anglican women's communities are known for their spotless and shining sacristies,
and perhaps the most profound lesson a priest can teach his altar guild is to take it
in a body to some convent for a demonstration and explanation of the sacristan's
arrangements and methods. The visitors may find the neatness, order, and efficiency
a little forbidding because their own practice falls so far short of this lofty standard,
but not even the most vigilant of them will be able to detect a candle half in and
half out of its box or a forgotten bottle of wine offensively standing where it has no
business to be. The tempo of a convent sacristy is equally impressive. From the sight
of nuns at work one can learn not to flit nervously about and not to chatter over

chalices and patens. The labors of the altar guild begin and end in prayer. This is praiseworthy, but a continuous accompaniment of prayer would be more so. Holy things handled with devout concentration advance the sanctification of those who participate in the service of the sacristy.

The choir room is another adjunct to the sanctuary, and our strictures on the sacristy apply with only slightly less force to the hall, chamber, or nook where the choir practices its music. In this department the personality of the choir-master must be accorded some latitude. To deal thus with him is usually not to put oneself or one's work in undue peril. The domineering musical genius of an earlier time survives only in an occasional eccentric. No longer does the comet-like performance of the choir blind the worshipers to the majesty of the liturgy and outshine the oratorical coruscations of the preacher. In an ever-growing number of churches the priest and the director of music have been transformed from competitors into collaborators, each appreciating and complementing the other's art and accomplishments. The choir still sings as a unit, but it is not an autonomous unit, as it used to be. This, at all events is the trend, and it is producing a deeper and deeper concord in worship. The time may come when choristers, grasping the totality of worship, will be conscious of their specific function and ready to accept its implications in discipline and personal dedication. Music is not the only thing that the choir needs to be taught.

Resolute adherence to a liturgical plan necessitates the recruitment of minor ministers, reliable acolytes make a daily celebration possible in churches where the priest cannot count on a weekday congregation, and when they have shown their sincerity by enduring an apprenticeship in these relatively inconspicuous duties they can be elevated to the prominence of a large Sunday service with little chance that their heads will be turned. A certain mild and realistic discipline should be prescribed for them, and their conduct both as servers and as Christians should be reviewed periodically. A just, firm, and reverent master of ceremonies or senior acolyte can relieve the priest of many minute worries and train the acolytes to a high pitch of efficiency. A master of ceremonies who is arbitrary and self-seeking will of course be poison to everybody who has anything to do with him, most of all to the priest who imprudently trusts him. The supervisor must himself be vigilantly supervised.

Apart from his personal character, which should be unimpeachable, the principal qualification of a lay reader is the ability to read, and, what is more, to read audibly, distinctly, intelligently, intelligibly, rubrically, and agreeably. Not many lay readers can meet these requirements in full when they are appointed. Given a basic aptitude for clear enunciation, there is every reason to expect that an earnest lay reader will develop into an efficient liturgical assistant and, if the opportunity occurs and he has the enterprise to seize it, a pastor of sorts, exercising a modest ministry in an obscure place for which provision could not otherwise be made. For the most part lay readers are docile, obedient, self-effacing persons to whom credit and applause are of scant interest. Occasionally an individualist among them tries somewhat too forcibly to transcend his limitations. The selection, indoctrination, and supervision of lay readers are rarely undertaken by the bishop. In practice, a lay reader is trained by the clergy with whom he is associated. They should direct him generously and sympathetically, for they are greatly beholden to him.

It is normal for minor ministers to gravitate, in an almost material sense, towards the priesthood. They spend much time with priests, admire them, envy them, and imitate them. All this is harmless enough, so long as it does not give rise to false vocations and presumptuous aspirations. Proficiency in serving or layreading is not an indubitable mark of a vocation to holy orders. It is, at the same time, no disproof of an alleged vocation. The parish priest pronounces the initial judgment on a supposed call to the priesthood. He must remember that he touches the aspirant's life only at a few selected points. He is under a grave obligation to gather information from other observers before he forms his own opinion, and the applicant himself ought to be searchingly examined for the requisite potentialities of will, mind, and hand. Has he established a degree of devotional and ascetical discipline in his private life? Can he work under orders? Is he a realist about himself or is he pursuing some pious mirage? Will he do the Church's work where the Church puts him or will he dedicate himself to self-aggrandizement? Is he bright enough to get degrees from a good college and a good seminary? Can he think, speak, and write clearly and consecutively? If not, is he capable of learning? How broad are his interests and his information and how varied his aptitudes and skills? Has he the promise of the versatility and virtuosity all congregations expect? Has he imagination, compassion, charity, and not too thin a skin? Is he adaptable without being a chameleon, energetic without being a beaver, sociable without being a sheep, and chatty without being a cat? Is he at his best now or will he be at his best a decade or two decades hence? What is his basic passion? What is his ultimate, quintessential, irreducible idea of God? What does he mean when he speaks of 'giving' his 'life to the priesthood'? Unless this inquiry issues in some assurance of a vocation, let us halt the applicant and, if we can, start him moving towards an objective he can reach. This is the point at which we can most painlessly prevent the tragedy of a futile priesthood and a miserable deposition. If our rejection is just, the illusion of a vocation will probably not persist. If we have made a mistake, God will rectify or overrule it.

The screening should be rigorous, but some will pass all the tests we can contrive, and to these we are ready to give help without stint. They will not be very dependent or demanding. In responding to their acute questions we shall often satisfy them with a hint or a reference, which they will follow up promptly and energetically. They will ask of us little but stimulation and a certain amount of reassurance. Ministering to a man whose vocation is new and unproved humbles us, who in our cynicism and fatigue have nearly forgotten our earlier clarity and courage. For any priest thus engaged the furtherance of another's vocation is the recovery and reinforcement of his own. He cannot teach arts that he does not practice himself, and if he has grown slack in his prayers, he will soon tighten up his interior life as he attempts to show somebody else how a priest ought to live. Neophytes make us ashamed of the shifts, evasions, and compromises into which we have been led. Fortunately they idealize us and do not see how far we have deviated from the pattern of faithful priesthood. So it is that in spite of our deficiencies and infidelities we can send them to seminary with a vocation already well advanced towards maturity.

We have wandered far from the main theme. Now we must return to it. Many hindrances to worship exist besides those already mentioned. One of them is the abruptness of the arrival and departure of the congregation. Immediately before the service the church fills up (we use the term relatively) with almost miraculous speed. The process is reversed, with somewhat less celerity, as soon as the service is over, and the reasons for the comparative slowness of egress are (1) post-liturgical conversations, (2) the hand-shaking rite, which compels the departing worshipers to form a single file, and (3) an unexpected shower, the failure of one's husband to turn up with the car, or some other fortuitous circumstance. Nevertheless, the congregation gets out of church as fast as it physically and morally can, showing as little inclination to linger as it does to arrive prematurely.

Customs of this sort can be eradicated only with the greatest determination and patience. The bare suggestion that they need to be eradicated will surprise, irritate, and offend a considerable number of the clergy. What harm, they will argue, is there in the last-minute arrival and the hasty departure, so long as people are present for the service itself? They are right if one can meet the obligation of worship in purely physical terms. We do not agree that a cardinal Christian duty can be so easily performed. We believe that it takes at least a few minutes to pass from absorption in the common (and legitimate) activities of life to undistracted participation in the common prayers of the Church. Nor should we rush away from public prayer as though our minds had all the time really been engaged in some quite different kind of effort. We are not urging a Pelagian program on harassed priests and uncomprehending congregations. We do not advocate the use of still more preliminary and supplementary vocal prayers than we have at present. We can say so many prayers that we do not speak to God at all.

The corrective of poor liturgical prayer is an increasingly delicate and perceptive awareness of what happens when the Church prays to the Father through the Son in the Spirit. We acquire and retain that awareness by concentrating on what happens before it happens and after it happens. As it is, our congregations are not ready for worship when worship begins, and they never overtake the liturgy, which neither drags nor drives, but moves evenly and surely towards its consummation. All they need is a little quiet teaching about getting to church in plenty of time, making at once for one's seat, pleading with God for the grace of an undivided mind, following the liturgy through each moment with no thought of other moments, and at the conclusion retiring with a certain fond reluctance. The atmosphere of worship is too quickly dissipated once the service has ended. Devotion is confined to church, and men continue to lead split lives. They cannot serve under two banners forever. God commands us in all things, and obedience is not to be limited to the hours of worship. Liturgical devotion that does not spread far beyond the liturgy soon vanishes from the liturgy itself.

Liturgical discipline is most effective and abiding when it begins in the early years of a person's life. The priest attaches his most ardent hopes to the children of the parish, who, unlike many of their elders, welcome his teaching and carry it out with a very satisfying directness. He sometimes thinks that if the parish consisted entirely of children the hindrances that now seem so serious would no longer exist. As it is, every course of religious instruction is beset with pitfalls and vexations.

Religious education is still widely regarded as a sort of parallel to worship: the children attend classes while the parents attend service. An attempt to integrate the children into the liturgical congregation is certain to irritate divers parishioners in divers ways. Some will object to the distracting behavior of the younger children, others will be upset by a slight simplification or other adaptation of the service, and still others will exhaust their ingenuity in a search for weaknesses, general or specific, in the theology that has produced so many unpalatable innovations. A number of children will be at your church or in church school for no better reason than that no other church is so handy. Parental assistance and encouragement will be minimal, and what the children learn from the priest will not be reinforced by anything they hear from their fathers and mothers. One of the greatest evils of all is the sense of impermanence that is the natural emotional accompaniment of the mobility and fluidity of society. No teacher, least of all a religious one, can hope to make more than a fleeting impression on most of his pupils. It is a highly favored child who has not been exposed, long before he attains maturity, to more diversity of religious teaching than he can safely handle. We have to cope with these disheartening conditions as best we can, and defeatism simply aggravates our woes. What God adds to our contribution always makes the total sufficient. Our principal obligation is to make our work as deep and thorough as possible. It does not take long to teach a child the technique of worship, and as he learns how to act in the Christian assembly he easily picks up the Creed, the Lord's Prayer, the Ten Commandments, and whatever else is requisite for a wholesome life in Christ. Furthermore, these are the things he will remember long after the philosophy, theology, ethics, and sociology we are now trying to impart prematurely to him evaporate from his mind. When he has worshipped a few times with the congregation under the expert guidance of a priest who knows how to point out to people the simple essentials of converse with God, he will be capable of making for himself all the indispensable acts of the human soul aspiring to be joined in faith and devotion with its Creator. The memorization of winged ejaculations in which we say to God all that he expects to hear from us is worth far more than the existential pabulum that is being provided in such abundance for young Christians these days.

With respect to language, style, bodily positions, ceremonial gestures, vestments, the utensils of worship, and numerous other things the liturgy is a process, though in most portions of Christendom an undeniably slow and conservative one. The Eucharist as it was celebrated last Sunday in the reader's parish church seems to him identical in every particular with the Eucharist as it was celebrated the Sunday before. Yet differences arise, and as they accumulate we become conscious of them. If our eyes are sharp, we are aware that in our short lifetime some ways have been abandoned and others have been introduced. This recasting of the liturgy is perpetually going on, and in general it appears to owe little to individual initiative. Novelties spread by suggestion, imitation, and the migration of Christians who have adopted them.

Two such phenomena can aptly be used here as illustrations because they have both sprung up within the last few years and therefore many Episcopalians are familiar with them and recognize that they are innovations. Who has not observed that often nowadays a clergyman officiating at the Eucharist raises the altar book on the completion of the gospel? What is the purpose of this ceremonial elevation of the book? Is it an emasculated Anglican form of the osculation of the book in the Roman rite? Is it a signal to the congregation, an example of bibliolatry, or an offering to God of our attention to the wisdom of the gospel? Whatever may be the intention, the effect frequently verges on the ludicrous. Some clergymen heave the book with such vehemence that the more timorous spectators must expect to see it rise spectacularly towards the ceiling. Occasionally an officiant lifts the book above the level of his eyes and for a moment contemplates the congregation. So odd a trick is susceptible of equally odd interpretations. Here we have an instance of a kind of liturgical caprice for which it is difficult to make a convincing apology. This abrupt gesture adds neither beauty nor intelligibility to the liturgy. It is simply a fad we have taken up without noticing how artificial and meaningless it is.

In contrast with the custom just described, the practice of taking non-communi-cating children to the altar rail can be traced to a healthy Christian instinct. They cannot safely be left behind. When they accompany their parents to the altar they should receive something, and the obvious thing to give them is a blessing. To see a couple coming forward with disciplined, reverent children of assorted ages is an ex-perience in which every pastor rejoices. The family reaffirms its unity and solidarity in the Eucharist and is joined with other families, thus escaping exclusiveness. Any departures from liturgical precedent are defensible if they facilitate this eminently Christian fellowship.

"Elizabethan English" is the term we commonly use for the language of our Book of Common Prayer, and if this is a permissibly loose way of designating it, our use of the antique idiom is reprehensibly loose –slovenly, in truth, to the point of being chaotic. No longer, for example, do we recognize any difference between the second and third person singular archaic endings of the verb. Whether we say *–est* or *–eth* is now almost wholly a matter of chance. The sight of an *–est* or an *–eth* frightens the wits out of us. This makes us deal blindly and fatalistically with these linguistic ghosts. We do not see the letters; we see only an alarming and demoralizing blur. Hence it comes out *–est* when it should be *–eth* and *–eth* when it should be *–est*. Sometimes, of course, we get it right, but this is no comfort to us, since we are not aware of it.

When the ending of a collect is only partly printed and we have to remember the rest of the standard form, it is easy to lose the connection and an occasional lapse deserves only the mildest blame. We are far more culpable when we misread, as we frequently do, the same suffixes printed in type so large that it would seem to preclude all mistakes. There they are in a text so well phrased and punctuated that accuracy appears all but inevitable. There they are, and we are perversely unable to recognize them.

The root of our inefficiency cannot, however, be plain funk. We are scared for a rea-son or perchance for several reasons. Two very readily occur to us. We are indiffer-ent to language as such, and we have an antipathy to Prayer Book language because we suspect that it is no longer a vital medium of communication.

We are not a superlatively literate nation. The studied, disciplined use of language is distasteful and tedious to us. We find precision in machines, not in our mother tongue. Its resources are a neglected heritage. Writing a term paper in seminary was an ordeal for us, and our present attempts at preaching are chores rather than adventures. Our lack of language sense closes many worlds to us (among them the world of the subtle Greek tongue, which most of us have studied in vain). We handle our language so badly that we deny our people most of its graces and beauties. Our awkwardness with –est and –eth is merely one manifestation of an extensive deficiency.

Moreover, we sometimes come close to resenting the Prayer Book. To a dejected priest it assumes the aspect of a stiff and heavy robe of state that embarrassingly restricts the movements of the wearer. We chafe under this ancient garment and in extreme moods would gladly exchange it for something modern. The Prayer Book commits us to a vocabulary that modern man does not understand, to careful, ceremonious periods that strike him as grotesque in their intricacy, and in general to much that seems to belong more to history than to religion. The Prayer Book ties our hands, and these days we cannot spare a finger. We seem to be deliberately putting ourselves out of action.

Superficially reasonable, such reflections are fundamentally a recognition of our appalling incompetence in a realm where the clergy were once supreme. The fault lies not with an outmoded liturgy, but with men who shrink from the enterprise and the industry by which they could acquire a creative mastery of words. If we slaved over our sermons with the courage and effort that honest writers put into the practice of their craft, the homiletical word would interpret the liturgical word and once again human beings would find the liturgy speaking directly and pertinently to them. If we took the pains to become pliant mouthpieces of the liturgy, it would lose much of its apparent obscurity. Worship still has the power to redeem, to restore, and to recreate. It is our hollowness that makes the liturgy sound empty. It is our lifelessness that makes the liturgy sound dead.

Memorization, if we made more diligent and devotional use of it, might help us to be more precise about the wording of the liturgy and therefore more concentrated and attentive. Learning a prayer by heart forces us to deal with its smallest units, and so we not only master the text to the last detail but also become acquainted with the meaning, the logic, and the sequences underlying the language. We apprehend the prayer as a single, though perhaps elaborate, act of the spirit, connected with other acts, yet distinct. We perceive how the worshiping person, passing from prayer to prayer, assumes a succession of inner attitudes ranging from penitence to adoration. A memorized prayer is eventually absorbed into the life of the person who memorizes it and is charged with his own devotional impulses. This is as far removed as possible from praying by rote. Prayers that we can repeat without hesitation free us for worship and guide us in worship.

What is good for us is good also for our people. Lay worshipers will never speak up in the liturgy, as we incessantly exhort them to do, unless they have over-learned their lines. In an ordinary congregation the occasional unannounced interpolation of a little practice in dialogue will not be seriously offensive or distracting and certainly cannot fail to arouse people from the droning lethargy into which they so readily fall. One hesitates to interrupt the liturgy for any reason or in any circumstances. The necessity for some measure of the sort does, however, exist when the people are so mute that their participation is a fiction. The shock of a brief workout over a few lines of the liturgy will keep them alert for some time to come. The device has to be used judiciously and with transparent charity. The result of a proper application of this discipline will always be a greater diligence on the part of the people to master the lines that the Church has appointed to be said by them. Eventually, if we prod them lovingly, they will have the whole thing by heart.

There are, of course, other times when we can exercise them in their responses. Confirmation lectures can advantageously include a few minutes of liturgical drill. When the rector addresses the church school, he can sometimes put the children through the *sursum corda* or the versicles and responds in the choir offices instead of asking them what Sunday it is. Marriages and baptisms might well be verbally rehearsed with the prospective participants. Our object throughout is to make the words an aid, and not a barrier, to man's converse with God. People will not find God through the liturgy until they stop stumbling over the words. The only thing that will avail is a basic liturgical education for the laity.

The best school of the liturgy is, of course, the liturgy itself, but only when the liturgy is completely alive is it self-explanatory, and seldom is a stranger converted by his first sight of an Anglican service. The truth we must convey to our sadly passive congregations is that the gestures, postures, and utterances of the liturgy spring from the depths of human life. Until a man discovers himself in the liturgy and transcends the chaos of his psyche in the freedom and self- fulfillment that become possible through the liturgy, the things we do and say in the sanctuary will continue to offend and puzzle him.

Man reaches his full stature and therefore is most himself when he worships, weaving the manifold threads of his life into a pattern of praise and gladness. This supreme truth about man can be formulated theologically, philosophically, psychologically, sociologically, historically, or in any other manner that is currently pertinent and convincing or, to put it more simply, effective *ad hoc*.

A resourceful priest will unceasingly search for means of improving his presentation of the liturgy to his people. He will preach sermons, he will conduct institutes, he will lecture, catechize, and demonstrate. His methods, efforts, and expedients will alter with the tides and swells of interest, feat, and desire that move his congregation. This will not matter, for the undeviating intention and the steadfast devotion will be evident from his youth to his age in all the instruction he gives. Man's minister is first God's minister, shining with the eternal light that is unbearable to the wicked, but renews the life of God's true servants. He says most about the liturgy when he celebrates it with radiant reverence and utter self-oblivion. A worshiping priest is an irresistible preacher.

CHAPTER IV

Instant in Prayer

ANCIENT distinctions are breaking down in our time, and many a Christian commentator rejoices in their dissolution. The Church is decreasingly contrasted with the world; we are advised to discard the terms sacred and secular; and a sharp division of Christian people into clergy and laity is now widely viewed as mischievous and misleading. The present trend towards the abandonment of all antitheses and antinomies may be an assertion of the unity of life, but there are moments when it looks more like a mere reluctance to think. The old distinctions have served us well, and if we jettison them irretrievably, we may someday miss them most acutely.

Some distinctions are absolute or so nearly absolute that we cannot do without them. Others are pragmatic and instrumental –valid and worthy of preservation only insofar as they are useful. In the latter class we must place the differentiation we are accustomed to make between the individual's participation in the public prayers of the Church and his pursuit of private devotion. These two activities cannot be kept completely apart without calamitous consequences. They are, in fact, nothing but the same prayer uttered under different conditions, most of them external. We always pray to the same God, with the same presuppositions, in essentially the same language, for the same things. Private prayer must be linked with the liturgy as closely as possible, and we must at no time permit ourselves to believe that any kind of prayer, even the most sublime and the most 'mystical,' is beyond our reach in the liturgy itself. Nevertheless, it is profitable to deal with non-liturgical devotions separately, and that is the way we are going to treat of them in this chapter.

Offhand, one can hardly conceive of an unprayerful priest. Granted that prayer is not easy for anybody, the priest has, superficially, a certain advantage over laymen in the practice of it. The seminary must have trained him in prayer, if it has trained him in anything at all, and in consequence he knows more than a layman usually does about the technical side of prayer. Books on the subject abound in his library, and periodically he and his fellow clergy are exposed to further teaching. He has more occasions for prayer, both formal and informal, than non-professional Christians are likely to have; he lives in what many people take for an atmosphere of prayer; and he is perpetually exhorting and counseling his parishioners to pray. He promotes schools of prayer and schemes, programs, and cycles of prayer. Prayer, prompt, pertinent, and potent, is expected of him, be the circumstances normal or abnormal. In a word, prayer is his main business. How then can he himself be unprayerful?

Few, we trust, are the priests who no longer pray at all save in the performance of their professional functions and therefore never utter a personal prayer. Much more numerous, we fear, are those who have lapsed into torpor, slackness, or indifference, but at least fitfully repent and try to return to their earlier fervor. The selfish, the lazy, the weak, and the weary are found in every calling, the clerical not excepted. Priests can be unprayerful because they are human.

It has recently been suggested that there is another reason for the trouble a priest may have with his prayers, and this time we have in mind not a sluggard, but a responsible, earnest, disciplined cleric who really wants to pray, but after years of trying still cannot. The suggestion, though not wholly original with Bishop Robinson, is made and developed in his *Honest to God*. His argument, in brief, is that we are taught to look upon prayer as "disengagement," whereas we ought to conceive of it as "engagement." "Our Victorian grandparents," he recalls, "believed in the constitutional, in the time-table, and above all in keeping accounts, almost as religiously as some priests now prescribe a rule of life. But one wonders whether there may not for some types be as much liberation in their abandonment as in their observance, and in the end no less discipline."[1] Bishop Robinson acknowledges that retirement is helpful and on occasion indispensable. At the same time he inclines towards the view that prayer is "to be *defined* in terms of penetration through the world to God rather than of withdrawal from the world to God."[2] We become contemplatives

1. The Rt. Rev. John A.T. Robinson, *Honest to God*, 103
2. *Ibid.*, 97

"by unconditional love of the neighbour, of 'the nearest *Thou* to hand.'"[3] "God can then be apprehended as "the 'depth' of common non-religious experience,"[4] and we perceive that "prayer is openness to the ground of our being."[5]

Bishop Robinson expresses himself in the familiar theological cant of the present day, and the origins of his theology are no mystery. Of course, the way he prays is related to what he believes. Similarly, the way he fails to pray is related to what he does not believe. Nevertheless, the empirical element in prayer can be decisive for the individual. Nobody will persevere forever in prayer that issues in nothing but aridity, paralysis, and despair. Such prayer may rest on unexceptionable dogmatic premises, but if it merely pains us and, so far as we can see, does us no good, we eventually give it up. This, it appears, is what has happened to Bishop Robinson and various persons with whom he has talked. The devotional practices they have inherited, if not totally otiose, have so limited a value and so tenuous a vitality that they cannot be relied on for any sustained converse with the Almighty. People so constituted either do not pray at all or pray, habitually and ordinarily, through their "involvement" in their environment.

Bishop Robinson does a fair amount of wondering in his book, and perhaps he will not mind if we do some wondering too. We wonder how numerous the people he has described actually are, and we wonder how just it is to say that prayer, as tradition represents it, is abstraction from the world, the very opposite of that rich life of personal relationships in which prayer becomes possible for Bishop Robinson.

That many seminarians and priests are dissatisfied with their interior condition scarcely anybody will venture to deny. One sees among them humble ones, who do not know how much they have accomplished; proud ones, who are annoyed with themselves for not accomplishing more; clever ones, who defeat grace by trying to rationalize all its operations; slovenly ones, who are not systematic about anything; volatile ones, who never give any method a thorough trial; lazy ones, who shrink from even the lightest labors of devotion; and bewildered ones, who are listening to everybody and following nobody. Any of these could very easily convince himself

3. *Ibid.*, 100

4. *Ibid.*, 62

5. *Ibid.*, 102

that Bishop Robinson had diagnosed his malady. For every Christian who might be right in this judgment upon himself there are at least several who would be rushing to an unwarranted conclusion. How many persons have, in fact, exhausted the resources of traditional spirituality without finding a manner of prayer that suits them? Self-deception in too obvious a hazard to be disregarded. Selfishness rather than congenital unfitness may be what ails us. Perhaps we reject all forms of the mechanics of prayer because at the very "ground of our being" we do not want to pray.

Moreover, the world, in all acceptations of that term, has never been the object of hostility on the part of normal Christians, to be sure, when we speak of 'normal,' 'orthodox,' or even 'Catholic' Christians, we are begging the question unless we attach a precise sense to each of these words, and Anglicans instinctively hesitate to be absolutely, rigidly, and exclusively precise. Here we shall have to be content to express ourselves loosely, for we are dealing with a vast range of history and all of the known gamut of human personalities. Prescinding from all eccentricities and extremes, which we concede are very numerous, we maintain that an awareness of 'mission' has always been an inescapable concomitant of the Christian's personal intercourse with God through prayer. Ultimately every praying Christian addresses himself to the life that encompasses him. He does not need to get involved in it, because to be human is to be involved, deeply, gladly, and vulnerably. It is sheer nonsense to pretend that the determination to live while one prays is confined to a handful of avant-garde prophets belonging to the last few decades.

The world is, to begin with, creation, society, doing one's work, earning one's living, and sharing the resources of nature and culture with other people. Flying and crawling away from this world are equally impossible for us. We must live in it, if we are going to live at all; so we stay in it, whether or not we also pray in it. Next, the world is the people to whom we are sent, the strangers whom we try to persuade to listen to the Christian evangel. We do not shun this world, because we are uninterruptedly telling it about Christ.

In still another guise, the world is the seat of evil, the abode of lethal mischief and boundless malevolence and menace, the abyss that invites us to a never-ending fall. This is the world we eschew or withstand, alternating between arts offensive and arts defensive in our endeavor to meet the emergencies that the wicked universe creates for us. Here is a world with which we can pursue no 'dialogue' and to which the truths entrusted to us have no 'relevance.' The only 'involvement' open to us is the involvement of foe with foe. To the world in its satanic character we have no mission save one of denial, defiance, and destruction. Christians who parlay with the third world, in the hope of saying something relevant to it, are almost at once outwitted by it. Then the relevance begins to flow in the opposite direction.

Nobody is exempt from the attrition of mundane interests upon whatever ideals, convictions, and principles he has. A carefully initiated and indoctrinated layman can practice his religion quietly without being involved professionally in ecclesiastical business, and this is a defense that the priest may well envy him. A faithful layman never quite loses his youthful awe of clergy and churches as representative of God; deep in him lies a reverence that no disenchantment can corrupt. That is not the case with a priest. He is close to all the sordid jobbery of church life. Unless he is diligent in the use of countermeasures, eventually the very core of his vocation is worn away by the persistent tides of ambition and frustration. Malice, chagrin, and envy resound within him like waves penetrating a cave at the edge of the sea, and all prayer is drowned in the tumult. Evil defeats us because we do not take the trouble to fight it, and our reason for not fighting it may be that we are not sharp enough to recognize it. If 'involvement' is necessary, so also is wariness.

A priest who has never used, or no longer uses, any of the devices and exercises of traditional piety is an odd man indeed, and he will need some extraordinarily positive arguments to justify his negative position. The majority of his less radical brethren do not take refuge in self-justification or rationalization. The problem for them is their clumsiness in the application of inherited techniques or their reluctance to put themselves to any strain in the nice adaptation of the old wisdom to their own apparently unprecedented difficulties. Laziness, ineptitude, and stupidity are not incurable. Nobody's predicament is unique, and this becomes plain to us when we contemplate the continuity and uniformity of human experience.

Each of us has a bias –possibly several of them– that if undetected and uncurbed produces a dislocation of more or less grave proportions in the whole of his spiritual character and practice. Every predisposition overemphasizes some part of Christian truth and perforce slights the complementary truth, which then loses its creative and corrective power, to the impoverishment of the Christian life as a totality. This is the essence of heresy, an evil that can readily be identified in its collective manifestations, but may escape notice when it arises spontaneously in particular Christians. Our contention is that every Christian's individuality inclines him towards some type or other of pernicious error.

A predisposition to Pelagianism is sometimes attributed to Anglo-Saxons. Whatever may be the truth of so sweeping an allegation, the Anglican clergy are certainly more activistic than fatalistic, and if self-reliance is a vice, one can scarcely deny that they are very vicious indeed. They may not actually hold the main Pelagian tenets in any of the crass formulations that are to be found in the literature of the Pelagian controversy. They do not believe that man's own exertions suffice for the attainment of perfection. They are sounder than they used to be on the question of original sin. What is Pelagian about them is their attachment to action and attainment, and this, if it were coupled with cheerfulness, would be, much of the time, so mildly Pelagian that it would deserve no reproof. Unfortunately, we strive without confidence. Anxiety divides our energies, and we insure the failure we make such efforts to escape. We are pitiably unrelaxed and frustrated Pelagians, incurring the guilt of heresy, but capturing none of its advantages. We worship an illusory self- sufficiency, but find no joy in it and almost never feel that we are achieving anything by it. The Pelagian is always trying to make the situation right for himself. The plain Christian, without being passive, is chiefly interested in what God will do to make him right for the situation.

Theoretically, the modern Pelagian is a hard-working, responsible person who has fully earned the respect that most people give him. His friends lean on him, and he has an assortment of splendid traits, every one of which he has acquired by sedulous cultivation and improvement. His progress in Christian virtue has never been seriously interrupted, nor has he ever been impeded by those curious interior difficulties that haunt so many Christians of his acquaintance. One of his few faults is his impatience with his jittery brethren, who in his opinion deliberately make things harder than they need be. He cannot help contrasting his own firmness with the irresolution that surrounds him, and try as he will, it is simply beyond him to account for all this instability. Sustained by self-approval, he matures, mellows, and expands, and the older he grows, the less qualified is his conviction that he is the author of his own perfection.

This, we repeat, is a theoretical description. We have never encountered a person who completely corresponds to it, and we hope we never shall. If such a person were possible, he would be unendurable. Fortunately the uncertainties of our existence prevent the attainment of the superlative priggishness here depicted. Unfortunately they do not prevent an approach to it. All men have their Pelagian moments, their Pelagian fits, and their Pelagian phases. Our ideals, our expectations, and our aspirations are deeply tainted with Pelagianism, and that is why they are never more than relatively fulfilled. We are perpetually trying to do with mere creaturely resources what grace alone can accomplish. We can cooperate with God, but we cannot dispense with him. A priest who proves that truth to himself in everything he does will not forever remain a Pelagian.

Another perennial heresy is Gnosticism, a name that covers a vast confusion of ideas. Gnostics covet, and try to procure for themselves, an esoteric knowledge or illumination. Everybody likes to belong to an 'in-group,' and the tightest of all in-groups is the one that gives its members an opportunity to share secret knowledge. Thus we find, in seminaries and dioceses, the liturgical faction, with its contempt for those who do not use its enlightened ceremonial; the doctrinal faction, which builds walls and ramparts for the protection of its theological opinions; and the pastoral faction, the possessor of arcane techniques and obscure neologisms. They are all exclusive, divisive, and sectarian, each laying claim to a knowledge that God is supposed to have withheld from other men. Such coteries form gospels within the Gospels, and it is always the narrower faith that triumphs when a choice has to be made. A priest's partisan loyalties restrict his ministry. They also cramp and weaken his prayers. Gnosticism is a protean and pervasive heresy, and few of us are uncontaminated by it.

There are many articles in the Gnostic creed, and some of the others are as injurious as the one we have just considered. Morality cannot be securely rooted in a system that attributes so much efficacy to knowledge as such. A logical Gnostic will relegate conduct to a secondary position. He himself may live strictly, but at bottom he is indifferent to morals; and if he remains indifferent long enough, it will be very strange if he does not discard them. This indifference can quite consistently be extended to the total earthly life of a human being. Our struggles, our victories, and our defeats are then regarded as fundamentally meaningless. With the *gnosis* we inevitably win, and without it we inevitably lose. Man's original sin, the Gnostics declare, is his involvement in matter. From this servitude only an insight superior to that of his fellows can deliver him. It is unthinkable that matter should be susceptible of any redemption or invested with any power to convey grace to man. Salvation is accomplished, not by the conquest of time, but by escape from time. The Gnostic attitude towards matter precludes real sacramentality in worship. Whenever we feel completely alienated from our material environment, an unacknowledged Gnosticism may be our trouble. We can recall what has happened to our prayers at such times.

Current interest in glossolalia and similar phenomena will justify a brief inspection of Montanism. The deviations and excesses of Montanism have a single source in an exaggeration-and thus also a distortion-of the pneumatic element in Christianity. The only real Christians in this dispensation of the Spirit are the 'pneumatic' Montanists. The 'psychics,' i.e. non-Montanists, are an inferior breed. Christianity is not complete in the Incarnation. There is a third dispensation, which logically must produce a third testament. Montanism and other pneumatic movements preach salvation through inspiration, and inspiration, like gnosis, is a privilege and a favor by which some men are elevated above others. It gives rise to a snobbery that can defend itself against all assaults by invoking the authority of the Spirit.

The evils of naive inspiration are so well known to the generality of clergy these days that every priest should be on the alert for symptoms of this malady in his own spirituality. The pride, the obstinacy, the presumption, and the superficiality of the uncritical inspirationist repel us, and the sight of them should inspire in us a craving for the authentic wisdom of the spirit, in whom we confront ourselves and ultimately know ourselves, as the wisdom of the Greeks bids us do. It is the Spirit himself who teaches the priest in his prayers and in his temptations that the inspired life is not the convulsed life, but the guided life, in which we gradually learn to hear what the Spirit has always been saying to every body.

In prayer, as in all things besides, the priest is required to be a Christians' Christian. His prayer do not have to be advertised; their effect on him and on his cure prevails over all derision and indifference. He is a devotional leader as well as a liturgical leader, even if he is modest and reticent, as he normally should be, about his own prayers. He need not be more 'advanced' in prayer than any other person in the parish, but he should persevere when others give up, endure when others collapse, trust when others suspect, and be instant and persistent with God when others relax. For the priest, in a distinctive way, prayer is something to be done –an assignment, a commission, a charge, a task that is at once a worry and a joy, an onerous and yet precious responsibility. He is glad that prayer is a work, because he is a working man and if prayer were not a work and his volition had nothing to do with it, he would be capable of it only at long intervals and perhaps not at all. To him prayer is less a gift than it is to anybody else, or if it is a gift, it goes with his priesthood, which is also a gift, but a gift that imposes duties. The prayers of a priest are conscientious, unpretentions, and dull to behold in their plodding fidelity. The lack of glamor is a blessing to him; if he were a man of raptures, ecstasies, and levitations, he might be a dangerous priest. Recognition would surprise and confuse him. After all, is he not doing what he was engaged to do? He is a man under obedience, a servant, a functionary whose most constant function is prayer. The prayers of a good priest are, above all, simple, and simplicity is the brightest and rarest virtue of Christian prayer.

We all know that works have no efficacy apart from the grace that makes them possible and the love of the creature who offers them. Ours is not a quantitative religion, and a priest does not count his works in the hope of building up a comfortable balance for himself. He is just as existentially isolated and impotent as anybody else, the universe showing him no special amiability. The priest's secret is that he knows how to make capital of misery, desolation, and humiliation, which his patient acceptance transforms into powerful works of devotion. We have something else in mind when we contrast works with grace or faith.

The priest is a busy man, and it is ordinarily supposed that alertness to detail precludes contemplation. It does nothing of the sort. The essence of contemplation is the elective centrality of God in our interests and affections. The contemplative lives with God. We ought to look upon contemplation as normal for the clergy. They spend their time with things that represent God, and it should not be difficult for them to go a little farther and enter into an abiding fellowship with God himself. A priest is driven to simplicity in order that he may remain a priest amidst a throng of bewildering pressures. Not every simple man is a contemplative, but every contemplative is a simple man.

To anybody who agrees with us that prayer is a concrete work, usually of manageable size, the desirability of a rule to govern it and ancillary devotions is clear beyond question. Things that can be done can also be regulated, and so long as we do not make idols of the regulations, our pious tasks are performed the better for the regularity that discipline gives them. We do not propose to expatiate on the self-evident utility of a rule. We take this as recognized, even if the clergy do not always act on it.

The character and content of the rule are dictated by its purpose, which is to implement our ordination vows. Our rule simply elaborates the promises we have made and insures our fidelity to them. It takes us to the altar and keeps us ready to serve there blamelessly and undistractedly. It locks us in our study and slowly shapes us into masters of theology. It dispatches us to the hundreds who need us and makes certain that we pray for the recipients of our ministrations. It leads us into the pulpit and prevents our arriving there with nothing to say. If we can take no higher view of it, we are obliged to admit that it increases our professional efficiency, for a priest must indeed be dispirited not to covet greater competence. An ambitious ecclesiastic who adopts a rule on utilitarian grounds may rise, in the practice of it, to devotion. The alternative for everybody who does not belong to the emancipated elite is to blunder, to flounder, and finally to founder.

Rule or no rule, we are all tortured by an interior cleavage, a schizophrenia that confuses our best and most demanding moments. When we ought to be most conscious of God, the occurrence of some proud, sensual, or vain image in our minds darkens our devotions and makes us doubt our allegiance. The greater our alarm, the more severe and prolonged the combat is apt to be. Here is a hint as to the origin and aim of the attack. Its immediate source is undoubtedly within us, and that is why we feel identified with the very evil we are trying to repel. Our vulnerabilities are, however, constantly being exploited in a cosmic contest between good and evil. Whatever may be a fitting name for the powers that labor to accomplish our undoing, we know their magnitude and their strength.

Man does not exist in order that he may surrender to these powers or accommodate himself to them, but in order that he may triumph over them; and this he can do, both in the most unremarkable incidents of his life and in its rarest and most extraordinary temptations. At a crucial point in his career, Bishop Henson exclaimed, "How hard it is to realize the greater factors of life!" and deplored his failure to banish "the squalid anxieties as to ways and means," which should have yielded to concern for what he calls "the continuing paradox of my inner life."[6] We are all similarly in peril of being smothered by the details of living, but this never actually happens to anybody whose life moves consistently and perseveringly in one direction. If the powers cannot grind us down, they will inflame us, and we shall have sharp encounters with naked evil. In these struggles, too, we prevail by the wholeness, the integrity, of our persons and our service. We consecrate an entire life, and God defends us in its crises, for we are now indivisibly his. We shall not have to endure the ambivalences and ambiguities of our existence forever, and we do not have to succumb to them now. We are delivered by the grace of integrity.

Priestly integrity has its roots in theological integrity, and the most useful of its fruits is intellectual integrity. Entirety of mind is our testimony against fragmentation, the distinctive evil of our time. Our contemporaries have abandoned themselves to pluralistic thinking. Truth has ceased to be a totality, and partial truth is no truth at all. Nor is the universe really a universe if it did not originate with God and is not run by God. The purely intellectual realization of this verity is now impossible; we can believe in the relatedness of things, but we cannot demonstrate it. The only way to experience all reality as one is to join ourselves by prayer to the

6. Rt. Rev. H.H. Henson, *Retrospect of an Unimportant Life*, Vol. II, 24-15

Living God who is the author of creatures and their multiplicity. The task that is too large for the mind is within the compass of a priest's devotion. Praying as one to One, he helps make all men one and enables them to perceive the singleness of creation. Prayer so directed is a priceless service to a centrifugal society. When he prays, when he reads, and when he preaches, the priest must specialize in not being a specialist. In the present world he is the sole universal interpreter.

A disjointed world is also an unstable world. We are responsible to an excessive number of competing authorities, and it is not strange that we should be fully loyal to none of them. There is no hard spiritual currency in such a world, where values forever emerge, fluctuate, and vanish, and none is permanently recognized. The objectives are too numerous and too scattered to permit a concentration of the will in any all-embracing enterprise. Few things remain important long enough to shape a life, to form a character, or even to lend purpose to a long series of actions.

The terms of our vocation preclude uncertainty as to our ultimate reason for doing what we do. Instability is a particularly unpriestly fault. We are not free to flit about from one occupation to another; our time already belongs to Another, our days are designed, and our way is charted. We may follow the appointed path unimagina- tively and woodenly, we may at times lose it and at other times monopolize it; but we cannot long be deceived about the path itself. It is the road that all priests have had to tread, and we recognize it by its directness, its varying breadth, its fatiguing length, and above all its alarming difficulty. Much of the time the most we can do is to stay on it, making sure that we do not get disoriented and turn our backs on our destination. No stability more heroic than this is demanded of us, but at least we should have the predictability that comes from an unfailing awareness, and an unreserved acceptance, of our vocation. Every time we pray we recollect what a priest is and why we are priests. These things do not change, and if we are good priests, neither do we.

The basis of a priest's stability –and of his adaptability– is the readiness with which he relates new situations to the enduring elements in his life: his vocation, his re- sponsibilities, and his faith. Adaptability is merely the complement of stability; as we move from task to task in the Church we change our rules of devotion and the matter of our prayers to suit the circumstances, but throughout we serve the same God with the same single-minded fidelity. The adaptability that adorns the character of a priest is not the spinelessness of a man who is determined to be liked at all costs. The priest adapts himself to people's weaknesses, not in order to gain any advantage for himself, but in order to minister, and this he knows he cannot do by ostentatiously bending down to those who are already sufficiently humiliated. He has to partake of their infirmities without falling into those infirmities. He does not get drunk with alcoholics, but he does contrive somehow to be with them in their elation and depression and to feel, as more than a spectator, their irresponsibility and their self-contempt. He is as chaste as grace can make him, but he is not a stranger to the torment of ungoverned lust. By the very intensity of his love he experiences the devastating pain of the obdurate hater. He knows all these things by com- passionate participation in them, and his participation could not be compassionate if it were in any wise guilty. His fellow-feeling mysteriously embraces the worst and the best and embraces them both redemptively. By his prayers, which are infinitely penetrating, adaptable, and resourceful, men rise and grow, lifted and sustained as by the hand of Christ himself. And, of course, it is the hand of Christ, for when a priest identifies himself with those for whom Christ died he identifies himself with the Christ who died for them, and in the travail of the priest's still very human prayers to the divine, saving power is mediated to all degrees of men. The priest can safely be a thousand different persons in a thousand different situations because in this multitude of diverse particulars he is always making the same fundamental offering of himself. The more he renounces his personal will in all changes the more he fortifies his mediatorial and intercessory character.

Prayer is the exercise that keeps a priest teachable. Every morning he invites God to speak to him, and if this is a sincere invitation, he clears his mind of preoccupations and quietly awaits a reply. Some of the replies he gets are incredibly apposite. Pastoral riddles that have defeated human ingenuity are reduced, in prayer, to their elements, and we are immediately certain of the action required. Prayer shows us which of two nicely balanced duties is the one to follow at the moment. The mollifying word, the comforting word, and the electrifying word are given to us in prayer. The homiletical punch line for which we groped last night in vain is whispered to us this morning as we pray. We strain with no result; then we relax, and the work is done for us. This hap- pens, however, only to those who are teachable.

Teachability is the willingness continually to return to the beginning; in his daily defeats the priest is, so to speak, unceasingly being annihilated and recreated, and therefore he passes through times when he must be content to confess that he is nothing at all –less than a child, less than a tyro, less than a neophyte. He dies daily and daily lives again. Every morning he starts to learn once more the things he thought he knew already. The course of salvation in the universe is recapitulated in his daily experience. His prayers have cosmic effect because he is so often thrown back into the chaos from which the cosmos has arisen. Only so can he intercede for, and minister to, all men.

Time takes the bloom from prayer as it does from everything else. Underneath is the substance, and that is ours forever, if we have the courage to cling to it. Even the courage is a gift, and if we cannot earn it, we still have the will to seek it and the proof that God does not deny it. His body is sometimes sluggish, and his mind is often reluctant, yet the priest who is really a priest remains eager for the moment when he can pray unhindered. The most indifferent of us can testify that those moments are multiplied beyond all expectation.

Chapter V

In Your Chamber and Be Still

I N O R D E R to study we must have time, and time is hard to get. The clergy are perpetually lamenting their lack of it. They would, of course, have more of it for cerebration if they devoted less of it to complaints about the absence of erudite leisure from the life of a modern parochial priest. Room for really indispensable leisure can be made in the most cluttered life.

Freedom for study is not a luxury, and it is not for us to choose whether we are to study or not. A heavy list of appointments does not justify neglect of study. Among those appointments should be one with Wisdom itself. If we may so express it, the priest has a daily rendezvous with the Holy Spirit, and the only way to keep it is to reserve certain hours for reading and thinking. It is a poor priestly life that is destitute of such hours. No schedule, no condition of life totally precludes them. We may have to forgo them one, two, or three days a week at some seasons, but, unless we are not organized at all, there will never be a week when we are entirely without an interval for study, to which we are bound no less than to prayer and active works. We must recognize, and our people must recognize, that study is not only work, but also –and not in a figurative sense– prayer. The Church has coupled prayer and study in one of the ordination vows, and we have promised to strive, with God's help to "be diligent in Prayers, and in reading the Holy Scriptures, and in such studies as help to the knowledge of the same, laying aside the study of the world and the flesh."[1] That suffices to define our obligation.

The fulfillment of our obligation begins with the preservation of silence, so far as duty permits, during the guarded hours we spend in our chambers. Our silence is expectant and alert, and there are moments when, like Elijah, we hear "the sound of a tenuous stillness."[2] God utters truth to us as he has done to his prophets since

---

1. See *The Form & Manner of Ordaining Priests.*
2. I Kings 19:12

he framed the universe. God spoke and the world was made, God commanded and the hosts of heaven and earth were created. God's word does not return to him empty: it does his will, it is his will, in a manner of speaking it is himself. Nor do our words return to us empty. After many days they are spoken back to us, intensified, amplified, multiplied. Like God's word, due allowance being made for the finite minds that conceive and produce them, they have creative power.

Man's life is a vast verbalization. He is the speaking creature, the articulate animal, the master and the slave of words. His existence is an always failing but always renewed struggle to express perfectly something that cannot be known until it is expressed perfectly. Man is thus forever occupied with the riddle of himself, and the answer, the formula that summarizes his essence and his purpose, eludes him again and again. Each time he utters a definition of himself, in a sentence or a book, in an act or in a life, some vital word is missing. For all the power of his words, man cannot speak the decisive word about himself.

Our frustration takes us back to the myth of the defeat of the human word in Genesis 11:1-9. Originally the "one language and few words" (RSV) sufficed: the essentials of man's life are simple and not very numerous. The myth, like many myths, is tangled and obscure, and its logic is not our logic. God is represented as being alarmed at man's display of power, and indeed if God had anything to fear from man, it would be precisely in the realm of words. God thwarts man by destroying the unity of speech, but even this crude myth makes it clear that the blame is man's. Man tries to be God and so loses the universal language that has kept human beings conscious of their solidarity. Hence, Babel is of man's making, and when he stepped out of the bounds of his creaturehood, he forgot the simple speech that comes spontaneously to the lips of one made in the image of God. Ever since, the only words he has been capable of uttering are words that hinder and confuse communication. He has been trying to recover the mythical lost tongue, but by his own exertions he can never recapture the primeval language of peace and understanding. We spread our languages by conquest, military, economic, or cultural. The language of the vanquished eventually fades out. Even the enlightened, sincere, disinterested, and internationally-minded cannot agree on an artificial language, since this is a compromise that seems to dehumanize man.

Consequently, we have to go back to the original silence for the word that makes us one. Revelation emerges from the silence out of which creation emerged. The word of revelation is not shouted at men. The heavens declare the glory of God, but only attentive and obedient ears can hear what the heavens are saying, and by itself it is unintelligible. Silence is the non-existence of speech, but it is also the possibility of speech, the not-yet-existence of speech. In silence there is an infinite potentiality. For this reason, the prophet, in order to be a speaker, must first be a listener.

Silence, then, refreshes and renews us, and when it envelops us as we and write at our desks, we are not disappointed in our expectation of hearing the concrete word of God that is right for this historical instant. Much of the work men do would be better done if it were surrounded with silence. We ought to offer our responsive silence to the eloquent, vibrant, boundless divine silence out of which the word of salvation comes. The preacher has to close his ears to all the loud discords of the moment if he is to catch the elusive murmur of truth and repeat it for the redemption of the moment. He needs all the aid that a well-ordered life can provide for him, but more than anything else he needs a minimum of inviolable silence.

Of course, the mere acceptance of our obligation to study settles little with regard to the material and direction of our studies. The primacy of Scripture in our post-ordination development puts an initial curb on our predilections. Scripture comes first, and we should be as conversant with it as the Arab with his desert and the Mississippi pilot of former days with the stream he navigated. We should live with it, breathe it, think it, reproduce it. Its subtleties and difficulties should be a frequent theme in our conversations with fellow clergy and a matter of constant exploration and reflection when we are alone. We should be expert and resourceful interpreters, practiced in all the legitimate devices of hermeneutics. Scripture should be our business and our recreation. We should find in it the solemn truths about which we preach and the humor and the beauty that refresh us. We do not submit to Mosaic restrictions, but we derive the principles of our lives from the Bible, and our communion yields to no other in its reverence for, and devotion to, the Bible.[3]

---

3. "Holy Scripture containeth all things necessary to salvation: so that whatsoever is not read therein, nor may be proved thereby, is not to be required of any man, that it should be believed as an article of the Faith, or be thought requisite or necessary to salvation." (*Article VI*)

This, at all events, is true officially, but in this respect as in others official teaching is having a less and less obvious effect on the clergy all the time.

The discreditable realty of the situation is that we do not read Scripture, cannot explain it, rarely quote it, and do not resort to it in our perplexities. Our crass ignorance of Scripture is incomprehensible in men who hear it so constantly. In direct violation of one of their ordination vows, the Anglican clergy have developed a peculiar deafness to Scripture.

Nothing could be more stupid in an era when the professional study of the Bible is more necessary then ever. The text of Scripture belongs to everybody, and in the study of it scholars of all persuasions meet and fraternize. All savants make much the same use of archeology, versions, historical and literary criticism, and exegetical methods. The restoration of unity has already been partially accomplished by a new scriptural accent and interest throughout Christendom and a mighty revival of biblical theology. The meagerness of our contribution to all this is a measure of our apathy toward Scripture. It may also indicate that we do not really care very much about the eventual fulfillment of our oneness with brethren of other opinions. It suggests that we are less profoundly Christian than we pretend to be. The Church wants our intellects to be steeped in the Bible. We choose to steep them in something else.

When due provision has been made for biblical studies, priority should be accorded to the theological sciences in which the individual has shown himself to be deficient. Seminary examinations, canonical examinations, the sermons we preach, the instruction we give, and the discussions in which we engage are tests of our attainments, and wherever we detect a weakness the place should be marked, instead of being covered up with cowardly defenses and vague apologies. If we are ignorant of something we ought to know, let us seek the necessary counsel and do the necessary reading. Large numbers of our clergy could advantageously take leave, for a time, of contemporary theology and pastoral psychology and treat themselves to excursions into patristics, moral theology, and ascetical theology. Seminary curricula are always somewhat out of balance. We have to make adjustments after graduation.

This seems to be a good place to slip in a word about the judgments of the seminary.

The seminary is neither irresponsible nor infallible, its opportunities for observation do not embrace a student's entire life, and the atmosphere of a seminary sometimes brings about a temporary deterioration in a good man. In a word, the faculty's estimate of a seminarian has value, but nobody, least of all the seminarian under scrutiny, need take it as final. Hundreds of men who have failed to gain the unreserved approval of the teachers under whom they studied have proved to be acceptable, and even remarkable, parish priests or have filled a difficult non-parochial post with a virtuosity for which the seminary had provided no outlet. The intellectual criteria of a seminary are possibly more reliable than its measures of character, piety, and general effectiveness, but mediocre grades are not incontestably the mark of a mediocre man, and the unsympathetic presentation of a subject can have an inhibiting effect on a person of genuine talent.

We are wise to begin anew on graduation, whether we have done well or ill hitherto. The worst of seminaries tells us something about ourselves, but the best does not tell us everything. We prejudice our future if we stop studying either because we have rejected ourselves as morons or because we regard ourselves as geniuses. Actually we are neither, and what nature has not given us diligence can acquire for us. Priestly study derives a peculiar fruitfulness from its relation to vocation. It is always guided study. It is guided by the Holy Spirit, sometimes directly, at other times through Scripture. Intention, interest, plan, and discipline also contribute guidance. Insofar as we require a mind for the due exercise of our priesthood, grace will make possible what the natural intellect cannot achieve. There will be no miraculous rise in our I.Q., but as in our prayers and our ministrations, so in our studies, we shall be able to apply all our resources to a single present act, and that is something that merely brilliant persons are likely to be able to do only in their happiest and most favored moments. What we lack in power we make up in co-ordination.

Conscientious, realistic study is too demanding to be hazardous. It is painful, as all creative enterprise is painful. Therein lies our protection. For intelligent and inquisitive priests study can be, if this control is absent, an escape or an indulgence. Moderate light reading, so far from being a sin, is an eminently proper clerical pastime. As a rational and rationed recreation, it helps to keep us in touch with the human race and so fortifies our ministry. At the same time, any reading, whether light or weighty, that is primarily a gratification of our personal tastes can end in a ruinous, un-clerical dilettantism. An unsanctified enjoyment of snide wit can become an addiction into which a priest retreats because he is bored with his chores or frightened by his people.

The problems of a pastor can be forgotten in the more manageable problems or the vain ramifications of some odd line of study. Reading of this type, though legitimate enough for people whose lives would otherwise be totally without purpose, is not for us, who have far more purpose than we can ever fulfill. Excessive or indiscreet use converts a stimulant into an opiate. Without trying very hard, a dejected cleric can contract the habit of doping himself with study that at first takes his mind off his work and later keeps it off, so that he no longer wants to return to his assigned business. Engrossed in his chosen distraction, he lavishes upon it an industry and a perception that deserve to be applied to objects less trivial. He fails where he could easily succeed and succeeds where he should not be working at all.

It is a curious perversity that makes us do, even in study, everything except that to which we are bound. It is possible to study frivolities seriously, and this is almost as reprehensible as frivolous inattention to solemnities. Both courses are to be avoided. Studying bad things by good methods is not a corrective for studying good things by bad methods or refusing to study them. The motivation of our studies is equal in importance to the studies themselves. If they are properly motivated, they are integrated into our vocation.

We must distinguish between the systematic study of something that does not merit any kind of study and carnal, indiscriminate study, a perpetual 'browsing' among books and 'dipping into' them. Priestly study is never a desultory matter. We shut ourselves up in vain if, when we are alone, we limit ourselves to riffling through a shelful of books and read no more than a few pages in any of them. Aimless reading is demoralizing and wasteful, weakening our capacity for concentration and contributing nothing to our stockpile of information. At least, let us always have a serious book in hand and another in reserve.[4] Then there will be no idle intervals, and we shall not squander irretrievable time by sampling a host of books and settling

---

4. See Appendices, page 254. The Rev. Dr. Pusey gives the same advice.

down to none of them. We must not be in the position of the man who perished from lack of sleep because he could not decide which pajamas to wear.

An ordinary priest needs, above everything else, a good basic theological education. This he cannot acquire merely by obtaining a degree or bringing some prodigious labor of the mind to a conclusion. He cannot do it by allotting a stated amount of time to study, nor will his education be furthered solely by the adoption of an intricate and rigid plan of reading and reflection. Education does not consist primarily in reading books, writing papers, or doing any other specific thing. It is an attitude rather than an array of attainments, and one may have multiple doctorates without being recognizably educated. Unassimilated learning is simply something for a priest to stumble over as he gropes for vital contacts with human beings. We must learn to view problems theologically and to handle material in a theological way. It is this, and not the mastery of a theological curriculum, that makes us theologians.

To put content in its right place is not to say that one cares nothing about it. The only way to cultivate theological competence is to grapple with the stuff on which the theologian has to work. But what is this content, this material? In Scripture, it is the divine word communicated to man; in history, it is events; in theology straitly understood, it is propositions about the ultimate nature and meaning of the world; and in pastoral theology, it is the sum of the situations that call for ministry. For a theologian there cannot be any absoluteness about the divisions of the theological field. He makes distinctions as sharply as anybody else, but it is the unity of theology that he prizes. If we are dealing with content in a genuinely theological manner, we discover that we cannot imprison it. The real content of every theological discipline and every theological course is everything that man experiences and knows. The theologian has to continue to speak the universal tongue because he is occupied with nothing less than the universe.

With these hints, a priest will not be in much doubt as to what he ought to study. He is, however, likely to persist far beyond his seminary years in an abortive search for some sovereign technique of study, for which he longs because he has been taught that every difficulty yields to the proper procedure. Much that we have said above is calculated to discourage him from this arduous and unrewarding quest.

One becomes a scholar or, if one is less ambitious, a sound student by being realistically loyal to one's nature and capacities. The art of study is as manifold as the endowments of the people who practice it. What aids one man hinders another. Appropriate methods commence to emerge from study itself the moment we become concretely engaged in it. Imitation and borrowing may furnish the initial impulse, but it is ruinous to remain dependent on them as we continue. Method comes to us spontaneously as we discover who we are and what we can do. How idle therefore to worry about method as though it were a separate problem! We do not study well until we get so engrossed in the subject that we forget about method.

Nevertheless, the disciplined use of certain devices is not to be despised. Indeed, the benefits of discipline, if it is not rigidly and unreasonably exercised, are likely to be felt in everything the mind does. Thus an advance in mathematics may lead to an improvement in Latin, and the care we have taken to examine the historical setting of a controversy may make us more competent to deal with the theology involved. We have been insisting that it is always the same mind that thinks and the same person that acts. The gains made in one sector are often transferable to another.

The control of notes, for example, is a matter in which the disciplined utilization of other people's experience can be of immense service to us, but only if we really appropriate what we learn. There is a trick to writing notes from which we can recover the results of a course of reading when the material we studied has passed out of our conscious memory. It is instructive to see how physicists, historians, and anthropologists record their observations and findings, review and sift them, classify them, index them, relate them by means of cross-references, and keep them accessible. Watching how others work will suggest to us a multitude of improvements in our own technique, and sometimes we shall feel ashamed at our failure to perceive, without prompting, what was needed.

Eventually, of course, the volume of our notes exceeds the space we have for storage and the time we have for retracing our intellectual steps. Happily, before we reach that point we have become so familiar with the whole range of priestly lore that we can dispense with files, except in an emergency. Notes are meant to be outgrown, if not discarded. We owe them much for keeping us aware of things that we should otherwise forget, but we are even more indebted to them for teaching us to isolate the things that most deserve to be re- membered. Notes assist us in a critical selectivity. They analyze, they eliminate, they emphasize, they simplify; and without them the sheer mass of material would be unmanageable. We all do much the same things with notes. Yet nothing more precisely indicates a man's individuality than the expedients he has invented for recording what he has learned and handling the record. These are as intimately his as his handwriting.

Notes and the labor they represent are both a backlog and a sacrifice. A priest's life is replete with sudden invitations and unpredictable appeals. We are repeatedly being asked to stuff the cracks of a loose, misconceived program, and often we are told that, so far from being the first choice for the occasion, we are the last hope. It is perhaps pardonable to be irritated with the bunglers who produce this sort of situation, but if one can be humble enough to fill in where others have refused and to perform the oratorical chores that strike us as futile even when we know that nobody has declined them before us, an audience will sometimes be rocked and galvanized by a shot of unexpected eloquence. This, at any rate is an opening for the use of a great deal that, but for such providential demands, would rot away in our minds or our folders.

It is remarkable how apt and provocative so innocuous a thing as an invocation, a benediction, or an introduction can be. Christianity gets a meager hearing compared with other interpretations or misinterpretations of life, and we must seize whatever advantage comes to hand. Whenever we have access to an ear we should be ready to talk. A well-stocked and well-kept mind knows how to turn to brilliant account the drabbest task allotted to it in a public program.

A large portion of what we know is never actually produced, but remains in reserve. If we genuinely feel that we have lost time and vainly exhausted ourselves in acquiring it, we can regard it as a sort of offering; but in reality it is a great deal more than a bootless sacrifice we shall always regret. In order to say one thing convincingly we have to leave a number of other things unmentioned. There is an unmistakable difference between the man who tells us all he knows and the man who makes us feel, when he has finished, that he could tell us far more were it not that he has already said enough. For every proof we adduce, there should be at least one that we keep to ourselves. Each fact we cite should have behind it facts to which we make no reference. Our illustrations should suggest that we could multiply them interminably if we were less considerate of our listeners. The shadows of the mind should be as well filled as the lighted area of immediate consciousness. All that we have learned lurks somewhere within us, and none of it is wasted. God accepts and utilizes our feeblest apprehension of truth.

For the rest, the priest will get his discipline by an honest, discriminating search for perfection in communication. This will be pursued chiefly in the domain of words, but a priest should be conversant with other symbols, and in general communication he ought to possess his own kind of *expertise*.

In an earlier day the priest as often as not was the most learned man in his community. He might not be an omnicompetent polymath, but he knew something about everything and carried his burden of knowledge with a certain elegance. In his humane mind there was hospitality for all sincere thought and all righteous aspiration. His role was to reconcile in Christ the multitude of conflicting ideologies that men produced and the multitude of separate interests that agitated them. This is still his work, no matter how its difficulties have been aggravated by the fragmentation of learning. The reconciliation, of course, is far more than a pure affair of the intellect, but at least it has to include the mind, and often it begins there. A superficial, half-taught priest cannot render this vital service to his people or to people in general, and if he does not do it, nobody will do it. We expect many of our parishioners to surpass us in their respective specialties. That should not bother us, but a priest ought to be worried if specialists cannot talk to one another through him.

Study in America has become a regrettably competitive and individualistic pursuit. Learning, if often displayed, is at the same time hoarded. We look upon our ideas as our property, and we protect them and exploit them instead of sharing them. The rancor of rivalry long ago invaded the seminary and remains there to upset and divide men who could easily be at one in their common vocation. Later, we study to suit ourselves and so are further separated from one another. After some years our minds may lose much of their ardor and resilience for want of fellowship. Unstimulated and unfertilized, they will lapse into a lethargic indifference, for nothing is so fatiguing as one's own unbroken company. Anxiety about our intellectual individuality may deprive us of it entirely. At all events, our best chance of keeping it is to expose it constantly to encounters that will exercise, sharpen, and refine it. To think best we need the prodding that only companionship can administer.

All professional men tend to fraternize freely within the profession and to avoid challenging contacts, so far as possible, outside it. The clergy of a diocese or a deanery come together periodically on business, and their fellowship may be extremely refreshing. Nevertheless, it is an exclusively clerical fellowship, and its effect is to confirm us in our clericalism. A set of congenial parish clergy may, from time to time, spend a morning in discussion, but they either reach predictable conclusions or do not reach any conclusions at all. This inconclusiveness is indeed the bane of the discussions for which we have so insatiable a passion. We toss our opinions and, once in a long time, a bit of real knowledge into the crucible, and then suddenly the time is up and the fire goes out. We generate a quite promising heat, but we do not maintain it long enough to accomplish any fusion of ideas and purposes. Our discussions are commonly too short and too wary to be productive.

We might eventually settle something if we extended our conversation beyond the initial skirmish or clash and engaged one another in a sustained and unfeigned struggle of wills and minds. There would be some lacerations and contusions, if not actual fatalities, but at least our convictions would be put to the proof of battle, and the casualties would be reparable. As it is, we often raise the war cry, but we never launch an attack, to say nothing of pressing it to a decision.

If this proposal seems too bold, we might essay a little sensible collaboration. One can scarcely imagine a more profitable clerical project than a clearly defined task of research performed, say one day a week for some months, by a group of working priests. Pastoral situations and community problems could be examined unhurriedly and in the most searching fashion, with assistance from secular experts in matters beyond the competence of the clergy. In a similar way, a team formed on the basis of a common interest could explore some theological or historical question in a series of interlocking papers. The benefits of such fellowship in study are virtually infinite, both for the hesitant mind and for the lonely spirit. Besides, scholarship gains something, and its gain may not be negligible.

The reader may, if he likes, dismiss our remarks about corporate study as visionary and impracticable. If he prefers to study alone, we wish him enjoyment of his solitude. Every man shapes the ambiance of his work insofar as he has the power to indulge his tastes, humor his temperament, and select his associates. The one thing nobody can escape in true study is the exercise of judgment. Our final assertion about every enterprise of the intellect is that it is critical and for that reason productive. The ultimate force in all such endeavor is one's belief in one's own originality, and originality is simply the ability to recognize truth when one sees it. To have a mind at all is to possess this gift in some measure.

The rare originality that cracks all the codes of nature is perhaps not ours, but if we push ourselves we can write significant footnotes to the masterpieces of better minds. If this is all we can do, we need not be ashamed of our modest endowments. We too are scientists and scholars, and someday we shall speak the decisive word about something. We shall have the joy of grasping and enunciating some small truth that has eluded all other inquirers, and when that happens to us, we shall be glad that we are human. Our creative response to truth proves that we are the sons of God. The divine energy that made us also abides in us.

CHAPTER VI

Godliness with Contentment

F AITH itself is a decision, and it entails innumerable other decisions. If one is a priest, guidance towards soundness in these decisions is to be found in what may be called the ethics of priesthood. A complete formulation of sacerdotal ethics has yet to be produced. Even if we felt capable of the task, we should not undertake to perform it here. In any case, no exposition can capture all that the mystery of priesthood embraces. With the assistance of manuals, treatises, compendia, retreat addresses, sermons, biographies, canons, charges, and directives, supplemented by whatever we can glean from conversation and observation, we laboriously grasp the principles, criteria, standards, and patterns of priesthood. Yet such knowledge does not always tell us how to act in given circumstances. We sometimes have nothing to follow but our intuitive sense of what priesthood demands of us. When we can be precise about our duties, we are bound to a conscientious execution of them, but there are moments when precision is unattainable. At its deepest, the priesthood is a vocation from God and a relation to him. This is a stricter tie than any explicit law.

God is our portion, our wealth, our estate, and if he does not suffice, nothing will. Our felicity does not consist in doing a specific work or occupying a particular office. Nature has given us preferences, and it would doubtless be quixotic to ignore them; but we are not permitted to be dominated by them. All priests have a human desire for professional advancement. They have other appetites, superficially less creditable, and these they at least strive to curb. Lust and sloth would be condemned in any interpretation of the ethics of priesthood. In contrast, ambition for the most part is accepted as a legitimate motive, and eyebrows are raised the moment one asks, 'Is ambition in any degree compatible with the spirit of true priesthood?' To priests who are more worried about their brethren's ambition than about their own the question seems idle and naive. Exactly for this reason it requires ample and searching discussion.

One preliminary observation can be made flatly and boldly. The Church is the abode of truth and love. It is not a sphere in which power can lawfully be wielded against another human being simply because the wielder happens to possess it. It is a heinous thing to use an accidental advantage for our own selfish profit at the expense, and to the shame, of a person who lacks the means of resisting us. The bishop who ruthlessly rejects and gets rid of unsuccessful vicars, the rector who humiliates his curate, and the confessor who terrifies his penitents with his sadistic severity are guilty of flagrantly unchristian conduct. Sometimes it is a streak of meanness and cruelty that makes us act this way, but more frequently it is ambition or, especially with the junior clergy, frustration, which is ambition blocked and backing up on itself. In gaining our abominable little victories we are really disposing of rivals, and we are not innocent simply because we shed no blood. We cannot defend such behavior when we see it for what it is. Unprincipled ambition is reprehensible in a priest; on this point Christian opinion is unanimous. If clerical ambition is to be countenanced in any measure, it must confine its activities to unexceptionable methods and devices. If we must fight with others for rank and authority, let us shrink from kicking them in the groin and jumping on them when they are down.

The clergy of various persuasions still occasionally assault one another in the Church of the Holy Sepulcher in Jerusalem, and the spectacle is inexpressibly shocking to an observer who has Western standards of clerical deportment. Is this candid violence, however, the absolute nadir in clerical misconduct? We suggest that there are worse things. What, for example, does God think of the intrigues, combinations, and bargains that precede practically every episcopal election? Are we doing our best to demonstrate that Christianity is a spent religion? Are we helping to prove, by our machinations and chicanery, that the Church, as an institution containing people, is inescapably subject to the sordidness and deterioration from which every natural society eventually suffers? Perhaps, since we are so frail and stupid, we shall always have to tolerate a certain amount of horse-trading in the Church. If so, let it be horse-trading for which we need not apologize. The priest who ventures to be a politician at all must be at least an honest politician.

Having dissociated ourselves from corrupt, self-serving ecclesiastics, if there are any such, we can now survey the opinions that are current among our fellow-clergy. There are probably three distinct views. Many would argue that, short of actual wrong, a priest may be as aggressive as he likes in self-advancement. Others would grant him liberty to improve his condition only insofar as his needs and the needs of his dependents demand such effort of him. A few would deny him all initiative in the promotion of his own welfare, except in clear cases of misplacement. Where in all this confusion are the true Christian values to be found?

We begin by taking a close look at the permissible aggressiveness referred to just above. The more aggressive it is, the more perilously it approaches the unlawful. It requires a delicate awareness of conflicting good and evil to keep it in check, and a priest who is continually thrusting himself forward loses this sense very quickly. There is a kind of moral obtusity about the self-promoting ecclesiastic; he is crudely blind to much that more modest people see instantaneously.

Moreover, a careerist must scheme, calculate, maneuver, and manipulate; he is a politician, and that is the way politicians act. His friendships must be useful, his kindnesses must impose an obligation, his commitments must be conditional, and everything he does must propel him towards the consummation of his ambition. Such a person cannot be at the disposal of parishioners, penitents, and petitioners. Even the advice he gives must contribute to his glorification. Hence he cannot be wholly a priest. People will always perceive that he is subtly exploiting them by the very efficiency with which he serves them. He may do nothing manifestly wicked, but he will not progress beyond a negative estimability. He cannot hide his indifference to everything that militates against his own interests. Nobody regards him as a hero, and nobody imagines that he is seriously trying to be a saint. The most intimate confidences will be withheld from him, and men will guard themselves in his presence. He will never really know anybody else, because he refuses to know himself. His end is to get what he wants and to detest it when he gets it. He either attains his end and flourishes unloved and unfulfilled, or fails to attain it and has no comfort in his defeat. He has not been openly untrue to his vocation, but he has not fully embraced it either.

Last of all, the pusher is always at least faintly comic in his eagerness to be recognized. He never grows tired of nominating himself for dignities, distinctions, and decorations, and the result is that he is known more for his absurdity than for his merits. An invincible belief in oneself is the most ludicrous of human failings. The person who denies daily proof of his frailty and inadequacy is a bit of a monster, and if he is also a priest, he is doubly funny and grotesque in his infatuation. For all these reasons, a priest, even if he incurs no specific guilt, should not permit ambition to be paramount in his life. The passion to get ahead, if it is that and nothing more, submits to no permanent curb; it finally consumes the mind that is so misled as to yield to it.

A better position and a larger income become especially desirable when the older children of a sizable family are approaching college age. Here we are not dealing with raw ambition; rather it is a question of discharging one's responsibilities. There is in a priest's life a broad area where self-interest and the interests of one's flesh and blood coincide. Sometimes we have to help ourselves in order to help those who have a claim on us.

The Anglican clergy are at their best in this penumbra of clashing duties. Multitudes of them contrive to look after their cures and their families without any material neglect of either. The Church abounds in examples of cheerful and habitual unselfishness on the part of priests who have none of the usual reasons for being satisfied with their lot. Their present is unapplauded, their future is not assured, and they could easily become a prey to frustrations and anxieties. Their response to all this is to forget about themselves, and it proves to be a remarkably effective response.

What is more, good priests have to be prepared to recognize the moment when they need to forget about their families. Prudent provision for one's family is admirable and obligatory, but a priest has little to be provident with, and where others have resources on which they can draw, he frequently has to abandon himself and his family to the divine generosity. When the abandonment is neither a fiction nor a gesture, but an unreserved act of trust, the priest and his family are actually delivered from want and from the gnawing apprehensions that are far worse than want. It is incredible, but those who try it find that it is true.

Admittedly, perfect reliance on God's particular concern for us is difficult to acquire (if that is not a misleading word) and somewhat more difficult to retain. Much trouble springs from preconceptions concerning the clerical standard of living. When a priest's wife cherishes such preconceptions, she is apt to cherish them with formidable tenacity and rigidity. If she insists on amenities that many of her husband's parishioners have not the means of enjoying, she will at least appear to deny some of the things that he is constantly teaching. She may betray her husband into a destructive covetousness, with lamentable consequences to him and to herself. Out of loyalty to her he may seek or even demand a mode of life that he secretly regards as inimical to his vocation, and misery will certainly ensue for both of them.

Everything else in a priest's life is secondary to the vocation by virtue of which he has become a priest. A grasping wife is an impediment to a man who is contemplating ordination, and if a man is ordained first and looks for a suitable spouse after some acquaintance with the realities of parochial life, he is foolish not to examine all candidates for the trait we are now considering, an overweening social and economic ambition. Unfortunate is the priest who curbs this drive in himself only to find it out of control in the woman for whose support and welfare he is responsible. One sees no small number of clerical couples who should have had an understanding about this matter at the time of their engagement. A woman to whom the disabilities of a clergyman's existence are distasteful makes a hazardous wife for a priest. If he is already married to her when her character becomes evident, he will have to find some way of ministering to her, and this he will not accomplish by yielding to her. Presumably we do not marry unless we "judge the same to serve better to godliness."[1] A marriage so begun may require severe measures to keep it steadfast in conformity to its original design.

Certainly a priest without a private fortune cannot expect to provide lavishly for his children, even if he has few of them and his salary is unusually high. Nowadays a young priest has four or five children rather than one or two, and if his income is considerably larger than it would have been a generation ago, it still does not suffice

---

1. "Bishops, Priests, and Deacons, are not commanded by God's Law, either to vow the estate of single life, or to abstain from marriage: therefore it is lawful for them, as for all other Christian men, to marry at their own discretion, **as they shall judge the same to serve better to godliness.**" (*Article XXXII*)

to send all the girls to Smith and all the boys to Harvard. One gets the impression that often these limitations are boldly disregarded or not clearly foreseen.

A priest's family reaches a certain size, and only then does he ponder the complications that will plague him when his children are ready to be equipped for survival in a furiously competitive age. The benefits of a clerical rearing are not to be underestimated, but neither are the strains, hardships, and disappointments of a household in which there are never funds to spare. Not all clerical children have the capacity to obtain substantial scholarships. Most of them will depend on their parents for the payment of college bills, and their parents will depend on special consideration, of which there is less and less for the clergy all the time. Thus a modern Father Quiverful may have to make a business of procuring bounty for his family, and although he probably will not employ any really dubious means, his begging approach to people will distract and humiliate him and irritate them. What he gains as a parent by snatching at every possible cut, gift, and discount, he will lose as a priest. He will incur as much enmity as he would if he were concerned exclusively with his own advancement. To put oneself in the position of having to be ambitious is to choose ambition.

It remains true that the bare fact of marriage does not make a man less a priest. The godliness of a marriage consists in the exercise of restraint and self-denial as well as generous and unanxious love. All married Christians must maintain a rational relation between resources and responsibilities, for where there is no balance between the two there is after a time no integrity in the person. The deliberate increase of our responsibilities without a corresponding increase in our resources is either presumption or a laxity verging on imbecility, but it does little good, once a straitened situation has arisen, to talk about intentions and dispositions. Have we shouldered more than we can carry? If we cannot honorably lighten the load, let us stagger along under it with whatever dignity we can muster, in the hope (not a vain one) that God will not forever penalize us for our folly. Can we not, instead of importuning relatives, bishops, and headmasters for relief, tranquilly wait for God to intervene with mercy and understanding and so to save us from the shabby shifts of the habitual clerical mendicant?

By pointing out the perils and compromises involved in any guarded liberty we may give to ambition (unconditional liberty, we must understand, is forbidden), we have arrived at what seems to the writer the safest and truest stance for a priest to take. There is but one unobjectionable reason why a priest should look elsewhere for work, namely a conviction that he does not belong where he is. This has to be a total judgment, in which we have taken due account of the whole range of possible self-deception and rationalization. We do not move because we itch to be on our way, or do not like our associates, or prefer some other locality, or imagine that our great abilities are not being used in our present sphere of duty. We have to be able to say honestly that we are doing badly, and cannot help doing badly, the work in which we are engaged. Personal as well as professional difficulties can legitimately influence us: it may not be the job as such, but a climate that activates all our allergies, a community of rabid segregationists, a crushing weight of physical labor, or an antediluvian school system. It must be our sincere belief that we can further the mission of the Church more by departing than by remaining. In that case we are free to leave, and it is not ambition that drives us away. We have made the salutary admission that at least one place in the Church is better off without us. If we can really accept that knowledge and act appropriately, we have prevailed over the most persistent of man's inner foes.

Ambition involves us in pride, envy, anger, and covetousness, and we know what to do about specific acts of these and other sins. The pervasive and evasive discontentment that afflicts the ambitious is not so easily handled. Actually, the restless and dissatisfied priest is not always the victim of ambition; he may be an unintegrated Anglican or a volatile enthusiast. Therefore we have not exhausted the question.

Anglicanism is not a conspicuously restful variety of the Christian religion. It is too large to be a compact, exclusive ingroup, too small to convey assurance solely by its magnitude, too dogmatic to leave the individual wholly to his own tastes, and too accommodating in practice to spare him the pain and travail of frequent personal decisions. It has no approved philosophy, and its official theology is so presented as to encourage dissent in details and even an occasional earnest questioning of foundations. It has spread itself widely, but in most places much too thinly; nowhere is it the church of an entire society. There is no freemasonry among its adherents, and Anglicans do not instinctively seek out Anglicans. It gives substantial powers to its lay people, and yet those who exercise the powers are not altogether happy about them and often are not vitally involved in the government and mission of the Church. There is much familiarity between the laity and the clergy, but sympathy, confidence, and intelligent respect are not greatly in evidence. Authority is diffused and confused, and its applications lack precision and uniformity.[2] Our vernacular liturgy uses the vernacular of another age; our clergy take liberties, both small and great, with the text of the liturgy and its rubrics; liturgical schools suspect and shun one another; the chances are that a simple lay Anglican in a strange parish of his own communion will be more mystified by the service than edified; and whether a given parish has a coherent body of liturgical customs or is merely grappling with accumulated and uncomprehended innovations, the liturgy is probably still an enigma to the majority of its people. Although the Anglican clergy are diligent and skillful teachers, Anglican communicants in general know neither the principles nor the precepts of their religion.

We could extend this to oppressive length and still not make all the adverse observations that a contemplation of the scene suggests. We can sum it all up by confessing that contentment is hard for a zealous Anglican priest. He would like to contribute to a massive, homogeneous, enduring work. Instead, he often feels that the little he does stands by itself if it stands at all. Anglican priests experience deeply the desolation of isolation, and that is why a dangerous malaise underlies their prodigious activity. They are uneasy because they are lonely.

Now loneliness is not primarily a matter of physical separation from other people;

---

2. This present contention is a product of the age. It is true that there are divisions within our Communion, but legitimate schools of thought have always been sanctioned within the Christian Faith. Whether it was Antioch and Alexandria or the Franciscans and Dominicans, unity was preserved. See Bp. Jewel's *The Apology of the Church of England*, Part III, for an answer to the Romans on this point. With him we say that our internal divisions "will shortly be agreed... all causes and seeds of dissension shall be thoroughly plucked up by the root, and be buried, and quite forgotten for ever. Which God Grant."

On our part, we must heed the warning of Fr. Benson: "How people of opposite schools among ourselves regard writers as shallow, or cold, or unreal! Whereas the appearance of shallowness, coldness, unreality is because they do not read and regard those opposite writers or preachers from their own standpoint... All sects which humanize Christianity, beginning with the great Western Church, and going on to every little Puritan fanatic however insignificant, just agree in this: 'I am Catholicity, and all must be measured by me.'" (*Undated Letter to Fr. O'Neill*) it is, more fundamentally, a rejection of one's fellows and a refusal of fellowship. It is not Anglicanism or any of its deficiencies that the discontented priest repudiates. We do not reject ideologies and theologies; we reject human beings, and thereby we reject ourselves. The priest who cannot bear Anglicanism cannot bear anything else. The essential effort of priesthood is probably no more difficult, no more disagreeable, and no more discouraging in Anglicanism than it is in any other pattern of Catholic life. Whether it is or not, we must quit Anglicanism or learn to be loyal to it.

Being loyal to it means accepting it, working cheerfully within its confines when we cannot transcend them, and rejoicing in the providence that has made us Anglicans. Being loyal means serving without a cushion of reservations to protect us from the full impact of our duty.

We do not know exhaustively why God permitted Anglicanism to come into existence, how long he intends to let it survive, or to what end he is sustaining it. Complete knowledge of these things is not indispensable. If we were seriously in doubt of God's presence and activity in Anglicanism, alarm and dejection would be warranted. We cannot entertain such misgivings, for God has expressed himself to us and through us. Anglicanism is not the only vehicle of grace, but it is a true and effective descendant of the biblical community. If we do not perceive the power of the priesthood it has entrusted to us, the deficiency is in us. We are censorious talkers and self-indulgent laborers. Our uncertainties originate in the imperfections of our service. We have not embraced Anglicanism as an obligation and an opportunity.

One does not become integrated into a body without surrendering something to it. An Anglican priest surrenders everything that other Christians surrender; he offers himself, his endowments, and his possessions. One thing remains: the mind's bent towards the comfort of an assured, unambiguous, unassailable place in a perfect system. Here a distinctive sacrifice is required of the Anglican priest. He must reconcile himself to forgoing all the advantages of a clear, recognized position. He will have to learn not to be troubled and deterred by misunderstanding. Protestants will write him off as an odd, unruly Catholic. Other Catholics will dismiss him as a Protestant with a limited mastery of Catholic parlance and customs. He will have to explain himself to most of the people he meets, and still his position will be unintelligible. He himself will move within the Anglican range of opinion and practice, losing friends every time he alters his views or his habits. It is a setting in which the essential Christian values are conserved only by means of the most profound self-abnegation and self-oblivion.

In the main, the Anglican clergy cannot command; they are restricted to persuasion, and even the laws that support them have to be administered with a certain respect for personalities, though of course not with cowardly respect of persons. The Anglican priest rarely has the luxury of being satisfied with himself. The certitudes of rank, public character, and uncontested authority are denied to him. For him sanctity alone will suffice. If he can be positively thankful that he lacks all adventitious helps, he may count on receiving a power uncontaminated by pride, the power of an absolutely unreserved conformity to a cherished vocation. He will be literally, factually, and visibly a man of God, and with his godliness he will have contentment.

The priest who is not a guileless man of God will probably be an enthusiast, and the more empty and desperate he is within, the more effervescent his enthusiasm will be. Nobody minds his being energetic, if his energy is harnessed to his mission, but a capricious enthusiasm, darting from one object to another, can stimulate a parish to the point of satiety and yet effect nothing but a fragmentation of its essential interest. Enthusiasm is particularly regrettable when it compels the entire congregation either to follow the rector into immoderate devotion to a partisan cause or to withstand or forsake him. A priest may become so engrossed in work with delinquents, alcoholics, wayward girls, senior citizens, or some other specific group that he ceases to exercise a comprehensive ministry in his cure. He is guilty of a kind of self-indulgence, for he is doing what he prefers to do, and there is nothing priestly about that.

It is even less excusable to seek consolation for pastoral defeats in the pursuit of some unmistakably secular enthusiasm. A boat, a workshop, or a musical instrument can absorb our vitality and so virtually extinguish our priesthood. To remain a recognizable priest, one has to persevere in the characteristic labors of a priest.

We are protected so long as we remember that the work we do is not ours. We should not care excessively about surroundings, associates, satisfactions, or results. Priests whom adversity confirms in their vocation are invincible. Unless we are ruinous misfits, we can confidently stay just where we are. That is the substance of the ethics of priesthood.

Chapter VII

Compassed with Infirmity

I F contentment must accompany godliness, it must also be applied to godliness. We submit to the hindrances that our allotted place imposes on us, and at the same time we submit to the infirmities that make our witness and our service so meager and so miserable. We are not proud of the little we do, and we do not regard it as sufficient, but we do not fret about it and wish that we could think better of it. We do not resent the finitude of human capacity.

The most human thing about man is that nothing he ever does is completely right. He continues, for all that, to hold himself to, and to measure himself by, perfection, but it is not the same perfection for everybody. For one it is perfection in art, for another perfection in morals, for a third perfection in prayer. The nearest we get to perfection is to brush against it as it eludes us. We do not actually know what it is, yet we cannot stop pursuing it. We cannot ignore it because we were created to strive after it. A perfect God has made us in order that we may seek him by reflecting his perfection. Even the criminal's effort to achieve a perfect crime can be referred to an ideal that God has implanted in us. In its most perverted and distorted forms the desire for perfection remains genuinely human.

Absolute natural perfection can only be imagined. It is manifestly not for us in the world we now inhabit, where miscalculation, error, and failure are more conspicuous than their opposites. Moreover, their opposites are relative; one is merely better or worse at something than one's neighbor, and we know that this proves nothing. It is the fate of all achievement to be surpassed.

Priests, like other men, have their plans and their aspirations, and the objective of these is often the subject's own peculiar image of natural perfection. All such images are more or less illusions. There is no refuge from mischance. Thousands of planes take off and land every day under the control of pilots with practically

180

perfect reflexes, but the reflexes are not quite perfect, and occasionally an accident occurs. The coordination of military bodies in combat is never without fault. The best of priests will, once in a while, be unaware of a first evensong, read a wrong lesson, or muff the ending of a collect. No sermon wholly fulfills the design of its creator, no word of consolation altogether fits the situation, no intricate ceremony is performed without a hitch. For a day, a week, perhaps even a fortnight, we maintain a semblance of perfection, and then a tired muscle or a sluggish eye betrays us into committing an enormous blunder. We regret the lapse, but we do not need to repent of it. Mistakes are not totally avoidable.

We sometimes comfort ourselves by comparing ourselves with people who are demonstrably worse than we are, but, although this flatters us, we are as far as ever from absolute perfection. The fact that my colleague mispronounces seven times as many words as I do accentuates our common ignorance more than it accentuates the relative purity of my diction. He may manage a parish of nine hundred with almost no administrative slips, while I fail to keep a parish of two hundred in order, but neither of us is a flawless executive. We cannot perpetually solace ourselves with comparisons unless we rather myopically and dishonestly limit them. A general comparison will reveal so many points of inferiority in us that we shall find further study of comparative perfection a trifle unpalatable. Suppose we escape all these ordinary lacerations of the ego. It is still impossible for us to be so good at anything that our record is never threatened. We have to die early to preserve it.

The judgments that men pass on one another are as unpredictable as the distractions that mar our prayers. Where do our odd, grotesque thoughts come from, and where do men go for the criteria by which they assess one another? Most judgment is vitiated by arbitrariness and animosity. The authority is the self of the moment, and if the self is cross- grained, capricious, and vindictive, what is the value of the pronouncements? We can eliminate malice from our estimates of others, but a certain irreducible residue of infirmity continually defeats us. We do not see everything, and we misinterpret what we see.

People can be egregiously wrong about a priest, and a priest can be fantastically wrong about himself. Inside the Church as well as outside it, critics have divergent standards of clerical worth. The standards themselves are relative, and their application is fallible, inconstant, and inconsistent. Everybody who thinks about priests at all has picked up somewhere some simulacrum of a praiseworthy priest. People who are addicted to discussing themselves demand a priest of untiring sympathy and patience. Servicemen look for a 'good Joe,' humanists for a man of subtle taste, politicians for a demagogue or spellbinder, and men of business for a man of business. Vestrymen prize an active priest. Rectors value submissiveness. Bishops expect efficiency. No individual could meet every one of these frequently conflicting requirements, and if by some *tour de force* he made himself acceptable to all his judges, it would be only for a moment. The judges themselves do not really know why they prefer one man to another, and nobody retains their favor indefinitely. The phrase 'a good priest' has a thousand meanings, and a sufficiently mobile and flexible mind can run through them all in a lifetime. Even priests change their patterns of priesthood.

Therefore the verdicts of men are provisional. God reviews and corrects them, and for the present we are in ignorance of his judgment. St. Paul indicates the stand that a Christian must take: "So pass no premature judgment; wait until the Lord comes."[1] For all of us, particularly those who are priests, it is salutary to judge ourselves severely and others leniently, but we must stop short of self-rejection, which is also a rejection of the salvation God offers us. Our vision is blurred, but we can still see, and we still know the difference between light and darkness. Relative perfection, the only kind of perfection God requires of us, is not beyond us.[2]

How do we attain this relative perfection? We begin by finding out what we mean by relative perfection. It is relative only because it could be worse. If deterioration is possible, improvement also is possible, and we are instinctively conscious that this is the case with us. Human perfection therefore is motion, and so long as we are moving and our orientation is correct, we are entitled to call ourselves relatively

---

1. 1 Corinthians 4:5

2. See William Law: "As the law to angels is angelic righteousness, as the law to perfect beings is strict perfection, so the law to our imperfect nature is, the best obedience that our frail nature is able to perform. (*A Serious Call to A Devout and Holy Life*, Chapter III.)

perfect.[3] Our destiny is to be united with God, and that union presumably will enable us to participate in his absolute perfection, but the participation will not make us absolute ourselves, and the gift of union will consist essentially in the removal of the possibility of failure. Because of our destiny, absolute perfection must be the measure of all that we do; only by perpetual reference to it can we maintain relative perfection. If this involves a paradox, it is an indispensable paradox. We attain perfection by not attaining it. Knowing that we have not attained it and cannot attain it, we yet interminably pursue it and are never satisfied with our present condition. To be thus engaged is to be perfect in the only manner that is now open to us.

Such reflections as these should lead to unqualified gratitude for our creaturehood, with all the contingencies and infirmities that belong to it. If we can cherish the amicable imperfections of others, we need not be excessively resentful of our own. Avoiding narcissism and everything reminiscent of it, we must nevertheless be glad to be what we are: sloppy administrators, inept pastors, stammering preachers, and blundering human beings. We are bound, it is true, to correct all that is corrigible; yet our limitations will persist, and we can laugh at them and love them for God's sake.

We shall use a very clerical illustration to sharpen these observations. A young vicar, resident in the diocese only a few months and therefore sure neither of himself nor of his new environment, invites the bishop to confirm a class of creditable size, and, in the vicar's partial judgment, sterling character. The bishop's wife is expected, since she is known to accompany her husband on every such expedition. The vestry and their wives have been asked to dinner, the bishop's liturgical and culinary tastes have been exhaustively investigated, and the confirmands have been elaborately coached in the intricacies of the confirmation ceremonial. Nothing that can conceivably help to insure a perfect visitation has been omitted.

The vicar and his wife are virtually prostrate with fatigue and apprehension. They are racked with fears of what they may have forgotten, what they will find to say to their visitors, and what the less reliable members of the class will do when they are

---

3. "And by all the declaration of St. Paul, it is evident, that the true, lively, and Christian faith, is no dead, vain, or unfruitful thing, but a thing of perfect virtue, of wonderful operation or working, and strength, bringing forth all good motions, and good works." (*Homily on the True & Lively Faith*)

inescapably face to face with the bishop. The day comes, and none of these fears is more than vaguely realized. The calamities that do occur are seemingly the antics of invisible powers. The bishop's wife does not appear with her husband, and the reason for this turns out to be that she was not explicitly included in the invitation. Obviously the bishop thinks that this is a prime piece of gaucherie on the vicar's part. Babbling to keep from collapsing, the vicar passes the sherry and hopes that the two tardy vestry couples will arrive in time to permit an unhurried dinner. Naturally they do not, and with barely an hour left before service, the vicar herds his guests into the dining room, starts to ask a blessing, remembers that the bishop is there, and clumsily tries to save the situation by grinning unhappily and nodding a bit brusquely to his superior, who by this time is decidedly not delighted with the way things are going.

Somehow they all sit down, and the bishop, with truly episcopal aplomb and urbanity, reactivates the conversation; but the talk begins to languish as the guests observe that the vicar is about to be thrown by the turkey he is supposed to be carving. This fowl, bought at a high price and unconditionally guaranteed to be superlatively tender, is proving to be inexplicably tough and, for an indubitably dead bird, curiously uncooperative. The vicar's trembling hands cannot guide the knife to the joints, and never afterwards will he be able to recollect how he contrived to hack a few shreds of white meat from the defiant breast. After ghastly suspense, everybody gets something to eat, but there is now scarcely time to eat it. The vicar and the bishop dash off without dessert, both hungry and both dyspeptic.

Two of the confirmands send word that they are ailing and cannot come, a third falls out of the procession in a fainting condition, and the survivors make the responses inaudibly. The bishop gets away as soon as he can, and the vicar, tossing all night beside his weeping wife, waits for the moment when he can carry his woes to the altar in quest of some comfort for the mishaps of an unfavored day.

Not all days will be like this regrettable one, from which the vicar derives lifelong profit. There are certain mistakes that he will never make again. He cannot, however, anticipate all trouble, and some disasters will come upon him because of the infirmity of his intelligence and the dimness of his foresight. It is then that theology, if he is willing to live by it, will be his deliverance. If he really understands what it is to be a creature, he will not be discouraged about himself.

Man does not have to resign himself to his natural weaknesses. He suffers them patiently, but does not perforce sink abjectly under them. Some semblance of direction can always be maintained, and our purposes can be firm, sound, and true, no matter how we bungle the execution. People as limited as ourselves see what we do. God sees what we intend. In the divine judgment we have all the vindication we need.

The very knowledge of an infirmity can make us more steadfast than we should have been if we had been born stronger. Victorious inner power often springs from weakness candidly recognized, accepted for what it is, and valiantly overcome. Religious orders have rarely been founded by geniuses, and few of the Church's illustrious pastors have been men of superlative gifts. Again and again significant work has been done in the Church by a person with some grave defect, who instead of being depressed by it has used it as a stimulus and grown immensely strong by the proper treatment of it. The bulk of the clergy may not be capable of much really creative thought, but many of them have the deep wisdom that enables a man to do something creative with his deficiencies. If we genuinely intend to please and serve God, our mistakes cannot crush us. It fortifies us to know that our purpose is not chosen, but given, wherefore our weakness can be at least a negative aid to the divine energy on which the effort ultimately depends. People who are conscious of their fallibility are less likely than the irrepressibly confident to be misled with regard to vocation and the various drives and impulses that seem to belong to vocation and yet may not be consistent with it. People who are humbly aware of their weakness have to ask for the grace of perseverance, and this, rather than mere human talent or aggressiveness, is the power that builds the Church. We cannot always see the value of what is being done while it is being done. God alone sees the merit of the things we sincerely do for his sake, and they are good in his eyes. No other judgment should matter to us.

Realizing that God will salvage and utilize, in his providence, whatever deserves to survive, we cannot fail to perceive that works done are to be offered and surren-

dered. We allow them to rest with God until the reckoning, and then we shall know
how well they were done. We do not improve them by brooding over them long
past the time of action. The memory of last Sunday's wretched sermon may fill us
with shame and regret, but next Sunday's will be even more wretched if we permit
the shame and regret to interfere with our preparation.

The discontinuity of priestly work in the Anglican Communion is one of the great
Anglican mysteries, and we are constrained to live with it. All my visible achievements can be undone by my successor. I cannot allow this threat to paralyze me,
and really it is not a threat, for beneath the superficial clash of methods and programs and the vexation of man's infirmities the things we do for God endure because we abandon them to him. We have an obligation to our predecessors, and
when we discharge it we help to insure our own considerate treatment on the part
of our successors.

It is a mean sort of weakness that makes us minimize the good accomplished by
those who held office before us. We do not magnify ourselves by denigrating or
patronizing them. Their mistakes plead for our compassion, and what they did well
is entitled to our appreciation. Their notions of priesthood and ministry may not
be identical with ours, their emphases and enthusiasms may be distasteful to us,
and we may think that their blind spots still show up in the life of the parish. We
may justly feel that they have left us a difficult heritage. It is irritating to be fettered
by the past, as one so often is in a parish, and our resentment of the influence that
former rectors still exert and our contempt for their antiquated ways too readily
make us forgetful of their struggles, which in essence are scarcely distinguishable
from ours. They too fumbled, floundered, and failed. Like us, they read books,
subscribed to periodicals, went to clergy conferences, and listened with respect to
their intellectual betters. They fol- lowed the prevailing theological and ecclesiastical fashions, precisely as we do, and just as timorously and unoriginally. They were
sons of their respective ages, as we are of ours —sons and also prisoners. Strip them
of the rags that time has put upon them and you lay bare members, organs, and
drives that are universal.

Those who once served where we serve exhibit in various combinations the debility and the fortitude that mingle in human life. Too faithfully they reproduced the presuppositions and prejudices of the *Zeitgeist*, not knowing what they were doing any more than we do when we are engaged in the same activity. Their surplices, their sermons, and their prayers were longer than ours. Their years of schooling and their lives were shorter. They did not, on those accounts, belong to a different species. They were our brothers in their uncertainties, their efforts, their aspirations, and their limitations. Like us, they often implemented their faith badly, but they had the faith, and they helped to make us what we are. All honor, then, to them for their loyal wills and their warm love and no shame for the things that are less to their credit.

Can we not also manifest graciousness and forbearance towards our successors? A reluctance to do this is one of the gravest weaknesses of the clergy. There should be a complete disengagement when a man leaves a post; he should be careful even about the friendships he retains. The severance of emotional bonds is imperative. So long as our ego identifies itself with the job it will matter to us a great deal how the job is done, and if we show how we feel we may injure our successor. We must work on ourselves until we have produced an interior submission to the change. We relinquish the responsibilities we had in our former place, turn into other courses the energy we once expended upon it, and presumably transfer our interest in it from action to prayer. We are sorry Christians if our act of detachment is a sham and we covertly regard our successor as an intruder and usurper.

The shabby behavior that results from such a view is familiar enough. We maintain a formal correctness, but we encourage complaints, give comfort to malcontents, contrive to embarrass our successor, emit snide observations on his policies, gloat over his failures, and use the device of reserved and grudging applause to reduce the satisfaction he may feel in his undeniable successes. One retiring dignitary, seated beside his successor at a farewell dinner, declared coarsely, "I cannot bear to see another cock on my dunghill." He said bluntly what all of us feel like saying when we are supplanted. It is not wrong to feel the purely involuntary pangs of this bitterness, but it is wrong in the extreme to make our successor pay for our pain. With curious perversity, we invoke the Golden Rule against our predecessors, but flagrantly neglect to observe it in our relations with our successors.

The distress we experience at being adequately replaced is an indication that we have not wholly extricated ourselves from the jungle. Mistrust and envy of our successor are relics of a primitivity that we have partially outgrown and from which, insofar as it is evil, we have been redeemed. In a brute this response to a threat would be eminently natural, but it does not become us, with our rationality, to behave in so savage a fashion. The spectacle of another busy with our former duties should not inflame us, and in allowing such a thing to disturb us we are being unjust to ourselves. It would be far more rational to discern in our successor's success a delicate compliment to our own efficiency. Had we been less effective, he would not have been able to improve on our work so quickly. Our deeds have not been forgotten; they have been absorbed, and in this we have proof that they have been accepted.

All the positive things we have said in this chapter reach splendid fruition in the life of a priest who died a couple of decades ago. None of our readers would recognize his name. He was not renowned in his day, and there is nothing in his memory to inspire a cult. It is his obscurity that commends him as an example of self-effacing priesthood.

Indeed his power to forget himself was his greatest gift. He was not a brilliant ecclesiastic, and his charm was not the aggressive sort that asserts itself in the most brief encounter. People who had known him for years suddenly discovered him and found themselves venerating him. His admirers, however, constantly had to apologize for him to less penetrating observers. Not everybody perceived the pathos in him, and what his friends prized in him was not obvious to strangers. When he preached, his voice was soporific, his gestures were wooden, and his language was colorless and full of clichés. Nevertheless people were sustained and matured by his sermons. As a pastor, he was shy and unresourceful, rarely achieving rapport with a new parishioner on his first visit.

Still, the townspeople gradually became conscious of his broad and gentle ministry, and in time he was welcome at all levels. He did not excel as an administrator, nor was he conspicuously bad. He was conscientious rather than energetic about business, and occasionally a vestryman would be exasperated with him for some minor lapse in the conduct of the affairs of the parish. Yet every organization in that parish was solicitously, unremittingly, and unobtrusively supervised. It was a town of middle size, and a gathering of women for any purpose was apt to resolve itself quickly into a malicious supplement to the town's two newspapers. People soon noticed that this did not happen when the rector was there or even when he was anywhere around. After a time he did not need to attend every meeting; the bare possibility of his appearing in the midst of an unhallowed conversation had a deterring influence on the gossips. Administration, for him, was never its own justification.

Whatever other kinds of proficiency a priest is expected to display he displayed –*practiced* would be a better word– unspectacularly. His leadership was never flamboyant; his financial operations were conservative, honest, and circumspect; and he was a scholar to the extent of being able to listen intelligently to the theological dialogue of his day. Exceptional in no particular, he was saved from mediocrity and ineffectuality by a certain tranquil inner balance, part of it temperamental and part the work of intense discipline. He possessed a completely unobsequious humility.

He had come to the parish to assist an aging rector under a delicate and hazardous arrangement. The rector had announced that he would retire, but he had not said exactly when or to what extent. He had, however, intimated that his new associate would be the next rector. Finally the rector decided on a partial retirement. The terms were very advantageous to him: he remained in the rectory, drew a generous pension, and reserved to himself the use of the pulpit on the chief feast days, including the first Sunday of the month, which was a high Sunday in that parish. The title of rector he magnanimously surrendered to his patient assistant, but there was almost no visible change in the parish. The rector emeritus, who had both a taste and a talent for preaching and a genius for getting his own way, continued to enjoy the kudos, the comforts, and much of the stipend that had long been his. To the new rector fell, as before, all the legwork, drudgery, and routine of the parish.

Years passed, and the old man lived on, growing constantly more cranky and more domineering and showing an ever deeper reluctance to hand over one shred of his irregular power to the nominal rector. The latter's preaching deteriorated under this unnatural competition, but there was no decline in anything else he did. Above all, he remained an industrious pastor, and the more galling his now senile predecessor became, the more he himself developed in the kind- ness, perception, and tact that characterize the supreme masters of pastoral care. He smiled gently when the clergy commiserated with him or his lay intimates ventured to indicate that they knew what he was suffering. He seemed to be well occupied and completely content where he was. Offers of other parishes came, but he declined them. He knew that no cure in the Church was essentially better or worse than the one he had. He had learned how to thrive on hindrances and imperfections. At the old man's death he moved at last into the rectory, but by that time he had long been, as people said, "the first citizen of the town." He was willing to be weak, and that was the basis of his strength.

Our invincibility begins the moment we lose our fear of weakness. Forty years of undistinguished and imperfect work may add up to a sanctity through which men actually see what God is like. Infirmities will hem us in, for we are born to them. It becomes us to be glad of them. If they restrain and sometimes frustrate us, they also protect us. A man who has accepted his limitations knows approximately where he belongs, and all that he needs to do for the rest of his life is to remain within the confines that nature and reason have fixed for him. He does not dissipate his vigor by expending it on unprofitable objects, and by his modesty and self-restraint he escapes the pitfalls of ambition, vanity, and presumption, in which he could suffer the exquisite tortures of disappointment and disenchantment. When a priest sees what men do with their strength and what their strength does to them, he recognizes how good God has been to him in compassing him with infirmity. He remembers all the people who would never have come to a radical understanding with God if they had not at some time been flat on their backs. The Christian is adept at turning a handicap into an advantage. Suffering often introduces us to beatitude.

CHAPTER VIII

A World of Iniquity

S IN is an anomaly in a Christian and a much more absurd anomaly in a priest. There have been clerical murderers, clerical adulterers, and clerical thieves –not many, to be sure, but enough to put all priests on their guard lest they abuse the confidence with which men so commonly approach them. The sin of a priest has interminable repercussions. The transgressions of one who is committed to a mortal struggle with sin carry in them a vicious treachery all their own.

Clerical adultery and clerical theft no doubt have their charms for the criminologist, but we have not found them half so instructive as clerical murder, which captivates us while it repels us. Murder is a direct negation of the very essence of priesthood. Above everything else, a priest cherishes and communicates life. When he deliberately extinguishes it, we are appalled at the peculiar enormity of his offense. The twisted route he has followed to the ultimate in sin becomes a matter of excruciating concern to us as priests, inasmuch as the same dark ruin is presumably possible for us.

We have lost our tempers, but not so calamitously as the Rev. Mr. Hackman,[1] whose disappointed love for Martha Ray, Lord Sandwich's mistress, betrayed him into shooting that lively lady outside Covent Garden Theatre in London on an April night in 1779.

We can sympathize with scholarly John Selby Watson, who in his old age committed a quiet Victorian murder upon his wife, his social inferior and an inveterate nag-

---

1. The Rev. James Hackman was ordained a Deacon in the Church of England in 1779 on the 24th of February, and Priest only four days later. On the 1st of March he was instituted as Rector of Wiveton, holding this office only a few weeks before murdering Martha Ray – the Earl of Sandwich's mistress – with a pistol on the 7th of April. He was hung for his crimes shortly after at Tyburn on the 19th of April.

ger.[2] Rev. Robert Foulkes, Rev. Franz Salesius Riembauer, Rev. Hans Schmidt, and Rev. Guy Desnoyers were clerical sex-murderers and somewhat unpleasant ones at that. Sometimes it is lust that predominates, but with greater or less frequency it is anger, pride, or covetousness. Behind all these recognizable sins is self-deception. To a priest who tells himself lies even murder at last becomes thinkable.

We are not, however, going to devote this chapter to the lurid story of clerical misconduct. Statistically, most of us are reasonably safe from the extremes, particularly while we remain mindful of our criminal potentialities. What of the unspectacular sins so peculiar to the priestly calling and so often indistinctly perceived? They originate mainly in exhaustion, pride, sloth, and an indiscreet exercise of the gift of speech. The ground to be covered in the discussion of these matters has already been traversed, but a return to it does not necessarily involve undue repetition.

Watson was a harassed man, tired, bored, and almost despairing after a life spent in grinding out books that were neither duds nor dynamite. His existence was an endless Lent, crushing in its monotony and austerity. Lent is an exhausting season for the clergy, and the more faithfully they have observed it, the more likely they are to be tempted to some excess as soon as it is over. Post-Lenten fatigue is to blame for some arresting examples of spiritual defeat. A vacation immediately after Easter is a dangerous thing for a clergyman; relaxation following so quickly upon mortification can easily be carried too far. Possibly one way of conserving the benefits of quadragesimal self-denial is to keep a perpetual Lent. It is true that some Anglican clerics meet the difficulty by not keeping Lent at all.[3] The course we recommend is to tame the will by judicious restraint, but not to stimulate the appetite by excessive abstinence.

We know that exhaustion is always partly frustration. We are wholesomely tired after hours on the tennis court or in the basement workshop. The things we like weary only

---

2. The Rev. John Selby Watson was ordained a Deacon in the Church of England in 1839, and was a notable translator and academic. On the 8th of October, 1871, he was found unconscious by his servant after taking Hydrogen Cyanide. A note in his pocket read: "I have killed my wife in a fit of rage to which she provoked me" – his wife was found shortly afterward in a bedroom, beaten to death with a pistol. He recovered from the poison and was sentenced to life imprisonment. He died at the age 80, on the 6th of July, 1884.

3. It ought to be noted that refusing to fast in Lent is not permissible (unless reasonably prevented) to any confirmed member of the Anglican Church in North America. The Canon's clearly state that all laity are to "observe the feasts and **fasts** of the Church set forth in the Anglican formularies" (*Title I, Canon 10 §2*)

the muscles of our bodies and our minds, and from such pleasant fatigue we recover in a single night. The tiredness we drag around with us is not so easily managed. It is not a simple condition admitting of quick and obvious treatment. We often cannot say with any accuracy why we are tired. Our spiritual director may be able to tell us. Psychiatry will have an explanation to offer. Whether or not we have recourse to them, we must find a way out of the trouble and devise some measures to prevent a recurrence. How do we protect ourselves from exhaustion?

We have written at length about the acceptance of limitations. The humble priest will also be a sensible priest. It will not pain him to recognize that he can sign up for only so much work with the expectation of getting it done, and he will fix the quantity with a certain shrewdness. Sharp foresight will preserve him from the predicament of the man whose calendar all at once proves to be hopelessly overloaded.

The frustrated priest must consider whether he is the author of his own frustrations. He can easily produce a situation in which frustration is inevitable. He can set himself too difficult a task, too large a task, a task in which he is not sincerely interested, a task demanding skill he has not acquired, or a task incompatible with an obligation he cannot escape. If he essays any of these, he will be disappointed, and maybe disappointment is really what he wants, because it enables him to luxuriate in self-pity and to deny his freedom and responsibility. His woes are of his own making, but this is the one thing he will not acknowledge. Hence he vilifies his vestry, derides his parishioners, and is touchy and unreasonable with everybody. He develops, in the art of self-justification, an ingenuity that, if applied to the pursuit of his vocation, would make him a celebrated pastor. He is perpetually worn out, and it is his own fault.

Plain, uncomplicated fatigue is not a thing to worry about, and a priest who has joyfully abandoned himself to his calling will welcome it. People will want to send him away on a vacation, but he will gently ignore their solicitude. He will relax as he works, and his recreation will spring from his occupation. Thousands who toil with no vision of anything beyond this earth are remade by their labors because they love them. Not to equal such people is shame to us. A priest's nagging desire to 'get away' from the routine of his cure is a symptom of an inward, and perhaps very sinful, failure to live with the grateful delight that should animate every Christian. Let us enjoy our holidays, but let us not multiply them and regard a period of work as merely an interval between one vacation and another.

What is more refreshing than just for one hour to be completely a priest: to administer a sacrament with perfect concentration and an earnest intention that makes one the recipient as well as the transmitter of grace, to listen to a history of sorrow or sin and every minute to hear the accents of God in the voice of the sufferer, or simply for once to pray as we have all our lives believed we should? Here is the freshness that eludes the dispirited clergy who chase it into the tropics on pre-Lenten cruises or into the ether on expensive jet-flights, which are never fast enough to enable the worn-out priest to leave himself behind. What most of us need is a really hard day on the job. Analyze your fatigue and watch it break down into pride and sloth.

Ordination confers authority and, by accident, a certain sociological status. Authority in the Church is an impersonal thing. Status is its subjective accompaniment. If we are courageous, we exercise authority without respect of persons. If we are obsessed with status, we are snobs or tyrants. Many a priest has been vanquished by a selfish misconception of his office. To 'pull rank' in the kingdom of God is at best a sin of impatience and at worst a challenge to God.

Pride in the ugly shape of snobbery is less frequent than pride that assumes the form of an imperiousness demanding abject obedience and servile conformity whenever the priest issues an order or emits a ruling. Under the rule of such a priest the faithful are not permitted to argue or even seriously to question. Those who do not fall into line are coldly cast off and left to look after themselves. The priest is interested only in the submissive souls who will do things his way, and everything that happens in the parish must happen under his direction. He is more likely to be suavely paternal or avuncular in his insistence than to be a gruff martinet, but in either case he has no respect for the freedom of his people. In the long run he wins and is master of a cowed remnant or the opposition wins and he retires in uncomprehended discomfiture. Somehow people will never understand that he has only been trying to give them what they need, and somehow he himself will never understand that this is not the way to do it. He is more stubborn than any of the cantankerous people whose heads he has longed to bang together, and he emerges from each crisis with his self-confidence essentially unimpaired. He would be astonished at the suggestion that pride had been his undoing. Pride is the most fundamental of sins. It is also the most easily disguised. How else could so many priests be so repulsively egocentric?

In spite of all that we have said in denunciation of this manifestation of pride, we do not consider it a serious scourge. The pride that really hurts the clergy is the pride that expresses itself in fantasies and fugues. Appalled at the magnificence and magnitude of the lot that has fallen to us in the economy of salvation, we shrink from it and embrace in its stead some illusory notion of our human importance. We fight for the possession of some symbol and demand that life give us incontestable proof of our worth and distinction. The symbol need not be a dazzling one, nor does pride arise solely from the choice of extravagant or illegitimate objects. It is the tenacity of our yearning that does the harm –the tenacity that craves one thing and is desolate if it cannot be had.

There was once a woman who was never wholly at ease in the Christian religion because she knew that she could not be ordained and therefore could not say mass, a thing that fascinated her. A priest may, should, and does say mass, but he may be an unhappy priest because he cannot say it in some preferred place or style. Perhaps he wants to pontificate, and this he cannot do unless he becomes a bishop –not the easiest of feats. He may dream of a locality, a diocese, a specific parish, an impossible composite ideal of a parish, an utterly correct altar, music that carries the worshipers away, people who adore him, a rapt hearing for his sermons, a certain salary, a cozy or palatial rectory, an honored and potent place in the community, academic, social, or artistic recognition, or anything else within or without his reach. He shows himself a proud man, not by wishing to have a given thing, but by refusing to believe that he is a fulfilled and complete man if he lacks it.

Most people who suffer from this malady do not call it pride and do not realize that it is pride. It is not easily detected, and one can be the victim of it for a lifetime without being conscious of what is wrong. All the more reason to search for it in ourselves and to expel it. Has our imagination tricked us into cherishing some trivial, non-significant tag or title as a sign that we have fulfilled some nebulous ambition? Do we have to be recognized by a particular person, group, or institution in order to be able to feel that we are recognized at all? Do we carry on an unceasing quarrel with our circumstances? Only the conviction of our uniqueness could make us clamor, as we untiringly do, for the right job and the right surroundings. We think that we are shabbily provided for if we do not receive a bounty that marks us as the manifest pets of providence. This false sense of our individuality is a claim on our part to be better than other people. How preposterous such a view is we readily see as soon as we put it into plain words. Here is another pernicious variety of pride. Each of us is in truth a rare and wonderful creature, but God is the author of the rarity and the wonder, and he has no favorites.

As pride at its deepest level is a misconception of one's place in the universe, so sloth can be defined as basically a reluctance to participate in the motion of the universe. This may seem a pretentious way of describing one of the most common vices, but we believe that it is correct to stress the cosmic aspect of sloth. Motion has made the universe what it is, and anyone who withholds his contribution of energy impoverishes the totality. We live by moving and being moved, and only because we were made free is it possible for us to curtail our motion and to resist the fundamental tides of existence. Sloth therefore may be said to be contrary to nature. It is not an amiable fault occurring most frequently in jolly fat men. It is a deep and destructive sin. It can sew us up in a strait jacket that is tighter than any addiction. Few free themselves from the bondage of sloth long indulged.

Most of the clergy are not subject to regimentation. They are in a position to waste almost as much time as they choose, and some of them develop quite a flair for idleness. Those who keep active are likely to be active only about the things they like, and this leads to a serious imbalance in their work. The priest more than other men needs a planned life and the will to vanquish sloth, whatever mask it wears.

Every priest knows the ordinary precautions he can take against falling into habitual sloth. He can show a virtuous promptitude in getting into, and out of, bed. He can frame a timetable and stick to it. He can tie himself to a schedule of services, join a clerical book club or discussion group, register for a graduate or extension course, establish a weekly minimum for his pastoral calls, and devote the freshest hours of Monday, and perhaps also Tuesday, to the composition of a really original sermon. Adherence to such a design of action will certainly prevent his becoming a notorious sluggard. Sloth will then attack him more insidiously.

It will creep into his prayers, filling them with echoes, automatisms, and vain repetitions, for these are less trouble than apposite reflections and relevant acts. It will invade his visiting, counseling, and letter-writing, and under its influence he will adopt and follow a routine of stereotyped cheeriness and synthetic solicitude. It will cast a spell over his reading and preaching and enslave him to clichés and formulas. One has to get well below the surface of all this activity to see the sloth that underlies it.

A man who is doing a great deal may be exerting himself very little. The worst sloth is to reject one's own creativity in favor of what one merely needs to learn and reproduce; in other words, to imitate when one can originate and to copy when one can compose. If our gifts are meager, we have to draw on the greater achievements of others, but we do this by first assimilating, and then adapting, the productions of more inventive minds, and it is always necessary to distinguish intelligent, perceptive borrowing from indiscriminate quotation and appropriation. An authentic artist may be dissolute, but in his art he is not slothful. He does not rest until he has said what is in him. We must not use the givenness of the Gospel as a pretext for lazy, mechanical service on our part. We convey the Gospel to others by living it ourselves, as persons and not as puppets. Passivity is not less slothful than negligence.

The title of this chapter refers to sins of utterance. The clergy are notorious for their irresponsible and mischievous talk. We are men of words, and we act in our off-duty hours as if we were unaware how potent words can be. We have to learn to handle them delicately.

Words are easily controlled at the source, but once they have left it, they are subject to nobody. By repeating malicious words we continually reinfect ourselves with malice and fill ourselves with iniquitous suggestions. Words make or mar an occasion, a mood, a reputation, a fellowship, or a marriage. A nation is a nation because it has become articulate about its common interests, and states are founded upon words and overthrown by them. Release a word, and you will never be able to recapture it. It may continue to speak for you long after you are dead. It may be misheard, misconstrued, or grotesquely distorted in transmission. You have sent it on its way, and you can no longer discipline it.

Let a priest, adept at words and familiar with them, ponder them before he dispatches them into the world to affect it and possibly to revolutionize it. The simple monosyllable yes can be given so many intonations and inflections that it can express almost any sentiment or frame of mind, and what it can express it can also produce. We are everlastingly altering the atmosphere with words and by their means framing and reframing the situation in which our work has to be done. The wrong word can be merely an unfortunate but harmless mistake, but it can also be poison, devastation, and death. It can injure beyond anybody's power to heal and anger beyond anybody's power to placate. From it can result the loss of a parishioner, the ruin of a parish, or the disruption of a diocese. There is nothing good or bad that words cannot either do or cause a man to do. A priest who tosses them around carelessly presumably knows what he is doing and is answerable for what may ensue. Fool is the gentlest name we can find for him.

Insofar as the evils we have mentioned are temptations and as yet only possibilities of sin, Christ was conversant with them and understood how to vanquish them. What are Christ's counter-measures? To find out we have only to read the synoptic accounts of the Temptation.[4] The Son of Man does not confound the Tempter with any mysterious, esoteric learning. He does not surprise Satan or us with subtle replies. He quotes a book of the Old Testament, and the simple truth he speaks is so familiar, so axiomatic, so obvious that no contemporary Jew would have questioned it,

We look in strange places for a way out of temptation, and we miss the escape that lies close at hand. It is ordinary fidelity, in the ordinary round, with the ordinary opportunities and the ordinary assistance, that saves us. We are assured that God will with the temptation make a way to escape, that we may be able to bear it. If

---

4. Matthew 4:1-11; Mark 1:12-13; Luke 4:1-13

we watch how he works, we shall perceive that he commonly contrives to do this without resorting to miracles. Our guarantee of protection is the Incarnation. In all our temptations, the Son of God has been there before us, and what he has endured for us he will give us the power to endure for him.

CHAPTER IX

A Teacher of the Gentiles

THE virtues and graces we have been analyzing and delineating can be practiced on a small scale, in the setting of a parish or mission in which pastoral intimacy between priest and people springs up spontaneously from daily intercourse. If the pastor has been led by prayer and providence to such a place and is not merely insulating himself in a homogeneous, congenial environment and shirking his exercise of the universal mission that belongs to the Holy Catholic Church, he need not be gravely uneasy about the narrowness of his ministry. What it lacks in range it will probably make up in depth and intensity. Concentrated priestly care is sometimes exactly what the spot and the time require.

Yet where these days would one look for the self-contained little communities that once were so trying, so delightful, and so satisfying to the clergy who looked after them? Modernity has overtaken the compact flock of docile, backward villagers who listened gratefully to the vicar's sermons, even though his quotations from the classics were often lost on them. No longer do the children of the slums troop to a catechism conducted by a respected priest who wields a mighty influence among their elders as a disinterested benefactor of the poor. Perhaps we are mistaken about the past and people have never so revered the clergy. At all events, much of the deference has disappeared: the rustics now seem more knowledgeable, the derelicts more skeptical, and the juvenile delinquents tougher. Their attitudes are not simple, and suggestions of strange ideologies occur in their conversation They are not altogether contemptuous of the clergy, but they do not automatically tip their hats at the sight of a clerical collar.

The old clerical approaches are outmoded, and one of the reasons for this change is that they often rather offensively accentuated the difference in status between the helper and the helped. Whereas we once shook our heads in grim reproof over the destitute drunkard, we now embrace him as a brother and are careful to call him an *alcoholic*. Marriage has so largely escaped the Church's control that even the most broad-minded canons cannot be straightforwardly applied to the actual involutions we encounter. Mental disease, family disturbances, sexual aberrations, and suicide –and, we may as well say, all other crimes, ills, and misfortunes– are handled more sociologically than theologically, even by the clergy.

The priest is a friend, a physician, and a teacher, but scarcely any longer a judge. We tell a man that he is a sinner only when we have exhausted the milder methods of pastoral care. At this point he ceases to understand what we are talking about and looks at us blankly; sin is an unintelligible word to him. The fulminating priest is extinct, and the admonishing priest is not far behind him. Soon the clergy will do nothing but advise, suggest, and unprotestingly repair the damage done by high-riding egomaniacs. We read more eagerly what penitents say to their confessors than what confessors say to their penitents.

The mischief inflicted on the individual by an education that has trained him for a circumscribed job but equipped him with no standards for the measurement of his personal behavior is aggravated by the life he is constrained to lead, whatever his habitation. Personalism is being so heavily emphasized in the social sciences because a personality is a harder thing to achieve than it used to be and the dangers that attend its formation and maintenance are feared almost as much as cancer and nuclear dissolution. Society in the suburbs is artificially personalized, and there personality perishes of excessive effort. In the cities a protective impersonality throttles it at the start. Persons who have no really personal commerce with themselves or others live in rootless fluidity and mobility year after year, until they become a prey to moral relativism and indifferentism. Their overstimulated, anxious condition is mitigated only by a relative affluence, which is never lightheartedly enjoyed because the possession of it is thought to be tenuous.

A man's ability to withstand the attrition of this life is one of his principal qualifications for employment. He preserves himself by not becoming too concerned about his neighbors. He knows that the taxes he pays will be used to defend and succor him and them, and if he is uncommonly public-spirited, he writes out a check for the community chest and, at the year's end, allows himself some special benefactions. The turmoil reported to him from distant portions of the world always mystifies his mind and sometimes disquiets his emotions, but he does not try with any determination to fathom it. Fundamentally he has no vigorous care for internationalism or any other of the nebulous causes promoted by zealots, towards whom he cherishes a congenital suspicion. His affections are unselfishly engaged only in the area of his family, and not very firmly there.

He feels himself forced into a kind of spiritual solipsism, and so far as he can he reserves to himself the authority to decide what is good for him and those dependent on him. His principles are few. He cannot tell you whence he derived them or why he clings to them. He probably would not cling to them if they threatened what he conceives to be his welfare. He hopes that he is not inhuman, and he does not claim to be superhuman, though he covertly envies those who grab what they want. He is a man who has never analyzed his humanity, a creature who only occasionally thinks of a possible Creator. He does not know how he got where he is or where he may be going. He cannot visualize eternal life and is pretty sure that he would not be excited by the certain prospect of it. The problem is not his to solve, and he is reluctant to consider it. If he expects anything of religion, it is consolation, but even this he will accept sparingly, lest he form the habit of seeking it.

The only way to get to this person or any of his relatives is to share something with him. Lawyers cram to win a case, and we might do the same to win a soul. A famous British pastor prepared for an interview with a worldly youth by reading up on the latter's hobby, and so started a dialogue that ended in the young man's conversion. This has to be done casually and with no touch of studied drama. It also has to be meant. Questions deftly phrased and sincerely directed towards a person's most cherished interests disarm him and encourage him to express his enthusiasms and later, when he knows that he will be understood, his uncertainties. Then the pastor's moment comes. Can he be humble enough to become, as it were, the mouthpiece of Christ to the man before him? Can he forget everything that separates him from this necessitous soul and permit himself to be quite specifically enlightened, directed, and inspired for this occasion?

Our ministry to an individual may have any beginning. He may come to us; we may seek him out; a third person may introduce us. We may bore each other or find each other enchanting. We may meet once or a hundred times. The circumstances, the course, and the length of the conversation are not of our making, and we are indifferent to them. What we care about exclusively is the chance we have to convey to him the particular truth he needs. Only to wise and godly priests is it given to speak, at every such opening, the penetrating word that fits the moment. We should be surprised at what we say, because of ourselves alone we could not say it. This is not facile inspirationism; it is obedience to the Spirit. We have authority to preach the word, and we should expect to preach it with pentecostal eloquence. God will not deny us the power to speak to every man in his own language. All we have to do is to clear the way by emptying ourselves of a multitude of vanities. The worst of them is the belief that our ingenuity is equal to all exigencies. A man who relies on his cleverness says too much, and most of it is wrong.

The ability to talk to all men as they present themselves to us does not presuppose our being in a state of omnicompetence, natural or acquired. We learn all we can, and all we learn aids us in the prosecution of our mission –this we have been saying throughout the book. Yet if we knew much more than we do, it would not suffice. Something has to be added. The priest who allows himself to be led by the Spirit gets the additional intelligence and power. If we are not exercising a guided ministry, we are imposing our own notions on helpless people, and that is usually ruinous.

It is no grandiose conception of our dignity and attainments that makes us dare to be teachers of the Gentiles. We address ourselves to the nations and the individuals in the nations because God's call admits of no exceptions. We are sent to the whole world. None of us reaches the whole world, and God can communicate with it as he wishes, but the effort and the scope are essential to our priesthood. Much of the world comes to every priest, and even in a single day we meet a number of persons who would heed us if we had the courage and imagination to speak. Let us cultivate the skill of discerning them, and let us not rest until we have spoken to the last of them.

In the consecutive chapters of this book we have examined the various aspects of priesthood, and if it is still a mystery, we at least know it well enough to do some-thing with it. That observation supplies the closing question: How do we apply our priesthood? In particular, what use do we make of our authority to administer sacraments? Do we reserve them for people who are qualified to receive them, and do we regard ourselves as the 'custodians' of the sacraments? Or do we give the sac-raments to anybody who asks for them, no matter what the extent of his conformity to Christianity may be? Are we prodigal or niggardly with the sacraments?

Properly we cannot be either. The sacraments do not belong to us. This is the prime consideration in any discussion of their worthy use. They are God's gifts to men through the Church. God gives them with wisdom, mercy, and under- standing, and he gives them for the sake of men. He does not, however, distribute them without reference to men's readiness and competence to receive. He does not in-dulge men and stultify himself by bestowing sacramental grace on those who only halfheartedly want it or even mildly reject it.

The nature of the sacraments is the key to their sound administration. The sacra-mental life, initiated by the rebirth of baptism, is continued and enlarged by other sacraments in the context of the sacramental community. Like Christian theology, the sacraments hang together, and to be eclectic about them is to misuse them. We receive them, not merely according to our need, and certainly not according to our fancy, but as the Church has commanded us to receive them, for they have been entrusted to her, and she dispenses them in the name of Christ.

We are therefore not at liberty to detach a sacrament from this whole and to offer it to the public independently of the totality in which Christ himself has placed it. When we 'feature' a sacrament or recklessly invite the ignorant, the unprepared, and perhaps even the unwilling to partake of it, we are false to our trusteeship and come close to a superstitious view of the sacraments. They are not irresistible, and we have no promise that they will work in the absence of the safeguards and checks accompanying them in full, obedient, and sincere Catholic practice. If the use of the sacraments seems to us lamentably limited by conditions that so few in our generation can fulfill, it does not follow that the conditions are oppressive and therefore we have leave to remove them. Such things are not for us to decide.

As a result of the price he pays for his faithfulness to the terms on which God has given the sacraments, the priest may be disposed to feel that his loyalty is an onerous thing, because it separates him from men. But the separation is superficial, and a sacrament refused with charity can be more efficacious than one given too leniently. Many a conversion has begun with what was at first taken as a rebuff. Kindness makes it clear that no rejection is intended and nothing is required but a simple obedience that is within everybody's power. Men will clamor for the sacraments when they understand them. We are priests, and we have the means of making them understand.

We have no final exhortation for the priests who have kept us company through these pages. Nobody will ever speak the last word about priesthood. It is an endless vocation, bringing us always new difficulties and new joys in this realm of time and suggesting to us a less impeded priesthood beyond our present infirmities. The contemplation of these things makes us glad that we are priests forever.

Appendices

It is evident unto all men, diligently reading holy Scripture, and ancient Authors, That from the Apostles time, there have been these Orders of Ministers in Christs Church; Bishops, Priests, and Deacons. Which offices were evermore had in such reverend estimation, that no man might presume to execute any of them, except he were first called, tried, examined and known to have such qualities as are requisite for the same; and also by public prayer with imposition of hands, were approved, and admitted thereunto by lawful authority. And therefore to the intent that these orders may be continued, and reverently used, and esteemed in the Church of England; No man shall be accounted or taken to be a lawful Bishop, Priest, or Deacon in the Church of England, or suffered to execute any of the said Functions, except he be called, tried, examined, and admitted thereunto, according to the Form hereafter following, or hath had formerly Episcopal Consecration or Ordination.

−1662 Ordinal

We recognise that God has called and gifted bishops, priests, and deacons in historic succession to equip all the people of God for their ministry in the world.

—Jerusalem Declaration, VII

O God, you led your holy apostles to ordain ministers in every place: Grant that your Church, under the guidance of the Holy Spirit, may choose suitable persons for the ministry of Word and Sacrament, and may uphold them in their work for the extension of your kingdom; through the great Shepherd and Bishop of our souls, Jesus Christ our Lord, who lives and reigns with you and the Holy Spirit, one God, for ever and ever. **Amen.**

–Book of Common Prayer, 634

QUALITIES OF THOSE WHO ARE TO BE ORDAINED

According to the Constitution & Canons of the ACNA

Title III, Canon 2 §1-3

EVERY Bishop shall take care that he admit no person into Holy Orders but such as he knows either by himself, or by sufficient testimony, to have been baptized and confirmed, to be sufficiently instructed in Holy Scripture and in the doctrine, discipline and worship of this Church, as defined by this Province, to be empowered by the Holy Spirit and to be a wholesome example and pattern to the entire flock of Christ.

In accordance with Holy Scripture, a Deacon must be worthy of respect, sincere, not indulging in much wine, not pursuing dishonest gain, and one who holds the deep truths of the faith with a clear conscience. They must first be tested, and then if there is nothing against them, let them serve as Deacons (1 Timothy 3:8-13).

In addition to the qualifications above, and in accordance with Holy Scripture, a Presbyter must be above reproach, not self-pleasing but self-controlled, upright, holy, disciplined, temperate, hospitable, not given to drunkenness, not violent but gentle, not quarrelsome, not a lover of money, not a recent convert, one who loves what is good and one who has a good reputation with outsiders. A Presbyter must be able to preach and teach, holding firmly to the trustworthy message as it has been taught, in order to encourage others by sound doctrine and to refute those who oppose it (1 Timothy 3:1-7; 5:17; Titus 1:6-9).

THE COUNTRY PARSON & HIS CHARACTER

The Rev. George Herbert

Printed 1652

§I. OF A PASTOR.

A PASTOR is the Deputy of Christ for the reducing of Man to the Obedience of God. This definition is evident, and contains the direct steps of Pastoral Duty and Authority. For first, Man fell from God by disobedience. Secondly, Christ is the glorious instrument of God for the revoking of Man. Thirdly, Christ being not to continue on earth, but after he had fulfilled the work of Reconciliation, to be received up into heaven, he constituted Deputies in his place, and these are Priests. And therefore St. Paul in the beginning of his Epistles, professeth this: and in the first [v.24] to the Colossians plainly avoucheth, that he fills up that which is behind of the afflictions of Christ in his flesh, for his Body's sake, which is the Church. Wherein is contained the complete definition of a Minister. Out of this Charter of the Priesthood may be plainly gathered both the Dignity thereof, and the Duty: The Dignity, in that a Priest may do that which Christ did, and by his authority, and as his Vicegerent. The Duty, in that a Priest is to do that which Christ did, and after his manner, both for Doctrine and Life.

§II. THEIR DIVERSITIES.

Of Pastors (intending mine own Nation only, and also therein setting aside the Reverend Prelates of the Church, to whom this discourse ariseth not) some live in the Universities, some in Noble houses, some in Parishes residing on their Cures. Of those that live in the Universities, some live there in office, whose rule is that of the Apostle; Rom. 12.6. Having gifts differing, according to the grace that is given to us, whether prophecy, let us prophecy according to the proportion of faith; or ministry, let us wait on our ministering, or he that teacheth, on teaching, &c. he that ruleth, let him do it with diligence, &c. Some in a preparatory way, whose aim and labour must be not only to get knowledge, but to subdue and mortify all lusts and affections: and not to think, that when they have read the Fathers, or Schoolmen, a Minister is made, and the thing done. The greatest and hardest preparation is within: For, Unto the ungodly, saith God, Why dost thou preach my Laws, and takest my Covenant in thy mouth?[1] Those that live in Noble Houses are called Chaplains, whose duty and obligation being the same to the Houses they live in, as a Parsons to his Parish, in describing the one (which is indeed the bent of my Discourse) the other will be manifest. Let not Chaplains think themselves so free, as many of them do, and because they have different Names, think their Office different. Doubtless they are Parsons of the families they live in, and are entertained to that end, either by an open, or implicit Covenant. Before they are in Orders, they may be received for Companions, or discoursers; but after a man is once Minister, he cannot agree to come into any house, where he shall not exercise what he is, unless he forsake his plough, and look back. Wherefore they are not to be over-submissive, and base, but to keep up with the Lord and Lady of the house, and to preserve a boldness with them and all, even so far as reproof to their very face, when occasion calls, but seasonably and discreetly. They who do not thus, while they remember their earthly Lord, do much forget their heavenly; they wrong the Priesthood, neglect their duty, and shall be so far from that which they seek with their over-submissiveness, and cringings, that they shall ever be despised. They who for the hope of promotion neglect any necessary admonition, or reproof, Sell (with Judas) their Lord and Master.

§III. THE PARSONS LIFE.

The Country Parson is exceeding exact in his Life, being holy, just, prudent, temperate, bold, grave in all his ways. And because the two highest points of Life, wherein a Christian is most seen, are Patience, and Mortification; Patience in regard of afflictions, Mortification in regard of lusts and affections, and the stupefying and deading of all the clamorous powers of the soul, therefore he hath throughly studied these, that he may be an absolute Master and commander of himself, for all the purposes which God hath ordained him. Yet in these points he labours most in

---

1. Psalm 50.16.

those things which are most apt to scandalize his Parish. And first, because Country people live hardly, and therefore as feeling their own sweat, and consequently knowing the price of money, are offended much with any, who by hard usage increase their travel, the Country Parson is very circumspect in avoiding all covetousness, neither being greedy to get, nor niggardly to keep, nor troubled to lose any worldly wealth; but in all his words and actions slighting, and disesteeming it, even to a wondering, that the world should so much value wealth, which in the day of wrath hath not one dram of comfort for us. Secondly, because Luxury is a very visible sin, the Parson is very careful to avoid all the kinds thereof, but especially that of drinking, because it is the most popular vice; into which if he come, he prostitutes himself both to shame, and sin, and by having fellowship, with the unfruitful works of darkness, he disableth himself of authority to reprove them: For sins make all equal, whom they find together; and then they are worst, who ought to be best. Neither is it for the servant of Christ to haunt Inns, or Taverns, or Ale-houses, to the dishonour of his person and office. The Parson doth not so, but orders his Life in such a fashion, that when death takes him, as the Jews and Judas did Christ, he may say as He did, I sate daily with you teaching in the Temple. Thirdly, because Country people (as indeed all honest men) do much esteem their word, it being the Life of buying, and selling, and dealing in the world; therefore the Parson is very strict in keeping his word, though it be to his own hindrance, as knowing, that if he be not so, he will quickly be discovered, and disregarded: neither will they believe him in the pulpit, whom they cannot trust in his Conversation. As for oaths, and apparel, the disorders thereof are also very manifest. The Parsons yea is yea, and nay nay; and his apparel plain, but reverend, and clean, without spots, or dust, or smell; the purity of his mind breaking out, and dilating it self even to his body, clothes, and habitation.

§IV. The Parsons Knowledge.

The Country Parson is full of all knowledge. They say, it is an ill Mason that refuseth any stone: and there is no knowledge, but, in a skillful hand, serves either positively as it is, or else to illustrate some other knowledge. He condescends even to the knowledge of tillage, and pastorage, and makes great use of them in teaching, because people by what they understand, are best led to what they understand not.

But the chief and top of his knowledge consists in the book of books, the store-house and magazine of life and comfort, the holy Scriptures. There he sucks, and lives. In the Scriptures he finds four things; Precepts for life, Doctrines for knowledge, Examples for illustration, and Promises for comfort: These he hath digested severally. But for the understanding of these; the means he useth are first, a holy Life, remembering what his Master saith) that if any do Gods will, he shall know of the Doctrine, John 7[:17]. and assuring himself, that wicked men, however learned, do not know the Scriptures, because they feel them not, and because they are not understood but with the same Spirit that writ them. The second means is prayer, which if it be necessary even in temporal things, how much more in things of another world, where the well is deep, and we have nothing of our selves to draw with? Wherefore he ever begins the reading of the Scripture with some short inward ejaculation, as, Lord open mine eyes, that I may see the wondrous things of thy Law. &c. The third means is a diligent Collation of Scripture with Scripture. For all Truth being consonant to it self, and all being penned by one and the self-same Spirit, it cannot be, but that an industrious, and judicious comparing of place with place must be a singular help for the right understanding of the Scriptures. To this may be added the consideration of any text with the coherence thereof, touching what goes before, and what follows after, as also the scope of the Holy Ghost. When the Apostles would have called down fire from Heaven, they were reproved, as ignorant of what spirit they were. For the Law required one thing, and the Gospel another: yet as diverse, not as repugnant: therefore the spirit of both is to be considered, and weighed. The fourth means are Commentators and Fathers, who have handled the places controverted, which the Parson by no means refuseth. As he doth not so study others, as to neglect the grace of God in himself, and what the Holy Spirit teacheth him; so doth he assure himself, that God in all ages hath had his servants, to whom he hath revealed his Truth, as well as to him; and that as one Country doth not bear all things, that there may be a Commerce; so neither hath God opened, or will open all to one, that there may be a traffic in knowledge between the servants of God, for the planting both of love, and humility. Wherefore he hath one Comment at least upon every book of Scripture, and ploughing with this, and his own meditations, he enters into the secrets of God treasured in the holy Scripture.

§V THE PARSONS ACCESSORY KNOWLEDGES.

The Country Parson hath read the Fathers also, and the Schoolmen, and the later Writers, or a good portion of all, out of all which he hath compiled a book, and body of Divinity, which is the storehouse of his Sermons, and which he preacheth all his Life; but diversely clothed, illustrated, and enlarged. For though the world is full of such composures, yet every mans own is fittest, readiest, and most savory to him. Besides, this being to be done in his younger and preparatory times, it is an honest joy ever after to look upon his well spent hours. This Body he made by way of expounding the Church Catechism, to which all divinity may easily be reduced. For it being indifferent in it self to choose any Method, that is best to be chosen, of which there is likeliest to be most use. Now Catechizing being a work of singular, and admirable benefit to the Church of God, and a thing required under Canonical obedience, the expounding of our Catechism must needs be the most useful form. Yet hath the Parson, besides this laborious work, a slighter form of Catechizing, fitter for country people; according as his audience is, so he useth one, or other; or sometimes both, if his audience be intermixed. He greatly esteems also of cases of conscience, wherein he is much versed. And indeed, herein is the greatest ability of a Parson to lead his people exactly in the ways of Truth, so that they neither decline to the right hand, nor to the left. Neither let any think this a slight thing. For every one hath not digested, when it is a sin to take something for money lent, or when not; when it is a fault to discover another's fault, or when not; when the affections of the soul in desiring and procuring increase of means, or honour, be a sin of covetousness or ambition, and when not, when the appetites of the body in eating, drinking, sleep, and the pleasure that comes with sleep, be sins of gluttony, drunkenness, sloth, lust, and when not, and so in many circumstances of actions Now if a shepherd know not which grass will bane, or which not, how is he fit to be a shepherd? Wherefore the Parson hath throughly canvassed all the particulars of humane actions, at least all those which he observeth are most incident to his Parish.

§VI. The Parson Praying.

The Country Parson, when he is to read divine services, composeth himself to all possible reverence; lifting up his heart and hands, and eyes, and using all other gestures which may express a hearty, and unfeigned devotion. This he doth, first, as being truly touched and amazed with the Majesty of God, before whom he then presents himself; yet not as himself alone, but as presenting with himself the whole Congregation, whose sins he then bears, and brings with his own to the heavenly altar to be bathed, and washed in the sacred Laver of Christs blood. Secondly, as this is the true reason of his inward fear, so he is content to express this outwardly to the utmost of his power; that being first affected himself, he may affect also his people, knowing that no Sermon moves them so much to a reverence, which they forget again, when they come to pray, as a devout behavior in the very act of praying. Accordingly his voice is humble, his words treatable, and slow; yet not so slow neither, to let the fervency of the supplicant hang and die between speaking, but with a grave liveliness, between fear and zeal, pausing yet pressing, he performs his duty. Besides his example, he having often instructed his people how to carry themselves in divine service, exacts of them all possible reverence, by no means enduring either talking, or sleeping, or gazing, or leaning, or half-kneeling, or any undutiful behavior in them, but causing them, when they sit, or stand, or kneel, to do all in a strait, and steady posture, as attending to what is done in the Church, and every one, man, and child, answering aloud both Amen, and all other answers, which are on the Clerks and peoples part to answer; which answers also are to be done not in a huddling, or slubbering fashion, gaping, or scratching the head, or spitting even in he midst of their answer, but gently and pausably, thinking what they say; so that while they answer, As it was in the beginning, &c. they meditate as they speak, that God hath ever had his people, that have glorified him as well as now, and that he shall have so for ever. And the like in other answers. This is that which the Apostle calls a reasonable service, Rom. 12 [:1]. when we speak not as Parrots, without reason, or offer up such sacrifices as they did of old, which was of beasts devoid of reason; but when we use our reason, and apply our powers to the service of him, that gives them. If there be any of the gentry or nobility of the Parish, who sometimes make it a piece of state not to come at the beginning of service with their poor neighbours, but at mid-prayers, both to their own loss, and of theirs also who gaze upon them when they come in, and neglect the present service of God, he by no means suffers it, but after divers gentle admonitions, if they persevere, he causes them to be presented: or if the poor Church-wardens be affrighted with their great- ness, notwithstanding his instruction that they ought not to be so, but even to let the world sink, so they do their duty; he presents them himself, only protesting to them, that not any ill will draws him to it, but the debt and obligation of his calling, being to obey God rather then men.

§VII. The Parson Preaching.

The Country Parson preacheth constantly, the pulpit is his joy and his throne: if he at any time intermit, it is either for want of health, or against some great Festival, that he may the better celebrate it, or for the variety of the hearers, that he may be heard at his return more attentively. When he intermits, he is ever very well sup- plied by some able man who treads in his steps, and will not throw down what he hath built; whom also he entreats to press some point, that he himself hath often urged with no great success, that so in the mouth of two or three witnesses the truth may be more established. When he preacheth, he procures attention by all possible art, both by earnestness of speech, it being natural to men to think, that where is much earnestness, there is somewhat worth hearing; and by a diligent, and busy cast of his eye on his auditors, with letting them know, that he observes who marks, and who not; and with particularizing of his speech now to the younger sort, then to the elder, now to the poor, and now to the rich. This is for you, and This is for you; for particulars ever touch, and awake more then generals. Herein also he serves himself of the judgments of God, as of those of ancient times, so especially of the late ones; and those most, which are nearest to his Parish; for people are very attentive at such discourses, and think it behooves them to be so, when God is so near them, and even over their heads. Sometimes he tells them stories, and sayings of others, according as his text invites him; for them also men heed, and remember better then exhortations; which though earnest, yet often die with the Sermon, especially with Country people; which are thick, and heavy, and hard to raise to a point of Zeal, and fervency, and need a mountain of fire to kindle them; but stories and sayings they will well remember. He often tels them, that Sermons are dangerous things, that none goes out of Church as he came in, but either better, or worse; that none is careless before his Judge, and that the word of God shall judge us. By these and other means the Parson procures attention; but the character of his Sermon is Holiness; he is not witty, or learned, or eloquent, but Holy. A Character, that Hermogenes never dreamed of, and therefore he could give no precepts thereof. But it is gained, first, by choosing texts of Devotion, not Controversy, moving and ravishing texts, whereof the Scriptures are full. Secondly, by dipping, and seasoning all our words and sentences in our hearts, before they come into our mouths, truly affecting, and cordially expressing all that we say; so that the auditors may plainly perceive that every word is hart-deep. Thirdly, by turning often, and making many Apostrophes to God, as, Oh Lord bless my people, and teach them this point; or, Oh my Master, on whose errand I come, let me hold my peace, and do thou speak thy self; for thou art Love, and when thou teachest, all are Scholars. Some such irradiations scatteringly in the Sermon, carry great holiness in them. The Prophets are admirable in this. So Isaiah 64:1. Oh that thou wouldst rent the Heavens, that thou wouldst come down, &c. And Jeremiah Chapter 10:23. after he had complained of the desolation of Israel, turns to God suddenly, Oh Lord, I know that the way of man is not in himself, &c. Fourthly, by frequent wishes of the peoples good, and joying therein, though he himself were with Saint Paul even sacrificed upon the service of their faith. For there is no greater sign of holiness, then the procuring, and rejoicing in another's good. And herein St Paul excelled in all his Epistles. How did he put the Romans in all his prayers? Romans 1:9. And ceased not to give thanks for the Ephesians.[2] And for the II Corinthians 1:4. And for the Philippians made request with joy, 1:4. And is in contention for them whither to live, or die; be with them, or Christ, verse 23. which, setting aside his care of his Flock, were a madness to doubt of. What an admirable Epistle is the second to the Corinthians? How full of affections? He joys, and he is sorry, he grieves, and he glories, never was there such care of a flock expressed, save in the great shepherd of the fold, who first shed tears over Jerusalem, and afterwards blood. Therefore this care may be learned there, and then woven into Sermons, which will make them appear exceeding reverend, and holy. Lastly, by an often urging of the presence, and majesty of God, by these,

2. Ephesians 1:6.

or such like speeches. Oh let us all take heed what we do, God sees us, he sees whether I speak as I ought, or you hear as you ought, he sees hearts, as we see faces: he is among us; for if we be here, he must be here, since we are here by him, and without him could not be here. Then turning the discourse to his Majesty, And he is a great God, and terrible, as great in mercy, so great in judgment: There are but two devouring elements, fire, and water, he hath both in him; His voice is as the sound of many waters. Revelations 1 [:15]. And he himself is a consuming fire, Hebrews 12 [:29]. Such discourses shew very Holy. The Parsons Method in handling of a text consists of two parts; first, a plain and evident declaration of the meaning of the text; and secondly, some choice Observations drawn out of the whole text, as it lyes entire, and unbroken in the Scripture it self. This he thinks natural, and sweet, and grave. Whereas the other way of crumbling a text into small parts, as, the Person speaking, or spoken to, the subject, and object, and the like, hath neither in it sweetness, nor gravity, nor variety, since the words apart are not Scripture, but a dictionary, and may be considered alike in all the Scripture. The Parson exceeds not an hour in preaching, because all ages have thought that a competency, and he that profits not in that time, will less afterwards, the same affection which made him not profit before, making him then weary, and so he grows from not relishing, to loathing.

§VIII. The Parson on Sundays.

The Country Parson, as soon as he awakes on Sunday morning, presently falls to work and seems to himself so as a Market-man is, when the Market day comes, or a shopkeeper, when customers use to come in. His thoughts are full of making the best of the day, and contriving it to his best gains. To this end, besides his ordinary prayers, he makes a peculiar one for a blessing on the exercises of the day, That nothing befall him unworthy of that Majesty before which he is to present himself, but that all may be done with reverence to his glory, and with edification to his flock, humbly beseeching his Master, that how or whenever he punish him, it be not in his Ministry: then he turns to request for his people, that the Lord would be pleased to sanctify them all, that they may come with holy hearts, and awful minds into the Congregation, and that the good God would pardon all those, who come with less prepared hearts then they ought. This done, he sets himself to the

Consideration of the duties of the day, and if there be any extraordinary addition to the customary exercises, either from the time of the year, or from the State, or from God by a child born, or dead, or any other accident, he contrives how and in what manner to induce it to the best advantage. Afterwards when the hour calls, with his family attending him, he goes to Church, at his first entrance humbly adoring, and worshiping the invisible majesty, and presence of Almighty God, and blessing the people either openly, or to himself. Then having read divine Service twice fully, and preached in the morning, and catechized in the afternoon, he thinks he hath in some measure, according to poor, and frail man, discharged the public duties of the Congregation. The rest of the day he spends either in reconciling neighbours that are at variance, or in visiting the sick, or in exhortations to some of his flock by themselves, whom his Sermons cannot, or doe not reach. And every one is more awaked, when we come, and say, Thou art the man. This way he finds exceeding useful, and winning; and these exhortations he calls his privy purse, even as Princes have theirs, besides their public disbursements. At night he thinks it a very fit time, both suitable to the joy of the day, and without hindrance to public duties, either to entertain some of his neighbours, or to be entertained of them, where he takes occasion to discourse of such things as are both profitable, and pleasant, and to raise up their minds to apprehend Gods good blessing to our Church, and State; that order is kept in the one, and peace in the other, without is disturbance, or interruption of public divine offices. As he opened the day with prayer, so he closeth it, humbly beseeching the Almighty to pardon and accept our poor services, and to improve them, that we may grow therein, and that our feet may be like hinds feet ever climbing up higher, and higher unto him.

§IX. The Parsons State of Life.

The Country Parson considering that virginity is a higher state then Matrimony, and that the Ministry requires the best and highest things, is rather unmarried, then married. But yet as the temper of his body may be, or as thee temper of his Parish may be, where he may have occasion to converse with women, and that among suspicious men, and other like circumstances considered, he is rather married then unmarried. Let him communicate the thing often by prayer unto God, and as his grace shall direct him, so let him proceed. If he be unmarried, and keep house, he hath not a woman in his house, but finds opportunities of having his meat dressed and other services done by men-servants at home, and his linen washed abroad. If he be unmarried, and sojourn, he never talks with any woman alone, but in the audience of others, and that seldom, and then also in a serious manner, never jestingly or sportfully. He is very circumspect in all companies, both of his behavior, speech, and very looks, knowing himself to be both suspected, and envied. If he stand steadfast in his heart, having no necessity, but hath power over his own will, and hath so decreed in his heart, that he will keep himself a virgin, he spends his days in fasting and prayer, and blesseth God for the gift of continency, knowing that it can no way be preserved, but only by those means, by which at first it was obtained. He therefore thinks it not enough for him to observe the fasting days of the Church, and the daily prayers enjoined him by authority, which he observeth out of humble conformity, and obedience, but adds to them, out of choice and devotion, some other days for fasting, and hours for prayers; and by these he keeps his body tame, serviceable, and health- full; and his soul fervent, active, young, and lusty as an eagle. He often readeth the Lives of the Primitive Monks, Hermits, and Virgins, and wondereth not so much at their patient suffering, and cheerful dying under persecuting Emperors, (though that indeed be very admirable) as at their daily temperance, abstinence, watchings, and constant prayers, and mortifications in the times of peace and prosperity. To put on the profound humility, and the exact temperance of our Lord Jesus, with other exemplary virtues of that sort, and to keep them on in the sunshine, and noon of prosperity, he findeth to be as necessary, and as difficult at least, as to be clothed with perfect patience, and Christian fortitude in the cold midnight storms of persecution and adversity. He keepeth his watch and ward, night and day against the proper and peculiar temptations of his state of Life, which are principally these two Spiritual pride, and Impurity of heart: against these ghostly enemies he girdeth up his loins, keeps the imagination from roving, puts on the whole Armour of God, and by the virtue of the shield of faith, he is not afraid of the pestilence that walketh in darkness, [carnal impurity] nor of the sickness that destroyeth at noon day, [Ghostly pride and self-conceit.] Other temptations he hath, which, like mortal enemies, may sometimes disquiet him likewise; for the humane soul being bounded, and kept in, in her sensitive faculty, will run out more or less in her intellectual. Original concupiscence is such an active thing, by reason of continual inward, or outward temptations, that it is ever attempting, or doing one mischief or other. Ambition, or untimely desire of promotion to an higher state, or place, under colour of accommodation, or necessary provision, is a common temptation to men of any eminency, especially being single men. Curiosity in prying into high speculative and unprofitable questions, is another great stumbling block to the holiness of Scholars. These and many other spiritual wickednesses in high places doth the Parson fear, or experiment, or both; and that much more being single, then if he were married; for then commonly the stream of temptations is turned another way, into Covetousness, Love of pleasure, or ease, or the like. If the Parson be unmarried, and means to continue so, he doth at least, as much as hath been said. If he be married, the choice of his wife was made rather by his ear, then by his eye; his judgment, not his affection found out a fit wife for him, whose humble, and liberal disposition he preferred before beauty, riches, or honour. He knew that (the good instrument of God to bring women to heaven) a wise and loving husband could out of humility, produce any special grace of faith, patience, meekness, love, obedience, &c. and out of liberality, make her fruitful in all good works. As he is just in all things, so is he to his wife also, counting nothing so much his own, as that he may be unjust unto it. Therefore he gives her respect both afore her servants, and others, and half at least of the government of the house, reserving so much of the affairs, as serve for a diversion for him; yet never so giving over the rains, but that he sometimes looks how things go, demanding an account, but not by the way of an account. And this must bee done the oftener, or the seldomer, according as he is satisfied of his Wifes discretion.

§X. The Parson in His House.

The Parson is very exact in the governing of his house, making it a copy and model for his Parish. He knows the temper, and pulse of every person in his house, and accordingly either meets with their vices, or advanceth their virtues. His wife is either religious, or night and day he is winning her to it. In stead of the qualities of the world, he requires only three of her; first, a training up of her children and maids in the fear of God, with prayers, and catechizing, and all religious duties. Secondly, a curing, and healing of all wounds and sores with her own hands; which skill either she brought with her, or he takes care she shall learn it of some religious neighbour. Thirdly, a providing for her family in such sort, as that neither they want a competent sustentation, nor her husband be brought in debt. His children he first makes Christians, and then Commonwealths-men; the one he owes to his heavenly Country, the other to his earthly, having no title to either, except he do good to both. Therefore having seasoned them with all Piety, not only of words in praying, and reading; but in actions, in visiting other sick children, and tending their wounds, and sending his charity by them to the poor, and sometimes giving them a little money to do it of themselves, that they get a delight in it, and enter favour with God, who weighs even children's actions.[3] He afterwards turns his care to fit all their dispositions with some calling, not sparing the eldest, but giving him the prerogative of his Fathers profession, which happily for his other children he is not able to do. Yet in binding them apprentices (in case he think fit to do so) he takes care not to put them into vain trades, and unbefitting the reverence of their Fathers calling, such as are taverns for men, and lace-making for women; because those trades, for the most part, serve but the vices and vanities of the world, which he is to deny, and not augment. However, he resolves with himself never to omit any present good deed of charity, in consideration of providing a stock for his children; but assures himself, that money thus lent to God, is placed surer for his children's advantage, then if it were given to the Chamber of London. Good deeds, and good breeding, are his two great stocks for his children; if God give any thing above those, and not spent in them, he blesseth God, and lays it out as he sees cause. His servants are all religious, and were it not his duty to have them so, it were his profit, for none are so well served, as by religious servants, both because they do best, and because what they do, is blessed, and prospers. After religion, he teacheth them, that three things make a complete servant, Truth, and Diligence, and Neatness, or Cleanliness. Those that can read, are allowed times for it, and those that cannot, are taught; for all in his house are either teachers or learners, or both, so that his family is a School of Religion, and they all account, that to teach the ignorant is the greatest alms. Even the walls are not idle, but something is written, or painted there, which may excite the reader to a thought of piety; especially the 101 Psalm, which

---

3. I King 14:12-13.

is expressed in a fair table, as being the rule of a family. And when they go abroad, his wife among her neighbours is the beginner of good discourses, his children among children, his servants among other servants; so that as in the house of those that are skilled in Music, all are Musicians; so in the house of a Preacher, all are preachers. He suffers not a lie or equivocation by any means in his house, but counts it the art, and secret of governing to preserve a directness, and open plainness in all things; so that all his house knows, that there is no help for a fault done, but confession. He himself, or his Wife, takes account of Sermons, and how every one profits, comparing this year with the last: and besides the common prayers of the family, he straitly requires of all to pray by themselves before they sleep at night, and stir out in the morning, and knows what prayers they say, and till they have learned them, makes them kneel by him; esteeming that this private praying is a more voluntary act in them, then when they are called to others prayers, and that, which when they leave the family, they carry with them. He keeps his servants between love, fear, according as he finds them; but generally he distributes it thus, To his Children he shows more love then terror, to his servants more terror then love; but an old servant boards a child. The furniture of his house is very plain, but clean, whole, and sweet, as sweet as his garden can make; for he hath no money for such things, charity being his only perfume, which deserves cost when he can spare it. His fare is plain, and common, but wholesome, what he hath, is little, but very good; it consisteth most of mutton, beef, and veal, if he adds any thing for a great day, or a stranger, his garden or orchard supplies it, or his barn, and back-side: he goes no further for any entertainment, lest he go into the world, esteeming it absurd, that he should exceed, who teacheth others temperance. But those which his home produceth, he refuseth not, as coming cheap, and easy, and arising from the improvement of things, which otherwise would be lost. Wherein he admires and imitates the wonderful providence and thrift of the great householder of the world: for there being two things, which as they are, are unuseful to man, the one for smallness, as crumbs, and scattered corn, and the like; the other for the foulness, as wash, and dirt, and things thereinto fallen; God hath provided Creatures for both: for the first, Poultry; for the second, swine. These save man the labour, and doing that which either he could not do, or was not fit for him to do, by taking both sorts of food into them, do as it were dress and prepare both for man in themselves, by growing them selves fit for his table. The Parson in his house observes fasting days; and particularly, as Sunday is his day of joy, so Friday his day of Humiliation, which he celebrates only with abstinence of diet, but also of company, recreation, and all outward contentments; and besides, with confession of sins, and all acts of Mortification. Now fasting days contain a treble obligation; first, of eating less that day, then on other days; secondly, of eating no pleasing, or over-nourishing things, as the Israelites did eat sour herbs: Thirdly, of eating no flesh, which is but the determination of the second rule by Authority to this particular. The two former obligations are much more essential to a true fast, then the third and last; and fasting days were fully performed by keeping of the two former, had not Authority interposed: so that to eat little, and that unpleasant, is the natural rule of fasting, although it be flesh. For since fasting in Scripture language is an afflicting of our souls, if a peace of dry flesh at my table be more unpleasant to me, then some fish there, certainly to eat the flesh, and not the fish, is to keep the fasting day naturally. And it is observable, that the prohibiting of flesh came from hot Countries, where both flesh alone, and much more with wine, is apt to nourish more then in cold regions, and where flesh may be much better spared, and with more safety then elsewhere, where both the people and the drink being cold and phlegmatic, the eating of flesh is an antidote to both. For it is certain, that a weak stomach being prepossessed with flesh, shall much better brook and bear a draught of beer, then if it had taken before either fish, or roots, or such things; which will discover it self by spitting, and rheume, or flegme. To conclude, the Parson, if he be in full health, keeps the three obligations, eating fish, or roots, and that for quantity little, for quality unpleasant. If his body be weak and obstructed, as most Students are, he cannot keep the last obligation, nor suffer others in his house that are so, to keep it; but only the two former, which also in diseases of examination (as consumptions) must be broken: For meat was made for man, not man for meat. To all this may be added, not for emboldening the unruly, but for the comfort of the weak, that not only sickness breaks these obligations of fasting, but sickliness also. For it is as unnatural to do any thing, that leads me to a sickness, to which I am inclined, as not to get out of that sickness, when I am in it, by any diet. One thing is evident, that an English body, and a Students body, are two great obstructed vessels, and there is nothing that is food, and not phisick, which doth less obstruct, then flesh moderately taken; as being immoderately taken, it is exceeding obstructive. And obstructions are the cause of most diseases.

Rules and Advices to Clergy

The Rt. Rev. Jeremy Taylor

Printed 1672

§I. Personal Duty.

Remember that it is your great Duty, and tied on you by many Obligations, that you be exemplar in your lives, and be Patterns and Presidents to your Flocks: lest it be said unto you, Why takest thou my Law into thy mouth, seeing thou hatest to be reformed thereby? He that lives an idle life may preach with Truth and Reason, or as did the Pharisees; but not as Christ, or as one having Authority.

Every Minister in taking accounts of his life, must judge of his Duty by more strict and severer measures, than he does of his People; and he that ties heavy burdens upon others, ought himself to carry the heaviest end: and many things may be lawful in them, which he must not suffer in himself.

Let every Minister endeavour to be learned in all spiritual wisdom, and skillful in the things of God; for he will ill teach others the way of godliness, perfectly, that is himself a babe and uninstructed. An Ignorant Minister is an head without an eye; and an Evil Minister is salt that hath no savour.

Every Minister, above all things, must be careful that he be not a servant of Passion, whether of Anger or Desire. For he that is not a master of his Passions will always be useless, and quickly will become contemptible and cheap in the eyes of his Parish.

Let no Minister be litigious in any thing; not greedy or covetous; not insisting upon little things, or quarrelling for, or exacting of every minute portion of his dues; but bountiful and easy; remitting of his right, when to do so may be useful to his people, or when the contrary may do mischief, and cause reproach. Be not over-righteous, (saith Solomon) that is, not severe in demanding, or forgoing every thing, though it be indeed his due.

Let not the name of the Church be made a pretence for personal covetousness; by saying, you are willing to remit many things, but you must not wrong the Church: for though it be true, that you are not to do prejudice to succession, yet many things may be forgiven upon just occasions, from which the Church shall receive no incommodity; but be sure that there are but few things which thou art bound to do in thy personal capacity, but the same also, and more, thou art obliged to perform, as thou art a public person.

Never exact the offerings, or customary wages, and such as are allowed by Law, in the ministration of the Sacraments, nor condition for them, nor secure them be-fore-hand; but first do your office, and minister the Sacraments purely, readily, and for Christs sake; and when that is done, receive what is your due.

Avoid all Pride, as you would flee from the most frightful Apparition, or the most cruel Enemy; and remember that you can never truly teach Humility, or tell what it is, unless you practice it your selves.

Take no measures of Humility, but such as are material and tangible; such which consist not in humble words, and lowly gestures; but what is first truly radicated in your Souls, in low opinion of your selves, and in real preferring others before your selves; and in such significations, which can neither deceive your selves nor others.

Let every Curate of Souls strive to understand himself best; and then to understand others. Let him spare himself least; but most severely judge, censure, and condemn himself. If he be learned, let him shew it by wise teaching, and humble manners. If he be not learned, let him be sure to get so much Knowledge as to know that, and so much Humility, as not to grow insolent, and puffed up by his Emptiness. For many will pardon a good man that is less learned; but if he be proud, no man will forgive him.

Let every Minister be careful to live a life as abstracted from the Affairs of the world, as his necessity will permit him; but at no hand to be immerged and principally employed in the Affairs of the World: What cannot be avoided, and what is of good report, and what he is obliged to by any personal or collateral Duty, that he may do, but no more. Ever remembering the Saying of our Blessed Lord: In the world ye shall have trouble; but in me ye shall have peace: and consider this also, which is a great Truth; That every degree of love to the world, is so much taken from the Love of God.

Be no otherwise solicitous of your Fame and Reputation, but by doing your Duty well and wisely; in other things refer your self to God: but if you meet with evil Tongues, be careful that you bear reproaches sweetly and temperately.

Remember that no Minister can govern his people well, and prosperously, unless himself hath learned humbly and cheerfully to obey his Superior. For every Minister should be like the good Centurion in the Gospel: himself is under authority, and he hath people under him.

Be sure in all your Words and Actions to preserve Christian simplicity and ingenuity; to do to others, as you would be done unto your self; and never to speak what you do not think. Trust to Truth, rather than to your Memory: for this may fail you, that will never.

Pray much and very fervently, for all your Parishioners, and all men that belong to you, and all that belong to God; but especially for the Conversion of Souls: and be very zealous for nothing, but for Gods glory, and the salvation of the World, and particularly of your Charges: Ever remembering that you are by God appointed, as the Ministers of Prayer, and the Ministers of good things, to pray for all the World, and to heal all the World, as far as you are able.

Every Minister must learn and practice Patience, that by bearing all adversity meekly, and humbly, and cheerfully, and by doing all his Duty with unwearied industry, with great courage, constancy, and Christian magnanimity, he may the better assist his people in the bearing of their crosses, and overcoming of their difficulties.

He that is holy, let him be holy still, and still more holy, and never think he hath done his work, till all be finished by perseverance, and the measures of perfection in a holy Life, and a holy Death: but at no hand must he magnify himself by vain separations from others, or despising them that are not so holy.

§II. OF PRUDENCE REQUIRED IN MINISTERS.

Remember that Discretion is the Mistress of all Graces; and Humility is the greatest of all Miracles: and without this, all Graces perish to a mans self; and without that, all Graces are useless unto others.

Let no Minister be governed by the opinion of his People, and destroy his Duty, by unreasonable compliance with their humors, lest as the Bishop of Granata told the Governours of Leria and Patti, like silly Animals they take burdens upon their backs at the pleasure of the multitude, which they neither can retain with Prudence, nor shake off with Safety.

Let not the Reverence of any man cause you to sin against God; but in the matter of Souls, being well advised, be bold and confident; but abate nothing of the honour of God, or the just measures of your Duty, to satisfy the importunity of any man whatsoever, and God will bear you out.

When you teach your people any part of their duty, as in paying their debts, their tithes and offerings, in giving due reverence and religious regards, diminish nothing of admonition in these particulars, and the like, though they object, That you speak for your selves, and in your own cases. For counsel is not the worse, but the better, if it be profitable both to him that gives, and to him that takes it. Only do it in simplicity, and principally intend the good of their souls.

In taking accounts of the good Lives of your selves or others, take your measures by the express words of Scripture; and next to them estimate them by their proportion and compliance with the public measures, with the Laws of the Nation, Ecclesiastical and Civil, and by the Rules of Fame, of public Honesty and good Report; and last of all by their observation of the Ordinances and exteriour parts of Religion.

Be not satisfied when you have done a good work, unless you have also done it well; and when you have, then be careful that vain-glory, partiality, self-conceit, or any other folly or indiscretion, snatch it not out of your hand, and cheat you of the reward.

Be careful so to order your self, that you fall not into temptation and folly in the presence of any of your Charges; and especially that you fall not into chidings and intemperate talkings, and sudden and violent expressions: Never be a party in clamours and scoldings, lest your Calling become useless, and your Person contemptible: Ever remembering that if you cheaply and lightly be engaged in such low usages with any Person, that Person is likely to be lost from all possibility of receiving much good from your Ministry.

§III. Government to be Used by Ministers in Their Cures.

Use no violence to any man, to bring him to your opinion; but by the word of your proper Ministry, by Demonstrations of the Spirit, by rational Discourses, by excellent Examples, constrain them to come in: and for other things they are to be permitted to their own liberty, to the measures of the Laws, and the conduct of their Governours.

Suffer no quarrel in your Parish, and speedily suppress it when it is begun; and though all wise men will abstain from interposing in other mens affairs, and especially in matters of Interest, which men love too well; yet it is your Duty here to interpose, by persuading them to friendships, reconcilements, moderate prosecutions of their pretences; and by all means you prudently can, to bring them to peace and brotherly kindness.

Suffer no houses of Debauchery, of Drunkenness or Lust in your Parishes; but implore the assistance of Authority for the suppressing of all such meeting-places and nurseries of Impiety: and as for places of public Entertainment, take care that they observe the Rules of Christian Piety, and the allowed measures of Laws.

If there be any Papists or Sectaries in your Parishes, neglect not frequently to confer with them in the spirit of meekness, and by the importunity of wise Discourses seeking to gain them. But stir up no violences against them; but leave them (if they be incurable) to the wise and merciful disposition of the Laws.

Receive not the people to doubtful Disputations: and let no names of Sects or differing Religions be kept up amongst you, to the disturbance of the public Peace and private Charity; and teach not the people to estimate their Piety by their distance from any Opinion, but by their Faith in Christ, their Obedience to God and the Laws, and their Love to all Christian people, even though they be deceived.

Think no man considerable upon the point or pretence of a tender Conscience, unless he live a good life, and in all things endeavour to approve himself void of offence both towards God and Man: but if he be an humble Person, modest and inquiring, apt to learn and desirous of information; if he seeks for it in all ways reasonable and pious, and is obedient to Laws, then take care of him, use him tenderly, persuade him meekly, reprove him gently, and deal mercifully with him, till God shall reveal that also unto him, in which his unavoidable trouble and his temptation lies.

Mark them that cause Divisions among you, and avoid them: for such Persons are by the Scripture called Scandals in the abstract; they are Offenders and Offences too. But if any man have an Opinion, let him have it to himself, till he can be cured of his disease by time, and counsel, and gentle usages. But if he separates from the Church, or gathers a Congregation, he is proud, and is fallen from the Communion of Saints, and the Unity of the Catholick Church.

He that observes any of his people to be zealous, let him be careful to conduct that zeal into such channels where there is least danger of inconveniency; let him employ it in something that is good; let it be pressed to fight against sin. For Zeal is like a Cancer in the Breast; feed it with good flesh, or it will devour the Heart.

Strive to get the love of the Congregation; but let it not degenerate into popularity. Cause them to love you and revere you; to love with Religion, not for your compliance; for the good you do them, not for that you please them. Get their love by doing your Duty, but not by omitting or spoiling any part of it: Ever remembering the severe words of our Blessed Saviour, woe be to you when all men speak well of you.

Suffer not the common people to prattle about Religion and Questions; but to speak little, to be swift to hear, and slow to speak; that they learn to do good works for necessary uses, that they work with their hands, that they may have wherewithal to give to them that need; that they study to be quiet, and learn to do their own business.

Let every Minister take care that he call upon his Charge, that they order themselves so, that they leave no void spaces of their time, but that every part of it be filled with useful or innocent employment. For where there is a space without business, that space is the proper time for danger and temptation; and no man is more miserable than he that knows not how to spend his time.

Fear no mans person in the doing of your Duty wisely, and according to the Laws:

Remembering always, that a servant of God can no more be hurt by all the powers of wickedness, than by the noise of a Files wing, or the chirping of a Sparrow. Brethren, do well for your selves: do well for your selves as long as you have time; you know not how soon death will come.

Entertain no Persons into your Assemblies from other Parishes, unless upon great occasion, or in the destitution of a Minister, or by contingency and seldom visits, or with leave: lest the labour of thy Brother be discouraged, and thy self be thought to preach Christ out of envy, and not of good will.

Never appeal to the judgment of the people in matters of controversy; teach them obedience, not arrogancy; teach them to be humble, not crafty. For without the aid of false guides you will find some of them of themselves apt enough to be troublesome: and a question put into their heads, and a power of judging into their hands, is a putting it to their choice whether you shall be troubled by them this week or the next; for much longer you cannot escape.

Let no Minister of a Parish introduce any Ceremony, Rites or Gestures, though with some seeming Piety and Devotion, but what are commanded by the Church, and established by Law: and let these also be wisely and usefully explicated to the people, that they may understand the reasons and measures of obedience; but let there be no more introduced, lest the people be burdened unnecessarily, and tempted or divided.

§IV. RULES AND ADVICES CONCERNING PREACHING.

Let every Minister be diligent in preaching the Word of God, according to the ability that God gives him: Ever remembering, that to minister Gods Word unto the People is the one half of his great Office and Employment.

Let every Minister be careful that what he delivers be indeed the Word of God; that his Sermon be answerable to the Text; for this is Gods Word, the other ought to be according to it; that although in it self it be but the word of Man, yet by the purpose, truth, and signification of it, it may in a secondary sense be the Word of God.

Do not spend your Sermons in general and indefinite things, as in Exhortations to the people to get Christ, to be united to Christ, and things of the like unlimited signification; but tell them in every duty, what are the measures, what circumstances, what instruments, and what is the particular minute meaning of every general Advice. For Generals not explicated do but fill the peoples heads with empty notions, and their mouths with perpetual unintelligible talk: but their hearts remain empty, and themselves are not edified.

Let not the humors and inclinations of the people be the measures of your Doctrines, but let your Doctrines be the measure of their persuasions. Let them know from you what they ought to do; but if you learn from them what you ought to teach, you will give but a very ill account at the day of Judgment, of the souls committed to you. He that receives from the people what he shall teach them, is like a Nurse that asks of her Child what Physick she shall give him.

Every Minister in reproofs of sin and sinners, ought to concern himself in the faults of them that are present, but not of the absent; nor in reproof of the times; for this can serve no end but of Faction and Sedition, public Murmur and private Discontent; besides this it does nothing but amuse the people in the faults of others, teaching them to revile their Betters, and neglect the dangers of their own souls.

As it looks like flattery and design to preach nothing before Magistrates but the duty of their people and their own eminency; so it is the beginning of Mutiny to preach to the people the duty of their Superiors and Supreme; it can neither come from a good Principle, nor tend to a good End. Every Minister ought to preach to his Parish, and urge their duty: S. John the Baptist told the Souldiers what the Souldiers should do, but troubled not their heads with what was the duty of the Scribes and Pharisees.

In the reproof of sins be as particular as you please, and spare no mans sin, but meddle with no mans person; neither name any man, nor signify him, neither reproach him, nor make him to be suspected; he that doth otherwise makes his Sermon to be a Libel, and the Ministry of Repentance an instrument of Revenge; and so doing he shall exasperate the man, but never amend the sinner.

Let the business of your Sermons be to preach holy Life, Obedience, Peace, Love among neighbours, hearty love, to live as the old Christians did, and the new should; to do hurt to no man, to do good to every man: For in these things the honour of God consists, and the Kingdom of the Lord Jesus.

Press those Graces most that do most good, and make the least noise; such as giving privately and forgiving publicly; and prescribe the grace of Charity by all the measures of it which are given by the Apostle, in 1 Corinthians 13. For this grace is not finished by good words, nor yet by good works, but it is a great building, and many materials go to the structure of it. It is worth your study, for it is the fulfilling of the Commandments.

Because it is impossible that Charity should live, unless the lust of the tongue be mortified, let every Minister in his charge be frequent and severe against slanderers, detractors and backbiters; for the Crime of backbiting is the poison of Charity; and yet so common, that it is passed into a Proverb, [After a good dinner let us sit down and backbite our neighbours.]

Let every Minister be careful to observe, and vehement in reproving those faults of his Parishioners, of which the Laws cannot or do not take cognizance, such as are many degrees of intemperate drinkings, gluttony, riotous living, expenses above their ability, pride, bragging, lying in ordinary conversation, covetousness, peevishness, and hasty anger, and such like. For the Word of God searches deeper than the Laws of men; and many things will be hard to prove by the measures of Courts, which are easy enough to be observed by the watchful and diligent eye and ear of the Guide of Souls.

In your Sermons to the people, often speak of the four last things, of Death and Judgment, Heaven and Hell: of the Life and Death of Jesus Christ, of Gods Mercy to repenting sinners, and his Severity against the impenitent; of the formidable Examples of Gods anger poured forth upon Rebels, Sacrilegious, Oppressors of Widows and Orphans, and all persons guilty of crying Sins: These are useful, safe and profitable; but never run into Extravagances and Curiosities, nor trouble your selves or them with mysterious Secrets; for there is more laid before you than you can understand; and the whole duty of man is, To fear God and keep his Commandments. Speak but very little of the secret and high things of God, but as much as you can of the lowness and humility of Christ.

Be not hasty in pronouncing damnation against any man or party in a matter of disputation. It is enough that you reprove an Error; but what shall be the sentence against it at the day of Judgment, thou knowest not, and therefore pray for the erring person, and reprove him, but leave the sentence to his Judge.

Let your Sermons teach the duty of all states of men to whom you speak; and particularly take care of Servants and Hirelings, Merchants and Tradesmen, that they be not unskilful, nor unadmonished in their respective duties; and in all things speak usefully and affectionately; for by this means you will provide for all mens needs, both for them that sin by reason of their little understanding, and them that sin because they have evil, dull, or depraved affections.

In your Sermons and Discourses of Religion, use primitive, known and accustomed words, and affect not new Fantastical or Schismatical terms: Let the Sunday Festival be called the Lords day; and pretend no fears from the common use of words amongst Christians. For they that make a business of the words of common use, and reform Religion by introducing a new word, intend to make a change but no amendment, they spend themselves in trifles, like the barren turf that sends forth no medicinal herbs, but store of Mushrooms; and they give a demonstration that they are either impertinent people, or else of a querulous nature; and that they are ready to disturb the Church, if they could find occasion.

Let every Minister in his charge, as much as he can, endeavour to destroy all popular errors and evil principles taken up by his people, or others with whom they converse; especially those that directly oppose the indispensable necessity of a holy life: let him endeavour to understand in what true and useful sense Christs active obedience is imputed to us; let him make his people fear the deferring of their Repentance, and putting it off to their death-bed; let him explicate the nature of Faith, so that it be an active and quickening principle of Charity; let him, as much as he may, take from them all confidences that slacken their obedience and diligence; let him teach them to impute all their sins to their own follies and evil choice, and so build them up in a most holy faith to a holy life; ever remembering that in all ages it hath been the greatest artifice of Satan to hinder the increase of Christs Kingdom, by destroying those things in which it does consist, viz. Peace and Righteousness, Holiness and Mortification.

Every Minister ought to be careful that he never expound Scriptures in public contrary to the known sense of the Catholick Church, and particularly of the Churches of England and Ireland, nor introduce any Doctrine against any of the four first General Councils; for these, as they are measures of truth, so also of necessity; that is, as they are safe, so they are sufficient; and besides what is taught by these, no matter of belief is necessary to salvation.

Let no Preacher bring before the people in his Sermons or Discourses, the Arguments of great and dangerous Heresies, though with a purpose to confute them; for they will much easier retain the Objection than understand the Answer.

Let not the Preacher make an Article of Faith to be a matter of dispute; but teach it with plainness and simplicity, and confirm it with easy arguments and plain words of Scripture, but without objection; let them be taught to believe, but not to argue, lest if the arguments meet with a scrupulous person, it rather shake the foundation by curious inquiry, than establish it by arguments too hard.

Let the Preacher be careful that in his Sermons he use no light, immodest or ridiculous expressions, but what is wise, grave, useful and for edification; that when the Preacher brings truth and gravity, the people may attend with fear and reverence.

Let no Preacher envy any man that hath a greater audience, or more fame in Preaching than himself; let him not detract from him or lessen his reputation directly or indirectly: for he that cannot be even with his brother but by pulling him down, is but a dwarf still; and no man is the better for making his brother worse. In all things desire that Christ's Kingdom may be advanced; and rejoice that he is served, whoever be the Minister; that if you cannot have the fame of a great Preacher, yet you may have the reward of being a good man; but it is hard to miss both.

Let every Preacher in his Parish take care to explicate to the people the Mysteries of the great Festivals, as of Christmas, Easter, Ascension-day, Whitsunday, Trinity Sunday, the Annunciation of the blessed Virgin Mary; because these Feasts containing in them the great Fundamentals of our Faith, will with most advantage convey the mysteries to the people, and fix them in their memories, by the solemnity and circumstances of the day.

In all your Sermons and Discourses speak nothing of God but what is honourable and glorious; and impute not to him such things, the consequents of which a wise and good man will not own: never suppose him to be author of sin, or the procurer of our damnation. For God cannot be tempted, neither tempteth he any man. God is true, and every man a liar.

Let no Preacher compare one Ordinance with another; as Prayer with Preaching, to the disparagement of either; but use both in their proper seasons, and according to appointed Order.

Let no man preach for the praise of men; but if you meet it, instantly watch and stand upon your guard, and pray against your own vanity; and by an express act of acknowledgment and adoration return the praise to God. Remember that Herod was for the omission of this smitten by an Angel; and do thou tremble, fearing lest the judgment of God be otherwise than the sentence of the people.

§V. RULES & ADVICES CONCERNING CATECHISM.

Every Minister is bound upon every Lords day before Evening Prayer, to instruct all young people in the Creed, the Lords Prayer, the Ten Commandments, and the Doctrine of the Sacraments, as they are set down and explicated in the Church Catechism.

Let a Bell be tolled when the Catechizing is to begin, that all who desire it may be present; but let all the more ignorant and uninstructed part of the people, whether they be old or young, be required to be present: that no person in your Parishes be ignorant in the foundations of Religion: Ever remembering, that if in these things they be unskilful, whatever is taught besides, is like a house built upon the sand.

Let every Minister teach his people the use, practice, methods and benefits of meditation or mental prayer. Let them draw out for them helps and rules for their assistance in it; and furnish them with materials, concerning the life and death of the ever blessed Jesus, the greatness of God, our own meanness, the dreadful sound of the last Trumpet, the infinite event of the two last sentences at doomsday: let them be taught to consider what they have been, what they are, and what they shall be; and above all things what are the issues of eternity; glories never to cease, pains never to be ended.

Let every Minister exhort his people to a frequent confession of their sins, and a declaration of the state of their Souls; to a conversation with their Minister in spiritual things, to an enquiry concerning all the parts of their duty: for by preaching, and catechizing, and private intercourse, all the needs of Souls can best be served; but by preaching alone they cannot.

Let the people be exhorted to keep Fasting days, and the Feasts of the Church; according to their respective capacities; so it be done without burden to them, and without becoming a snare; that is, that upon the account of Religion, and holy desires to please God, they spend some time in Religion, besides the Lords-day: but be very careful that the Lords-day be kept religiously, according to the severest measures of the Church, and the commands of Authority: ever remembering that as they give but little Testimony of Repentance and Mortification, who never fast; so they give but small evidence of their joy in God and Religion, who are unwilling solemnly to partake of the public and Religious Joys of the Christian Church.

Let every Minister be diligent in exhorting all Parents and Masters to send their Children and Servants to the Bishop at the Visitation, or other solemn times of his coming to them, that they may be confirmed: And let him also take care that all young persons may by understanding the Principles of Religion, their vow of Baptism, the excellency of Christian Religion, the necessity and advantages of it, and of living according to it, be fitted and disposed, and accordingly by them presented to the Bishop, that he may pray over them, and invocate the holy Spirit, and minister the holy Rite of Confirmation.

§VI. RULES & ADVICES CONCERNING THE VISITATION OF THE SICK.

Every Minister ought to be careful in visiting all the Sick and Afflicted persons of his Parish: ever remembering, that as the Priests lips are to preserve knowledge, so it is his duty to minister a word of comfort in the time of need.

A Minister must not stay till he be sent for; but of his own accord and care to go to them, to examine them, to exhort them to perfect their repentance, to strengthen their faith, to encourage their patience, to persuade them to resignation, to the renewing of their holy vows, to the love of God, to be reconciled to their neighbours, to make restitution and amends, to confess their sins, to settle their estate, to provide for their charges, to do acts of piety and charity, and above all things, that they take care they do not sin towards the end of their lives. For if repentance on our death-bed seem so very late for the sins of our life; what time shall be left to repent us of the sins we commit on our death-bed?

When you comfort the afflicted, endeavour to bring them to the true love of God; for he that serves God for Gods sake, it is almost impossible he should be oppressed with sorrow.

In answering the cases of conscience of the sick or afflicted people, consider not who asks, but what he asks; and consult in your answers more with the estate of his soul, than the conveniency of his estate; for no flattery is so fatal as that of the Physician or the Divine.

If the sick person enquires concerning the final estate of his soul, he is to be reproved rather than answered; only he is to be called upon to finish his duty, to do all the good he can in that season, to pray for pardon and acceptance; but you have nothing to do to meddle with passing final sentences; neither cast him down in despair, nor raise him up to vain and unreasonable confidences. But take care that he be not carelessly dismissed.

In order to these and many other good purposes, every Minister ought frequently to converse with his Parishioners; to go to their houses, but always publicly, with witness, and with prudence, lest what is charitably intended be scandalously reported: and in all your conversation be sure to give good example, and upon all occasions to give good counsel.

§VII. Of ministering the Sacraments, Public Prayers, & Other Duties

Every Minister is obliged publicly or privately to read the Common Prayers every day in the week, at Morning and Evening; and in great Towns and populous places conveniently inhabited, it must be read in Churches, that the daily sacrifice of Prayer and Thanksgiving may never cease.

The Minister is to instruct the people, that the Baptism of their children ought not to be ordinarily deferred longer than till the next Sunday after the birth of the child; lest importune and unnecessary delay, occasion that the child die before it is dedicated to the service of God and the Religion of the Lord Jesus, before it be born again, admitted to the Promises of the Gospel, and reckoned in the account of the second Adam.

Let every Minister exhort and press the people to a devout and periodical Communion, at the least three times in the year, at the great Festivals: but the devouter sort, and they who have leisure, are to be invited to a frequent Communion: and let it be given and received with great reverence.

Every Minister ought to be well skilled and studied in saying his Office, in the Rubrics, the Canons, the Articles, and the Homilies of the Church, that he may do his duty readily, discreetly, gravely, and by the public measures of the Laws. To which also it is very useful that it be added, that every Minister study the ancient Canons of the Church, especially the Penitentials of the Eastern and Western Churches: let him read good Books, such as are approved by public authority; such which are useful, wise and holy; not the scribblings of unlearned parties, but of men learned, pious, obedient and disinterested; and amongst these, such especially which describe duty and good life, which minister to Faith and Charity, to Piety and Devotion; Cases of Conscience, and solid expositions of Scripture. Concerning which learned and wise persons are to be consulted.

Let not a Curate of Souls trouble himself with any studies but such which concern his own or his peoples duty; such as may enable him to speak well, and to do well; but to meddle not with controversies, but such by which he may be enabled to convince the gainsayers in things that concern public peace and a good life.

Be careful in all the public administrations of your Parish, that the poor be provided for. Think it no shame to beg for Christs poor members; stir up the people to liberal alms by your word and your example. Let a collection be made every Lords-day, and upon all solemn meetings, and at every Communion; and let the Collection be wisely and piously administered: ever remembering, that at the day of Judgment nothing shall publicly be proclaimed, but the reward of alms and mercy.

Let every Minister be sure to lay up a treasure of comforts and advices, to bring forth for every mans need in the day of his trouble; let him study and heap together Instruments and Advices for the promoting of Every virtue, and remedies and arguments against every vice; let him teach his people to make acts of virtue not only by external exercise, but also in the way of Prayer and internal meditation.

In these and all things else that concern the Ministers duty, if there be difficulty you are to repair to your Bishop for further advice, assistance and information.

To a Mission Priest, Newly Ordained

The Rev. Richard Meux Benson, S.S.J.E.

Feast of St. Thomas, 1888

How full of marvel and power the life of a priest ought to be. Would that we could realize it more truly. What entire loss of self there should be if we recognize the presence of the Holy Ghost, Whom we receive, as accomplishing in us the work of the priesthood, so entirely beyond all human power –at once miraculous in its extent, and mysterious in its character– the spreading of the life of another world throughout the organism of the material creation. May we have grace to carry on this work faithfully. We of many years standing in the priesthood feel the need of much reparation for wasted powers. You who are just beginning must look to Him to uphold you, and assuredly He will. He never calls us to do anything for which He does not give the power. We accept His charge, and say with humble confidence in His help, "We are able."[1] May this blessed sufficiency of His grace be continually experienced by you.

---

1. "Jesus answered, 'You do not know what you are asking. Are you able to drink the cup that I am to drink?' They said to him, 'We are able.'" (*Matthew 20:22*)

LETTER TO CANDIDATES FOR HOLY ORDERS

The Rt. Rev. Charles C. Grafton

The Cathedral at Fond du Lac, Lent, 1892

MY DEAR SON IN CHRIST:
It was my expectation to have seen you and all my Candidates and Postulants this Lent, but I have been unable to do so, and in place, send to you all this circular letter.

Naturally, you will at this time, by special prayers and meditations, be striving to deepen your own spiritual life and get a more vigorous perception of your vocation.

It is a special act of love for God to call us out, not only from the world, but from the ranks of ordinary Christians, to become associated with Himself in the awful dignity of His Priesthood, and to become living examples, by the transformation of our characters, of the reality and power of Divine Grace. You are hereafter as Priests, to be associated with Him in His tremendous work of saving souls from the power of sin and delivering them from its thraldom. You are to take part, as soldiers of Christ, in the great conflict which enlists on one side or the other, all the powers of good and evil in heaven and earth. In union with Jesus Christ and through the power of His spirit, you are to save souls from being eternally lost, and to train them in holiness for union with God in glory.

There is no dignity so high, no responsibility so great, no work so noble, no reward so blessed, no life more full of beatitude, than that of a faithful Priest. It is a singular mark of God's predestinating love that He calls any of us into this association with Himself.

What I want you to make as the very fiber of your whole moral and intellectual nature, and to become stamped in on your mind and burnt into your will, that you will at all times be governed by it, is this fact, that your success as a minister of

Christ depends on the conformity of your life to His.

We are not merely teachers of truths, who perform our office chiefly by preaching. We are not like men of other professions, whose success may not be affected by their lives. Our success in delivering men from sin and making them holy, depends on the extent of our own self-victory and our own increasing sanctification. Natural abilities, learning, powers of speech or administration, make men popular. They help men to get on. They bring the reward that will perish. But they are not the sources of the Priest's real strength. To draw others to Christ, the Priest must be a spiritual magnet filled with divine energy. To deliver others, he must have fought a terrible fight with the world, the flesh, and the devil in himself. To win others to a real self-surrender, to a life separated from the world, he must himself be separated in life, aims, and conduct from it. To make men willing to submit to the mortification of true penitence, the Priest must preach the Cross from the Cross. His whole life must be united to Christ, not only as the Priest and advocate, but to Him as the Victim and the Lamb slain. He must become a Man of God and bear in every part of his life the brand of the Cross, if he is to compel others by the spiritual power in him, to be separated from the world and bear the Cross. You must put, my sons, nothing less than this before you, if you want the "well-done" at last and the eternal reward.

There are a number of clergy in our day, who do not put this high standard before them or seek to conform their lives to the life of Christ crucified. There are those who go in, as they say, for what they can get, whose lives are governed by secondary motives, who are popular, successful, and will probably be well spoken of when they die, but who will wake up to find the Master saying, "You lived for yourself, not for me, and you have had your reward."[1] They will say, "Lord, Lord, have we not prophesied in Thy Name, and in Thy Name done many wondrous works; built churches, presented large classes for confirmation, aided many charitable enterprises, preached the Gospel?" He will say, "I know you not,"[2] for it is true now, as it was in the days of St. Chrysostom and other fathers who declared that a large number of the clergy would certainly be lost, a larger proportion probably than of any other

1. See Matthew 6:2
2. See Matthew 7:21-23

profession.[3]

This is in itself very terrible to think of, but it applies to those who have no high aim concerning the Priesthood, no real purpose of self-consecration, who look away from the Cross and not to it, who do not realize to what Christ calls them and trust in His grace. For to aim high, to take the stricter line, to make sacrifice for Christ's service, is the way of safety. Christ's grace will never be wanting to those who have abandoned themselves to His protection. He loves men of great desires and aspirations as he did Daniel, and will provide all things necessary for their fulfillment. The only difficult and dangerous clerical line is that of half-hearted service and worldly conformity and prudential reserve. If our hearts are wholly with Him, His grace will be sufficient for us. His word "come" will sustain us in our venture on the water. The only thing you need fear, is the listening to some old and deceitful prophet, who bids you take a more comfortable and lower standard, or, if with generous devotion to our blessed Lord, you are determined to seek for nothing less than sanctity, dependence in any way upon yourself. The foundation of the saint is, distrust self. Grow in this distrust. Trust God. The sacraments are as full of grace now as when they made the heroes and the martyrs and the saints of old.

Another matter I wish to speak to you about is your life as seminarians. There is a danger, especially among men who have never been in any institution before, to look upon the seminary as if it were a college. Now, the spirit of a theological seminary should be very different from that of a college, not only in its discipline, good order, devotion, its sobriety in manners, its edifying conversation, and in the spirit of piety which should pervade it, but in the relation of seminarians one to another. We stand in very different and in closer relations to one another than the members of a college. The relation between college students is a temporary one. They are independent one of another. Each has come with his own ulterior aim in life, each is to use or waste by his choice, the provided equipment for his future life. The collegian is not therefore bound to feel concerned in the success of his fellow-student, or in any way to exercise supervision of his conduct. The latter he

---

3. There is a saying commonly attributed to St. Chrysostom that goes: "The road to hell is paved with the skulls of bishops." What he really wrote was: "I do not think there are many among Bishops that will be saved, but many more that perish" (3rd *Homily on the Acts of the Apostles*)

would rather regard as a dishonorable thing. But it is very different in a seminary. We are united together by a divine call to be trained as officers in the army of Christ. We are to form, thus, one body. As the success of an army depends upon the fidelity of all its different members, so any unfaithfulness to Christ on the part of any one works an injury to all. We are bound therefore by every principle of honor, by the trust Christ reposes in us, by our allegiance to Him and His interest to guard the discipline, the spirit, the devotion, the spiritual life, of the seminary. As in the army, an officer would deem it disgraceful not to report neglect of duty of which he was cognizant on the march or in the field, so that same spirit of honor should animate you when any one is known, as the Apostle says, to be walking disorderly. Let no mistaken sense of fellowship or good-nature or indifference blind you to your duty as an officer of the army, to your loyalty to Christ. By your own diligence and faithfulness, try to increase the spirit of devotion in your comrades, and with that high sense of honor which marks the military profession protest against everything in others which mars the effectiveness of the service. You are in training to be men of God. You are to be spiritual athletes. You are to be men of high moral character, men of firm resolve in matters of duty, men watchful over your own conduct, lest a world hateful of religion should be able in you to find any cause of offense. You are Christ-bearers. Christ trusts Himself to you by giving you the Blessed Sacrament; He trusts His Sacred Presence to your care. He relies on your honor to guard himself against insult. Guard His Presence in you. Like true Knights, determine to die, rather than do what is wrong. If thy hand or thy foot offend thee, cut it off, for it is better for thee to enter life maimed than, having both hands and feet, to be cast into hell-fire.

There is a third matter about which I want to speak to you. You are my Candidates for Holy Orders. In admitting you to the Sacred Ministry, I take a grave responsibility. It is a responsibility which weighs upon my heart when I think of the number who have been unpreparedly admitted to Holy Orders. It is not because I do not trust you all, but because I love you, and earnestly desire you may be most useful here and reach the highest rewards hereafter that I write this. When you came to me, I had not formulated the rules for my candidates, which I now must do. If any of you feel you cannot accept them, I will transfer you without blame, to any other

Bishop you may choose. But we are living at a time when the Church's faith and practice is assaulted within and without, when men are denying the inspiration of Scripture, the reality of our Lord's Resurrection in the flesh, the vicarious character of His offering on Calvary, and the oil and wine of the Priesthood and the Sacraments. The Church needs trained men, devoted men, faithful men, who will live and die for her faith, men who are willing to cast their lives at the feet of Christ, men who will answer back the love of Christ who died for them by the responsive love which gives themselves and all they are to Him. Only by such a spirit can this Church of ours be saved. If you have anything of this spirit, I ask you to follow me. I ask no man to do what I am not willing to do myself. I ask no man to make sacrifices in which I do not lead and share. I believe with my whole heart this Church of ours can be saved and the dead bones as in Elijah's vision come together and be filled with life. And I believe an outpouring of the Holy Ghost throughout the whole Church of Christ has already begun, and that men and women are giving themselves up to a consecrated life with such enthusiastic devotion to the interests of Jesus as to recall the Pentecostal days. It is a blessed privilege to fight for Jesus in such days as these. Fear nothing. Hope for everything. With God nothing is impossible. This is my motto and I pray it may be yours, "Jesus our All, and our all for Jesus."

Now, without asking you to consecrate your lives entirely to Christ's service as celibate priests, I do ask you to pray over it and ask God to give you the grace for the state of life which He Himself instituted, and to which He has given a special blessing. It is now as when "The ark, and Israel and Judah abide in tents; and the servants of my Lord are encamped in the open field"[4]; and it is to a self-denying priesthood, and the offering of the Daily Sacrifice that the conquest of the world is given. While a celibate consecration is what I want you to think and pray about, there are some other minor matters of sacrifice which I must insist upon. If you wish to continue my candidates, during your candidateship I must ask you to promise to abstain from the use of all intoxicating beverages, save as used medicinally and under direction; to give up the use of tobacco, not to dance, play cards, nor to visit saloons or theaters. At the seminary I wish you to wear your cassocks at

---

4. 2 Samuel 11:11

Church, in the refectory, and at recitations. I also request you, as it is more clerical, to remain shaven, if you do not wear full beards. Respecting these things I am only laying down rules for you while in training for the Priesthood.

If you will remember how the Disciples were trained by Christ for their work, how minute His rules were[5], and consider that your work is no different from theirs, *viz.* the advancement of a Kingdom upon which the eternity of souls depends, you will not deem these things either unwise or harsh. You will rejoice at every act of discipline which binds you closer to the Apostles and to the hero Saints of the Church. The Kingdom of Heaven suffereth violence, and the violent take it by force. The good soldier of Jesus Christ must learn to endure hardness. If St. Paul found it necessary to beat his body with blows in order to bring it into subjection, we cannot afford to miss any discipline which may advance us in sanctity. In this present time of distress, when the gates of hell are pressing against the Church, and she is calling for better-trained and more devoted warriors, let us not be cowards. As we realize how the heart agony of Christ is being prolonged and the Spirit's converting and convicting power hindered by the inefficiency of the Priesthood, let us try to mitigate that agony and further the Spirit's work, by casting ourselves and our little all of this present brief time on earth into the furnace fire of the Sacred Heart of our Blessed Lord.

With my love, prayers, and blessing,

Your Friend & Bishop.

---

5. Matthew 10

Reading in Preparation for Holy Orders

The Rev. Dr. Edward Bouverie Pusey

Printed 1898

I SUPPOSE one may take it for granted that any one who comes to ask for a course of theological study is, at least, well acquainted with the letter of Holy Scripture, such as might be acquired through the Daily Lessons, and the frequent reading of Holy Scripture in church. Otherwise, the first step would be a knowledge of the Holy Text itself, and especially a careful study of the Historical Books of the Old Testament. This presumed, the object would be to deepen the knowledge of Holy Scripture, of the substance of the Faith, and of practical wisdom, with some knowledge of the History of the Church.

In this we should begin with the Gospels as the center; and in this, I suppose, what persons would chiefly need, would be the deeper meaning of the whole, and of the several words as drawn out by the Fathers, rather than mere verbal criticism. It would then, probably, be best to begin to study the Gospels, either with the *Catena Aurea*; or each Gospel with some one Father who had commented on it: St. Matthew with St. Chrysostom and St. Hilary; St. Luke with St. Ambrose; St. John with St. Augustine and St. Chrysostom.

This study would not only bring out the context, and connexion, and meanings of Holy Scripture which people are not in the habit of thinking of, but would, incidentally, bring a person acquainted with a good deal of exposition of other parts of Holy Scripture. It is like reading Holy Scripture with a new sense. St. Ambrose, especially, brings one acquainted with a great deal of Holy Scripture. Besides, in this study of the Gospels, much might be learnt by way of meditating on them.

If the *Catena Aurea*; were used, it would probably be best to take two chief Fathers only at first, that a person might not be lost in the manifoldness and fullness of exposition. Other expositions might be reserved until afterwards.

The reading of the Fathers themselves has the advantage of their being a whole, and that their mode of practical teaching, in connexion with the exposition of Holy Scripture, is so learnt.

After, or with this, might be taken the *Exposition of the Psalms*, by St. Augustine, both as teaching the spiritual meaning of the Psalms (which it does even amid variance of translations, but much more when the translation is the same), the relation of their meaning s to our Lord and His members, and for the great value of its moral teaching.

For a first study of St. Paul, no work would perhaps give such a general view of the scope and connexion of the Epistles as St. Chrysostom. St. Augustine, again, beautifully unfolds St. John's Epistles.

Together with this, it would be best to take some hard book, which should be the subject of real study, in order to make it your own. Butler's *Analogy* may be presupposed. Then Hooker, Book V, ought to be turned *in succum et sanguinem*. The deep view of the connexion of the Sacraments with the Incarnation is probably hardly to be found elsewhere, save in the Schoolmen. Pearson *of the Creed* should follow, and later St. Athanasius *against the Arians*; with the notes in the Library of the Fathers. There is in these a very important doctrine, upon which people, if not instructed how to think, are continually thinking amiss, and even unconsciously falling into heresy. On the doctrine of Justification should be read Bishop Bull's *Harmonia*, or Mr. Newman's work

Bishop Bull's *Defensio Fidei Nicenae* should be taken later, if there is opportunity; and, as a great repertorium on all the questions which have been raised on sacred doctrine, *Petavius de Trinitate* and *de Incarnatione*.

For History it might suffice, in this stage, to read Eusebius and Collier's *English History*. Parts of Bingham's *Christian Antiquities* might also be read. Eusebius is a very suggestive book as to further questions.

On Moral Subjects, and as to practical teaching, I suppose he could hardly do better than take Bishop Andrewes' *Festival Sermons*, on account of his reverent and loving way of dwelling on the Divine Mysteries. Bishop Taylor's Sermons, *Life of Christ, Holy Living and Dying*, for personal practical experience. Newman's Sermons for deep moral and religious truth, and to read himself. Manning's Sermons for vivid realizing of things unseen, and the end of our being. St. Augustine's were named, and those on *Select Portions of Holy Scripture* (Library of the Fathers) might be added to them, as models of clear, affectionate, fatherly teaching. Perhaps on Penitential Subjects might be added the *Sermons at St. Saviour's, Leeds*. More direct spiritual guides are à Kempis, and the *Spiritual Combat, the Way of Eternal Life*; for Devotion one might name Bishop Andrewes, and the *Paradise of the Christian Soul*.

In this whole course of study it is best to prevent weariness by combining at least several portions of it. Especially every day should be taken one of the harder books, upon which, for some time, the whole mind should be concentrated, if but for a short time, half an hour or an hour ; and then the main extent of study be given to Holy Scripture, keeping always some time for Practical Reading, and that with a view, primarily, to the person's own soul.

Begin and end all study with at least a short prayer.

Advice for the Student Today

The Rev. Dr. Greg Peters

B ISHOP Klein was a realist when it comes to the priest-as-theologian. He suggests that many seminarians squander their opportunity at undivided studies, spending too much time talking about things of either little or no consequence and/or thinking of themselves and their intellectual endeavors in lofty terms. Klein also understands the perennial temptation to indulge the sin of *curiositas* whereas the seminarian (and future priest) ought to practice *studiositas*. Moreover, Klein is well aware of the temptation simply to repeat the thought of others rather than formulate one's own thoughts. And Klein is right in so many ways, including his comments that get at what is the current malady of many contemporary seminarians (and priests too), which is that they do not want to be theologians but rather consumers of "truth" distilled in digestible-sized bites that they can regurgitate to parishioners that no longer desire meat but remain content with milk.

My experience is that many seminarians today would like theological knowledge to come in the form of a blog or similar online means, for their lives are dominated by the use of social media and much of what passes for "knowledge" is trafficked on the internet. Why read a theology book when one thinks he can domesticate inexhaustible theological knowledge in an afternoon on his favorite website. Why read an accredited theologian whose education and experience qualifies him for the office when one can read a non-peer reviewed thought piece. What passes for "theology" these days often looks like one of the "thin, ugly cows" of Genesis 41 rather than the "plump cows."

Klein has a vision for the seminarian's life of study that is meant to carry him forward into his life in the Church. Thus, a weak life of study in seminary will, unfortunately, bear further bad fruit in one's ministry so much so that Klein suggests that the seminarian might not, in fact, have a genuine vocation to the priesthood: "The absence of a vigorous, untiring interest, embracing all aspects of theology though perhaps preferring one to another, renders a supposed vocation disturbingly questionable."[1] Klein rightly knows that one's theological formation does not end in seminary for no seminary (and no seminary professor) can exhaust the theological disciplines. Thus, "After ordination [the seminarian] shall go on learning," or at least they should go on learning. Rather, they *must* go on learning for his "intellectual enterprise will then become perhaps the supremely decisive factor in his ministry." Without a theologically deep well one's pastoral ministry remains shallow and the Church of God and the People of God pay the highest price for the priest's parched thought life.

What is particularly valuable is Klein's recommendation for priests to make space for "doing" theology and for establishing that pattern as a seminarian. Because the priesthood concerns divinity then it must be constantly undergirded and shored up by theology. Parishioners, vestries and staff alike are important but *not* at the cost of forgoing ongoing theological formation. Habits formed in seminary to this end will last a lifetime. To concretize the practice, let me make three suggestions. First, always be reading a difficult theology book, whether a primary text (like Thomas Aquinas' *Summa*) or a secondary study. Avoid the often unvetted drivel that passes for "theology" on the internet. Second, always be reading a "theological novel" like Fyodor Dostoevsky's *Brothers Karamazov* or Georges Bernanos' *Diary of a Country Priest*. These books will "entertain" while theologically educating. Lastly, find a theological mentor who will read and discuss theology with you and/or attend theological conferences. The life of the theological mind is nurtured best in community and common study. Seminary sets one on a path but it is up to the now-ordained priest to keep treading that road, the *via theologiae*, which leads in the end to "the gladsome hill" and not to the "brackish waters" (see George Herbert, *The Pilgrimage*) of an *a*-theological life and ministry.

---

1. See page 55

Advice for the Student Today

The Rev. Dr. Charles Erlandson

You have heard it said: "Physician heal thyself." Bp. Klein reminds all seminarians and priests: "Preacher hear thyself." For the heart of the gospel and the soul of Christian ministry is love, of which Bp. Klein speaks in Chapter II of *Clothed with Salvation*. This love must be manifest in the life of every Christian beginning today, whether a layman, seminarian, deacon, priest, or bishop.

Bp. Klein begins by reminding us that although the temptation for the seminarian and priest may be to retreat to the cloister or study, man is not made to live alone. However, the moment we enter human society the temptation is to self-interest instead of what is good for others. If we want to model loving relationships for our parishioners then we must order our relationships according to the principle of the Trinity or the One and the Many: "the individual human being finds neither in complete separation from others nor in complete fusion with them the self-fulfillment for which God has destined him."[1] We must, therefore, at one and the same time be individuals who employ their uniquely given gifts and talents and also use those same gifts in unity with others.

Crouching at our door, however, is the temptation to see the spiritual life, and even Christ's sacred ministry, as a competitive and not a cooperative endeavor. The temptation to selfishness doesn't magically go away just because a man is ordained or seeks ordination. In fact, as Bp. Klein warns us: "The selfishness of the righteous often looks so much like righteousness itself that only a saint can tell them apart."[2]

The necessity of loving our neighbor extends beyond a jovial cooperation and into the unpleasant realities of embedded human life. Holiness, the progressive measuring up to the stature of the love of Christ, takes place not in spite of but because

---

1. See page 15
2. See page 14

of the unlovable things we discover in others. As Bp. Klein says: "I must take it [God's love] with my brother's moldy jokes, his asinine opinions, his halitosis, and his maddening mannerisms . . . . God is the author of all idiosyncrasies, whether they exist in me or in my neighbor, and in each of them He has wonderfully and inimitably blended the elements of our nature."[3]

It's easy for seminarian and priest alike to mis-imagine just what it is that he has signed up for. Bp. Klein teaches us that: "We fall under the discipline of love the instant we cross the threshold of the seminary."[4] What we all, including every faithful Christian, have signed up for at our baptism is the cruciform ministry of Christ and His love. And love is a discipline, the ultimate discipline. It is the rod and staff of the Good Shepherd to lead, protect, and discipline His sheep, and it is the Cross by which we are mortified.

The Cross of Christ will usually come to us in small ways, with small beginnings, and we should not despise these small beginnings. Even Jesus had to begin life as a helpless infant, and only the last three years of His life were spent in public ministry.

Whether at home, in the office, at the seminary, or at the parish, God has providentially placed people in your life that you are to love as Christ with the love of Christ. Neglecting to learn to love fellow seminarians and professors in seminary, while acing all of the academic requirements, would be the ultimate act of hiding the God-given talent.

The lessons of love begin where God has placed you today with the people He has given you to love. Every Christian is bound to love and become more excellent at loving his neighbor, but the parish priest is to be the model of love. While the elder is, indeed, worthy of a double honor, he also has a double duty to love as Christ first loved him.

We were not made to live alone but to love.

3. See page 19
4. See page 20

PRAYERS FOR STUDENTS

From Several Divines

LORD make me chaste and temperate, humble and adviseable, diligent in my studies, obedient to my Superiours, and charitable to all men... Unto Thee, O my God, do I dedicate this day, and my whole life; O do Thou so bless and prosper me in my Studies, that I may every day grow more fit for Thy service. Hear me, O Lord, and pardon my failings, for the merits of Thy Son Jesus, in whose holy words, I sum up all my wants: *Our Father...*

–The Rt. Rev. Thomas Ken
For the Use of the Scholars of Winchester College

TEACH us, O Gracious Lord, to begin our work with fear, and to go on with obedience, and finish them with love; and, after all, to sit humbly down in Hope, and with a cheerful countenance look up to Thee.

–From the Nashotah Liturgy

BLESSED Lord, I devoutly thank thee for the gift of thy holy word. Help me now to read it with seriousness and attention, and incline me to love and practice whatever it commands. May thy law show me more and more of my sinfulness, and thy gospel fill me with love to the Redeemer, through whom alone I pray for the pardon of my transgressions. May the remembrance of what I shall now read, keep me from offending thee this day, so that by the teaching of thy Holy Spirit, I may daily grow in goodness and be made wise unto everlasting life. And this I ask for Jesus Christ's sake. Amen.

–Rev. Dr. William Augustus Muhlenberg
Tabella Sacra, Prayers for Students on Vacation

Printed in Great Britain
by Amazon